THOUGHTS

ON

REVELATION & LIFE

THOUGHTS

ON

REVELATION & LIFE

BEING

SELECTIONS FROM THE WRITINGS OF

BROOKE FOSS WESTCOTT, D.D., D.C.L.

REGIUS PROFESSOR OF DIVINITY, CAMBRIDGE, AND
CANON OF WESTMINSTER

ARRANGED AND EDITED BY

STEPHEN PHILLIPS, M.A.

READER AND CHAPLAIN OF GRAY'S INN

WIPF & STOCK · Eugene, Oregon

Wipf and Stock Publishers
199 W 8th Ave, Suite 3
Eugene, OR 97401

Thoughts on Revelation and Life
Being Selections from the Writings of Brooke Foss Westcott, D.D, D.C.L
Edited by Phillips, Stephen
ISBN 13: 978-1-55635-752-7
ISBN 10: 1-55635-752-4
Publication date 12/3/2007
Previously published by Macmillan and Co., 1887

PREFACE

THIS volume contains, besides selections from the well-known works of Dr. Westcott, passages from his occasional Sermons, Essays, and Addresses hitherto familiar only to a few.

To students of Divinity it is thought it will be an advantage to possess in a compendious form characteristic passages from Dr. Westcott's writings on the theological problems of our time.

The "Lessons of Literature and Art," with their unique teaching on the mission of poet and painter "to present the truth of things under the aspect of beauty," must have a special value to many.

There is much also in these pages that cannot fail to be acceptable to a wide circle of readers, whose interests centre rather in the course of ordinary life.

To all, it is believed, this volume will be welcome in proportion as they realise the truth which Dr. Westcott, throughout his writings, with so much force and beauty teaches—that "Christianity takes account of the whole nature of man, consecrating to its service the natural exercise of every power and the fulfilment of every situation in which he is placed."

For the choice of the passages selected the Editor alone is responsible.

CONTENTS

PART I

The Records of Revelation

	PAGE
THE VISION OF GOD IS THE CALL OF THE PROPHET.	3
THE OLD TESTAMENT SCRIPTURES	8
THE MEANING OF REVELATION	13
THE REVELATION OF THE FATHER	14
THE REVELATION OF THE RISEN LORD	29
THE GOSPEL OF THE RESURRECTION	40
THE HISTORIC FAITH	61
THE INCARNATION A DEVOUT STUDY	81
THE COMMUNION OF SAINTS	85
CHRISTIANITY AS THE ABSOLUTE RELIGION	93
THE BIBLE THE CHARTER OF HOPE	99

PART II

The Christian Society: its Office and Growth

	PAGE
THE TWO EMPIRES: THE CHURCH AND THE WORLD	105
CRISES IN THE HISTORY OF THE CHURCH	110
THE FAITH ONE AND PROGRESSIVE	118
MISSIONS AND THE UNIVERSITIES	125
INDIAN MISSIONS	131
THE COLONIAL CHURCH	136
THE INCARNATION INDEPENDENT OF THE FALL	139
COLLEGIATE LIFE IN THE ENGLISH CHURCH	141
OUR DEBT TO THE PAST	144
THE BENEDICTINE ORDER	149
KING'S COLLEGE CHAPEL, CAMBRIDGE	152
"YE ARE WITNESSES"	155
COMBINATION IN DIVERSITY	157
SOME THOUGHTS FROM THE ORDINAL	165
"FROM STRENGTH TO STRENGTH"	175
THE CONSTRUCTIVE WORK OF THE MINISTRY	183
WAITING FOR POWER FROM ON HIGH	187
THE SPIRITUAL OFFICE OF THE UNIVERSITIES	189

CONTENTS	ix
	PAGE
THE UNIVERSITIES AND THE TRAINING OF THE CLERGY	197
THE MISSION OF THE SCHOOLMASTER	200
THE MINISTRY OF THE LAITY	202
THE TRIALS OF A NEW AGE	205
DESTINY FULFILLED THROUGH SUFFERING	211
THE KING-PRIEST	215
THE UNIVERSAL SOCIETY	217

PART III

Aspects of Life

A POET'S VIEW OF LIFE—BROWNING	223
STEPS IN THE CHRISTIAN LIFE	233
THE INCARNATION AND CREATION	244
THE INCARNATION AND NATURE	247
THE INCARNATION AND LIFE	249
DISCIPLINED LIFE	250
LIFE CONSECRATED BY THE ASCENSION	258
MANY GIFTS—ONE SPIRIT	261
THE RESURRECTION AS INFLUENCING THE LIFE	263
SOCIAL ASPECTS OF CHRISTIANITY	265

	PAGE
ASPECTS OF LIFE	290
TYPES OF APOSTOLIC SERVICE	322

PART IV

Lessons of Literature and Art

THE DRAMATIST AS PROPHET: ÆSCHYLUS	331
THE DRAMATIST AS THINKER: EURIPIDES	336
VENTURES OF FAITH: THE MYTHS OF PLATO	342
DIONYSIUS THE AREOPAGITE	347
A CHRISTIAN PHILOSOPHER—ORIGEN	349
A CHRISTIAN PLATONIST—WHICHCOTE	353
THE LESSON OF BIBLICAL REVISION	356
THE RELATION OF CHRISTIANITY TO ART	363

PART I

The Records of Revelation

THE RECORDS OF REVELATION

Isaiah's Vision is Isaiah's Call

THE vision of God is the call of the prophet. Nowhere is the thought presented to us in the Bible with more moving force than in the record of Isaiah's mission (Isa. vi. 1-10).

Isaiah, a layman, as you remember, was, it appears, in the Temple court, and he saw in a trance the way into the holiest place laid open. The veils were removed from the sanctuary and shrine, and he beheld more than met the eyes of the High Priest, the one representative of the people, on the day on which he was admitted, year by year, to the dark chamber which shrouded the Divine Presence.

He beheld not the glory resting upon the symbolic ark, but the Lord sitting upon the throne high and lifted up; not the carved figures of angels, but the seraphim standing with outstretched wings, ready for swift service; not the vapour of earthly incense, but the cloud of smoke which witnessed to the Majesty which it hid.

This opening of "the eyes of his heart," was God's gift, God's call to him. Other worshippers about the young prophet saw, as we must suppose, nothing but "the light of common day," the ordinary sights of the habitual service—the great sea of brass, and the altar of burnt offering, and the stately portal of the holy place, and priests and Levites busy with their familiar work. But for an eternal moment Isaiah's senses were unsealed. He saw that which is, and not that which appears. For him the symbol of God dwelling in light unapproachable, was transformed into a personal presence; for him the chequered scene of labour and worship was filled with the train of God; for him the marvels of human skill were instinct with the life of God.

Such a vision, such a revelation taken into the soul, was for Isaiah an illumination of the world He could at last see all creation in its true nature through the light of God. So to have looked upon it was to have gained that which the seer, cleansed by the sacred fire, was constrained to declare. Humbled and purified in his humiliation, he could have but one answer when the voice of the Lord required a messenger, "Here am I, send me."

The Incarnation a fuller Vision of God

WHEN the prophet Isaiah looked upon that august sight, he saw, as St. John tells us, Christ's glory; he saw in figures and far off that which we have been allowed to contemplate more nearly and with the power of closer apprehension. He saw in transitory shadows that which we have received in a historic Presence.

By the Incarnation God has entered, and empowered us to feel that He has entered, into fellowship with humanity and men. As often as that birth rises before our eyes, all heaven is indeed rent open, and all earth is displayed as God made it.

For us, then, the vision and call of Isaiah find a fuller form, a more sovereign voice in the Gospel than the Jewish prophet could know.

The Reality of the Vision

THERE is nothing in life more real than such a vision. It is the pure light of heaven so broken by the shadows of earth that we can bear it. Do not then turn from it, or dismiss it as a dream. Meet it with the response of glad devotion.

It is easy, alas, to question the authority of the greatest thoughts which God sends us. It is easy to darken them and to lose them. But it is not easy to live on to the end without them. There is, happily, a noble discontent which disturbs all self-centred pleasure.

You are stirred with truest joy, and braced to labour best at your little tasks, while you welcome and keep before you the loftiest ideal of the method and the aim of work and being which God has made known to you. That is, indeed, His revelation, the vision of Himself. So He declares what He would have you do, what He will enable you to do. So He calls you to be prophets.

The Interpretation of the Vision

THE prophet's teaching must be the translation of his experience. He bears witness of that which he has seen. His words are not an echo but a living testimony. The heart alone can speak to the heart. But he who has beheld the least fragment of the divine glory, he who has spelt out in letters of light on the face of the world one syllable of the Triune Name, will feel a confidence and a power which nothing else can bring.

The Gospel a Growing Message, not a Stereotyped Tradition

LET us thank God that He has called us, in the fulfilment of our prophet's office, to unfold a growing message, and not to rehearse a stereotyped tradition.

The Gospel of Christ incarnate, the Gospel of the Holy Trinity, is new now as it has been new in all the past,—as it will be new, new in its power and new in its meaning, while the world lasts.

It was new when St. John at Ephesus was enabled to express its fundamental truth in the doctrine of the Word; new when Athanasius at Nicæa affirmed through it the living unity of the Godhead without derogating from the Lord's Deity; new when Anselm at Bec sought in it, however partially and inadequately, a solution of the problem of eternal justice; new when Luther at Wittenberg found in it the ground of personal communion with God; new in our own generation, new with an untold message, when we are bidden to acknowledge in it the pledge of that ultimate fellowship of created things which the latest researches in nature and history offer for consecration.

The Transformation of Life

WE, as we behold the Divine Image under the light of our own day, must labour to bring to our view of "the world"—the order for a time separated from God—that thought of God which makes it again a fit object of our love as it is the object of the love of God; to bring to our view of the present that sense of eternity which transfigures our estimate of great and small, of success and failure.

The transformation of life requires no more; it is possible with no less. And to us Christians the charge is given to bear this prophetic message to men.

The Power of Reverence a Measure of the Power of Rising

"HE that wonders shall reign;" "He that is near me is near fire," are among the few traditional sayings attributed to the Lord, which seem to be stamped as divine.

Awe, awe the lowliest and the most self-suppressing, is a sign not of littleness, but of nobility.

Our power of reverence is a measure of our power of rising.

As we bow in intelligent worship before the face of our King, His Spirit—a spirit of fire—enters into us. We feel that we are made partakers of the Divine nature because we can acknowledge with a true faith its spiritual glories, and lay ourselves

> Passive and still before the awful Throne . . .
> Consumed, yet quickened, by the glance of God.

The Vision at once Abasing and Elevating

IN the stress of restless occupation we are tempted to leave too much out of sight the inevitable mysteries of life. We deal lightly with the greatest questions. We are peremptory in defining details of dogma beyond the teaching of Scripture. We are familiar beyond apostolic precedent in our approaches to God. We fashion heavenly things after the fashion of earth.

If we are cast down by the meannesses, the sorrows, the sins of the world, it is because we dwell on some little part of which we see little; but let the thought of God in Christ come in, and we can rest in that holy splendour. At the same time let us not dare to confine at our will the action of the light. It is our own irreparable loss if in our conception of doctrine we gain clearness of definition by following out the human conditions of apprehending the divine, and forget that every outline is the expression in terms of a lower order of that which is many-sided.

The Prospect of one Purpose opened to us by the Old Testament

THERE are difficulties in the Old Testament, difficulties which perhaps we cannot explain. We have no desire to extenuate or to hide them. It would be strange if we had: for it is through these, as we believe, that we shall in due time learn to know better God's ways of dealing with us. But we are also bound to remember that the Old Testament offers to us something far higher, deeper, more majestic, more inspiring than materials for literary problems. The Old Testament, on any theory as to the origin of the writings which it contains, shews to us before all other books the philosophy of history in representative facts and in conscious judgments. It opens to us the prospect of one purpose variously reflected in writings spread over a thousand years: of one purpose moving onwards with a continuous growth among the barren despotisms of the East: of one purpose fulfilled in an unbroken national life which closed only when its goal was reached. The records in which this history is contained are strangely contrasted in style, in composition, in scope. They are outwardly disconnected, broken, incomplete: they belong to different ages of society: they are coloured by the natural peculiarities of different temperaments: they appeal to different feelings. But still in spite of this fragmentariness which seems to exclude the possibility of vital coherence: in spite of this variety which seems to be inconsistent with the presence of one informing influence, they show a continuity of progressive life which is found nowhere else, even in a dream. They enable us to see the chosen people raised step by step through failure and rebellion and disaster to a higher level, furnished with larger conceptions of truth, filled with nobler ideas of a spiritual kingdom, fitted at last to offer to the Lord the disciples who should be the first teachers of His Gospel, and to provide a home where, as we read, "Jesus increased in wisdom, and in favour with God and man." The world can show no parallel to this divine growth, no parallel to this divine narrative of a divine growth, in all the stirring annals of time. The great monarchies rose and fell around the little Jewish state. Other nations shone with more conspicuous glory, but the people of God lived on. They were not endowed with splendid gifts, which at once command the admiration of this world. They appealed to no triumphs of victorious enterprise; they showed no monuments of creative art. They were divided, oppressed, carried captive, "persecuted, but not forsaken, cast down, but not destroyed." By the power of their consecration they lived on; by the power of that "spirit of prophecy" which was in them they converted to the service of their faith the treasures of their conquerors; they lived on because they saw the invisible, and they were inspired to interpret, for all who should come after, the law of their life.

What then, we ask, are the characteristics of this Spirit of prophecy, of this Spirit of the Old Testament of which we speak? What are the main ideas by which Israel witnessed for centuries to the future advent of Christ? Briefly, I think, these: that Spirit witnessed to the unity of the human race as made by God in His own image; and it witnessed further to the belief that God would of His own love, and in His own wisdom, bring man and men into conformity with Himself. God is the one Creator of men: God is the one King of men. These thoughts breathe through the Old Testament from beginning to end. These thoughts Christ the Son of man fulfilled. By these thoughts "the spirit of prophecy," and "the testimony of Jesus" are shewn to be related as promise and accomplishment.

Judaism not Essentially Exclusive

NO view of Judaism can be more false than that which seems to be most common, that it was essentially exclusive. It was exclusive, and necessarily exclusive, so far as it was a beginning, a preparation, a discipline. But it was always pointing to a consummation. It was exclusive in its decay and fall, when general faithlessness had reduced it to the level of a sect. But from the first it was not so.

Uniqueness of Jewish History

IT is possible to find in the great teachers of other nations premature and fragmentary visions of truth, sometimes more attractive in themselves than the corresponding parts of the Old Testament; but they are visions premature and fragmentary. The Old Testament teaches by facts, by the organic and continuous development of a body. The Lord is not an abstraction, but a King, speaking, chastening, saving. The theatre of man's highest energies is not an imaginary Elysium of souls, but the earth with all its trials and contradictions. The prospect of the invisible future is almost excluded, lest men should forget that the world and all the powers of the world have to be conquered. One eternal counsel is carried forward, interpreted, applied, as those can bear it to whom its practical fulfilment is intrusted.

Let any one strive to concentrate his attention upon the life of which the Bible is the record, and not upon the record itself, and I venture to affirm that the thought will rise in his soul, to which Jacob gave utterance when he had seen in a vision earth and heaven united : *Surely the Lord is in this place, and I knew it not.*

If it is certain that the writings of the Old Testament offer to us many grave difficulties which we are at present unable to overcome, it is no less certain that they offer a revelation of a purpose and a presence of God which bears in itself the stamp of truth. The difficulties lie in points of criticism; the revelation is given in the facts of a people's life.

The Testimony we are to Bear

IT would have been hard—and we may thank God that we are spared the trial—to acknowledge a Galilæan teacher, as He moved among men in His infinite humility, to be the Son of God. It is hard still to find that He is with us, to discern His message in lessons perhaps as strange as those which startled His first hearers; to recognise His form in those whom fashion despises. Yet is it not the duty to which we are called? Is not this the office for which we have been furnished with a divine equipment?

The last voice of the Lord has not yet spoken: The last victory of the Lord has not yet been won.

We have known the facts of which all divine utterances are the exposition: we have looked upon the end in which all other ends are included. For us the dark and mysterious sayings of lawgiver, and seer, and psalmist have been changed into the simple message of that which has been fulfilled among men: for us the language of struggling hope has been changed into the confession of historic belief: for us, not only as the confirmation of our faith, but as the guide of our Christian effort, *the testimony of Jesus is the* spirit *of prophecy.*

The Glory of the Lord in the Old and New Testaments

THE glory of the Lord shall be revealed, and all flesh shall see it. These words give the theme of the gospel of the Old Testament, that "Gospel before the Gospel" which is contained in the second part of Isaiah, where prophecy finds its crown and consummation.

No possible conclusions of criticism can affect the unique majesty of the vision of great hope which rises out of them. Questions of date and authorship sink wholly into the background in view of the truths which the prophet declares.

Let any one read that Gospel of national life as a whole in its environment, and he will find what inspiration is: he will find what prophecy is; the sight of God and the living interpretation of the world in the light of His Presence. The situation is clear whether it be foreseen or only seen: the promise is clear; the fulfilment is clear.

The Bible is one widening answer to the prayer of Moses, *Shew me Thy glory*, which is the natural cry of every soul made for God.

The Jews a Prophetic, a Messianic Nation

FROM the date of the Return, the Jews fulfilled their office as a prophetic, a Messianic nation.

We do not, I think, reflect sufficiently upon the grandeur of their work. The old world has nothing to shew like it. It was given to other races to feel after and to unfold the broad sympathies of nature, the subtle attractiveness of beauty, the wise discipline of law, but the Jew received and witnessed to the idea of holiness which is the consecration of being.

Knowledge gained through Efforts

WE must use ungrudging labour. *The Son of God . . . hath given us an understanding that we may know . . .* He does not—we may say, without presumption, He cannot—give us the knowledge, but the power and the opportunity of gaining the knowledge.

Revelation is not so much the disclosure of the truth as the presentment of the facts on which the truth can be discerned.

It is given through life and to living men. It finds us men and it leaves us men. It is the ground of unending, untiring effort towards a larger vital apprehension of that which is laid open. It is not for the satisfaction of the intellectual part of our nature alone, but for the unfolding of our whole nature.

Men were made to seek God : that is the foundation of revelation ; to know Him as man : that is the condition of revelation ; to grow into His likeness : that is the test of revelation.

Holy Scripture Unexhausted and Inexhaustible

NO doubt we have used the Scriptures for purposes for which they were not designed. We have treated them too often as the one mechanical utterance of the Spirit, and not as writings through which the Spirit Himself speaks.

There is an immeasurable difference between making the Bible a storehouse of formal promises from which doctrinal systems can be infallibly constructed, and making it in its whole fulness the final test of necessary truth.

The Bible itself teaches us by its antithetic utterances that no single expression of the truth is co-extensive with the truth itself. And life proves beyond question that words gather wealth in the course of the ages.

It is not too much to say that no formula which expresses clearly the thought of one generation, can convey the same meaning to the generation which follows.

The language of the Bible grows more harmoniously luminous with the growing light. When its words are read and interpreted simply, as words still living, they are found to give the spiritual message which each age requires, the one message made audible to each hearer in the language wherein he was born.

Holy Scripture is unexhausted and inexhaustible. All later knowledge is as a commentary which guides us further into the true understanding of prophets, apostles, and evangelists: through old forms, old words, old thoughts—old and yet new—the Spirit of God speaks to us with a voice never before clearly intelligible as *we* can hear it.

Our Sonship

IF Christ be Son, then we who are in Christ are sons also. That relationship does not depend upon any precarious exercise of our own choice.

We do not determine our parentage. We are children of a heavenly Father by His will; and in that fact lies confidence which no failure can annul.

The Incarnation of Christ sets forth the reality of our

sonship: the life of Christ sets forth the duties of our sonship: the Passion of Christ sets forth, so that we tremble when we regard them, the privileges of our sonship.

If we are perplexed by the results and claims of physical or historical investigations, if opinions which have been handed down to us from early times appear to us to be no longer tenable, if we have to readjust our interpretation of the facts of the Faith: let us welcome the truths which are established as revelations offered to meet the requirements of a later age, untroubled by the hasty deductions which are made from them: let us welcome them with the earliest petition which we learnt to make: *Our Father, hallowed be Thy Name;* may every fresh discovery in the order of nature and in the life of men be so accepted as to shew more of Thy Glory of *Whom every fatherhood in heaven and on earth is named.*

The Word and the Christ

IF the thought of Christ as the Word fills us with courage, the thought of the Word as Christ fills us with patience.

It cannot have been for nothing that God was pleased to disclose His counsels fragment by fragment, through long intervals of silence and disappointment and disaster.

In that slow preparation for the perfect revelation of Himself to men which was most inadequately apprehended till it was finally given, we discern the pattern of His ways.

As it was in the case of the first Advent, even so now He is guiding the course of the world to the second Advent.

The Gospel of St. John from first to last is a record of the conflict between men's thoughts of Christ and Christ's revelations of Himself. Partial knowledge when it was maintained by selfishness was hardened into unbelief: partial knowledge when it was inspired by love was quickened into faith.

The Son of man came to fulfil all teaching of past history, to illuminate all the teaching of future history; and therefore He first revealed Himself by this title "Christ," the seal of the fulfilment of the Divine Will through the slow processes of life.

Waiting, Watching, and Hoping

Do not we assume that all things will go on as they have gone on for eighteen hundred years? And yet are not these centuries as full of divine warnings, of signs of judgment, of movements towards a kingdom of heaven, as the ages which preceded the first Advent?

Without hasting without resting let us move forwards with our faces towards the light to meet the Lord. *In your patience ye shall win your souls:* here is His promise.

There is the danger now which there was in old time, lest we mistake the reflection of our own imaginings for the shape of God's promises. We see a little, and forthwith we are tempted to make it all. We yield to the temptation, and become blind to the larger designs of Providence.

Our faith, our wisdom, our safety, lie in keeping ourselves open to every sign of His coming.

Life if we look at it in Christ is transfigured: Death if we look at it in Christ is conquered.

"Christ.—" That one word is a historic Gospel hallowing all time.

Not to a teacher of Israel, not to the disputants at Jerusalem, not to the eager multitudes who offered an army and a throne, but to a simple, sinful woman, an outcast from the Synagogue, an alien, the Lord declared Himself to be the Christ.

Christ is at once our remote and future aim, and our immediate and present stay.

The Bread of Life

THE phrase "to eat the flesh of Christ" expresses, as perhaps no other language could express, the great truth that Christians are made partakers of the human nature of their Lord, which is united in One Person to His Divine nature; that He imparts to us now, and that we can receive into our manhood, something of His manhood, which may be the seed, so to speak, of the glorified bodies in which we shall hereafter behold Him.

I am the Bread of Life.—It is equally wrong to regard the words as a simple prophecy of the Holy Eucharist and to dissociate them from it.

He in us, that we may never despair when we are beset by difficulties; we in Him, that when we have attained something we may reach forward to greater victories.

The Light of the World

I AM the Light of the World.—Any one who has watched a sunrise among mountains will know how the light opens out depths of beauty and life where but lately the eye rested on a cold monotony of gloom or mist. At one moment only the sharp dark outline of the distant ranges stands out against the rosy sky, and at the next, peak after peak catches the living fire, which then creeps slowly down their rocky slopes, and woods and streams and meadows and homesteads start out from the dull shadows, and the grass on which we stand sparkles with a thousand dewdrops.

Now all this represents in a figure what is the effect of the presence of Christ in the world when the eye is opened to see Him.

All that hath come into being was life in Him, before time, *and the life was the light of men.*

Let the thought of Christ rest on anything about us, great or small, and it will forthwith reflect on the awakened soul some new image of His power and love. Whatever is, was made through Him and subsists in Him.

And it is by the living apprehension of this truth alone that we can gain any deep insight into the marvels by which we are encompassed.

I am the Light of the World.—The light which reveals the world does not make the darkness, but it makes the darkness felt.

If the sun is hidden all is shadow, though we call that shadow only which is contrasted with the sunlight; for the contrast seems to intensify that which is, however, left just what it was before.

And this is what Christ has done by His coming. He stands before the world in perfect purity, and we feel, as men could not feel before He came, the imperfection, the impurity of the world.

The line of separation is drawn for ever, and the conscience of men acknowledges that it is rightly drawn.

Nothing is more truly one than light, yet nothing is more manifold.

For us the glory of heaven is tempered in a thousand hues, but we know even now that these thousand hues spring from and issue in the light which God is, and in which He dwelleth.

A Christian cannot rest in anything which has been already gained. New acquisitions of knowledge, new modes of thought, new forms of society, are always calling for interpretation, for recognition, for adjustment.

No one can mistake the problems which the present generation is called to face : no one who has felt in the least degree the power of Christ can doubt that he has in his faith that wherewith to illuminate them.

There are the trials of wealth burdened by an inheritance of luxury, which checks the growth of fellow-feeling, and enfeebles the energy of Christian love.

There are the trials of poverty worn by the struggle for bare existence, which exhausts the forces properly destined to minister to the healthy development of the fulness of life.

There is the separation of class from class which seems to become wider with increasing rapidity through the circumstances of modern labour and commerce.

There is the concentration of the population in crowded towns where the conditions of dwelling exclude large bodies of men from all share in some of the noblest teachings of nature.

There is the exaggerated extension of empires, which brings as its necessary consequence the crushing burden of military expenditure, and at the same time lessens the responsibility of the individual citizen.

There is the impatient questioning of old beliefs, which gives an unreal value to the appeal to authority and casts suspicion upon sympathetic efforts to meet doubt. But to meet all these dark problems, our light—the Light of Life—is unexhausted and inexhaustible.

And this only is required of us if we would know its quickening, cheering, warming energies, that we should follow it.

Only if we "cling to our first fault," if we pause when we are called to swift advance, if we faithlessly disbelieve that anything is offered to us which was not given to those before us, the darkness will overtake us, and our true road will be hidden.

We smile at evil, we dally with it, we do not confess in act that we hate it with a perfect hatred.

And the temptation to this false indifferentism is the more perilous because it comes to us in the guise of humility and self-distrust.

Christ the Door of the Sheep

THE fold which the Christian enters through Christ, the fold which gives safety to the flock, is a place for shelter, and not a place for isolation. He who has passed into it, and found in it his proper home, finds it also a vantage-ground for wider action. When the time comes he passes out, but he still observes the law that he passes out through Christ.

I am the door, by Me if any man enter in he . . . shall go in and go out and shall find pasture.

The world is a barren wilderness only to those who do not approach it through Christ.

The Christian then passes into the world, doing his Master's work there, by the way which his Master opens, but he does not remain in the world. He never wanders so far, he never is so deeply engrossed in the pursuits to which he is guided, as not to return to the fold when the darkness falls and the time of working is over.

Christ the Good Shepherd

OF all the images of Christ this is that which has ever appealed most forcibly to the universal instincts of men. It has been illustrated by art: it has been consecrated by history. When believers first sought to write the symbols of their faith upon the walls of the catacombs, they drew Christ as a Shepherd. And that earliest figure has never passed away from us.

Many who care little for painting must have hung with affection over the picture in which the Saviour is shown patiently and lovingly disentangling the lamb from the thorns by which it is imprisoned and torn. Many who care little for music must have been soothed by the air in which the office of Messiah the Shepherd has been described in universal language. All that we can imagine of tenderness, of endurance, of courage, of watchfulness, of devotion, is gathered up in the thought of the pastoral charge; and that charge Christ has taken over us.

From the earliest times men have felt the beauty and the truth of the image.

The oldest of Greek poets speaks of kings as "shepherds of men," but for the Jews this aspect of authority was set forth by living parables in each great crisis of their national growth. The patriarchs were shepherds; Moses was a shepherd; David was a shepherd.

Christ the Good Shepherd transfigured for ever the method, the conception, the fulfilment of leadership.

Nor can we forget that by consecrating this figure as the image of His power, Christ has given us a revelation of the character of all true government. While He tells us what He is to us, He tells us what we should strive to be to others. That which He makes known of His relationship to His people is true of all right exercise of authority. It does not matter whether authority be exercised in the Church, or in the nation, or in the city, or in the factory, or in the school, or in the family; the two great principles by which it must be directed are the same; and these are self-sacrifice and sympathy. Government which rests on any other basis is so far a tyranny and no true government.

False Views of Authority

PERHAPS the most urgent perils of our age spring from the forgetfulness of this divine theory of government. There is much of the spirit of the hireling among us; there is more of the affectation of the spirit. We hide ourselves, and we make but little effort to penetrate to the hearts of others. The nobility of leadership has been degraded in conception if not in act. The transitory accessories of popularity and wealth and splendour have obscured that absolute devotion to others which is its life. It has been supposed to end in lofty isolation and not in the most intense fellowship.

A truer View attainable for our Generation

BUT with all this, there are among us nobler strivings after a truer and more abiding order: there is an impatience of the unnatural ignorance by which we are separated from one another as classes and as individuals; there are generous impulses which move men with aspirations towards silent yet complete self-surrender; there is something of an awakened capacity to embody in the nation and in society the central truths of the Gospel. Here it seems lies the work of England in this generation; and while our thoughts are turned to the Good Shepherd, may we pray for ourselves and for

THE REVELATION OF THE FATHER 23

others that He will infuse the virtue of His Life and Passion into each office which we have to discharge for our families, for our country, for our Church; that He will lay the print of His Cross upon all the symbols of our power, and enlighten our counsels with the insight of His Love.

Christ the Resurrection and the Life

THE raising of Lazarus is nothing more than the translation of an eternal lesson into an outward and intelligible form.

The command of sovereign power, *Lazarus, come forth*, is but one partial and transitory fulfilment of the absolute and unchanging gospel, *I am the Resurrection and the Life*.

In these words Christ turns the thoughts of His hearers from all else upon Himself. The point at issue is not any gift which He can bestow, not any blessing which He can procure, but the right perception of what He is.

The Galilæans asked Him for the bread from heaven; He replied, *I am the Bread of Life*. The people were distracted by doubt; their leaders were blinded by prejudice; and He said, *I am the Light of the World*. Martha, after touching with sad yet faithful resignation upon aid apparently withheld, fixed her hope on some remote time, when her brother should rise again at the last day; and He called her to a present and personal joy. He revealed to her that death even in its apparent triumph wins no true victory: that life is something inexpressibly vast and mysterious, centred in one who neither knows nor can know any change; that beyond the earth-born clouds, which mar and hide it, there is an infinite glory of heaven in which men are made partakers.

Christ the Way to men Perplexed

ALL that Christ said to the apostles on the eve of His Passion He has said, and still says, to men in every great crisis of history.

The trial to which the first disciples were exposed was peculiar rather in its form than in its essential character.

It was the trial which belongs to every period of transition. It was a trial which presses, and will press, most heavily on our generation.

Men are perplexed. The infinite complexity and hurry and intensity of modern life confuses our perception of its general tendency. The old paths appear to be lost in a wild maze. Eager voices call us to follow this track or that. If we pause a moment we are at once left behind by our fellow-travellers. There is no repose, no strength of quietness, no patient waiting for fuller knowledge. We are almost driven to ask if there be any way, any end at all before us? And if there be, whether it is not hopeless for us to look for it?

At such times let us hearken to Christ's voice, *I am the Way*, and the purpose and order will come back to the world. We shall see that through all the ages there does run one way of self-sacrifice, and that way is Christ. All other ways soon disappear. They are drawn to this or lost in the darkness.

Christ the Truth for men Uncertain

MEN are uncertain. So much that has been held sacred for ages has been questioned or found false; so many social theories have been rudely scattered; so many noble traditions have been resolved into legends;

so many popular interpretations of Holy Scripture have been found baseless, that, when we look round on the ruin of old beliefs, we can hardly wonder that the question should arise whether there is anything on which faith can still repose.

When the trial is sorest the words of Christ, *I am the Truth*, at once lift us into that loftier region wherein no doubt or falsehood enters. Christ, the Son of God and the Son of man; Christ, the Uniter of the seen and the unseen; Christ, the Reconciler of the sinful and the Sinless—He is the Truth. In Him *is*, is essentially and eternally, all that is presented to us in the images of order and beauty and purity and love which surround us.

Christ the Life to those Bound by Sense

MEN are sense-bound. The claims of the world upon us are so many and so urgent: the triumphs of physical science are so unquestionable and so wide: the marvels of that which we can see and feel are so engrossing and inexhaustible, that it is not surprising that we should be tempted to rest on them: to take the visible for our heritage: to close our souls up against those subtle questionings whereby they strive after the knowledge of that which no eye hath seen or ear heard or hand felt, that life of the plant, of the man, of the world, which comes as we know not and goes as we know not.

But strong as the charm may be to lull to sleep that which is noblest within us, the words of Christ, *I am the Life*, can break it. We feel that that thought of a Divine personality underlying outward things, quickening them, shaping them, preserving through dissolution the sum of their gathered wealth, answers to a want within us.

Christ the True Vine

AMONG the parables of the Lord no one moved the people more deeply than that of the wicked husbandmen who would have made the Lord's vineyard their own by the murder of the true heir.

The thoughts of fifteen hundred years of beauty, of growth, of luxurance, of fertility, of joy, were gathered round the vine, and at the end Christ says that all those thoughts were fulfilled in Him: *I am the true*—the ideal—*Vine*.

Each living part of *the true Vine* is ideally the same, and yet individually different.

Our differences are given us to fit us for the discharge of special offices in its life. If, therefore, we seek to obliterate them or to exaggerate them, we mar its symmetry and check its fruitfulness.

We may have noticed how in a rose the coloured flower-leaf sometimes goes back to the green stem-leaf, and the beauty of the flower is at once destroyed. Just so it is with ourselves. If we affect a work other than that for which we are made, we destroy that which we ought to further.

Our special service, and all true service is the same, lies in doing that which we find waiting to be done by us.

We cannot compare the relative value of the leaves and the tendrils and the flowers on the vine: it is healthy and vigorous and fruitful because all are there. We cannot clearly define the minute features by which leaf is distinguished from leaf, or flower from flower, but we can feel how the whole gains in beauty by the endless combination of their harmonious contrasts.

From the figure we turn to ourselves; and when we look upon our own restless and ambitious strivings; upon our efforts to seem to be what we are not; upon our unceasing mimicry of those about us; upon our impatience of the conditions of our little duties; can we venture to think that we have learnt, as we may yet learn, the first lesson of the Vine?

The Unity between Past and Present

CUT down the tree, and you will read its history in the rings of its growth. We count and measure them, and reckon that so long ago was a year of dearth, so long ago a year of abundance. The wound has been healed, but the scar remains to witness to its infliction. The very moss upon its bark tells how the trunk stood to the rain and the sunshine. The direction of its branches reveals the storms which habitually beat upon them. We call the whole perennial, and yet each year sees what is indeed a new tree rise over the gathered growths of earlier time, and die when it has fulfilled its work.

And all this is true of the society of men. We are what a long descent has made us. Times of superstition and misgovernment and selfish indulgence have left, and ever will leave, their marks upon us. There are unhealthy parts on which the cleansing light has not fallen. There are distorted outgrowths which have suffered for want of shelter and want of care. And there are too, let us thank God for it, solid and substantial supports for developments yet to come: great boughs, as it were, towering heavenward, through which our little results of life may be borne aloft; ripe fruits which may be made the beginnings of wider vitality through our service.

The Human Conception of God given back and hallowed in Christ

IN the earliest ages God was pleased to satisfy man's instincts by transferring to Himself in a figure the senses and feelings of men. The saints of old time, with childlike minds, rejoiced to think that His "eye" was upon them; that His "ear" was open to their prayers.

The thought of His "wrath" or "jealousy" moved them with wholesome fear; the thought of His "compassion" and "repentance" raised them from hopeless despair.

It was as easy as it was vain for philosophy to point out that in all this they were extending finite ideas to an infinite Being. They could not surrender what was the soul of religion. And when the fulness of time came, all that had been figure before was made reality. Christ in His own Person reconciled the finite and the infinite; man and God.

God in Christ gives back to us all that seemed to have been lost by the necessary widening of thought through the progress of ages. We can without misgiving apply the language of human feeling to Him whom we worship.

We can give distinctness to the object of our adoration without peril of idolatry. The limitations of our being do not measure the truth, but they are made fit to express it for us.

The Revelation of a New Life

THE Resurrection, if we may so speak, shows us the change which would have passed over the earthly life of man if sin had not brought death.

Nothing perhaps is more surprising in the whole sum of inspired teaching than the way in which the different appearances of Christ after His Resurrection meet and satisfy the aspirations of man towards a knowledge of the unseen world.

As we fix our thoughts steadily upon them we learn how our life is independent of its present conditions; how we also can live through death; how we can retain all the issues of the past without being bound by the limitations under which they were shaped. Christ rose from the grave changed and yet the same; and in Him we have the pledge and type of our rising.

Christ Changed yet the Same

CHRIST was changed. He was no longer subject to the laws of the material order to which His earthly life was previously conformed. As has been well said: "What was natural to Him before is now miraculous; what was before miraculous is now natural."

Or, to put the thought in another form, in our earthly life the spirit is manifested through the body; in the life of the Risen Christ the Body is manifested (may we not say so?) through the Spirit.

He "appears," and no longer is seen coming. He is found present, no one knows from whence; He passes away, no one knows whither.

Thus Christ is seen to be changed, but none the less He is also seen to be essentially the same. Nothing has been left in the grave though all has been transfigured.

It is not that Christ's soul lives on, divested of the essence as of the accidents of the earthly garments in which it was for a little arrayed. It is not that His body, torn and wounded, is restored, such as it was, to its former vigour and beauty. But in Him soul and body, in the indissoluble union of a perfect manhood, are seen triumphant over the last penalty of sin.

In Him first *the corruptible puts on incorruption, and the mortal puts on immortality*, without ceasing to "be" so far as it has been, that in Him we may learn something more of the possibilities of human life, which, as far as we can observe it with our present powers, is sad and fleeting; that in Him we may lift our eyes to heaven our home, and find it about us even here; that in Him we may be enabled to gain some sure confidence of fellowship with the departed; that in Him we may have our hope steadfast, unmovable, knowing that our labour cannot be in vain.

The Revelation made of Necessity to Believers

THAT which is of the earth can perceive only that which is of the earth. Our senses can only grasp that which is kindred to themselves. We see no more than that for which we have a trained faculty of seeing.

The world could not see Christ, and Christ could not —there is a Divine impossibility—show Himself to the world. To have proved by incontestable evidence that Christ rose again as Lazarus rose again, would have been not to confirm our faith but to destroy it irretrievably.

The Revelation through Love

LOVE first sought the lost Lord; and in answer to love He also first revealed Himself.

Sursum Corda

NOT on the first Easter Morning only have those who have truly loved Christ, those who have felt His healing power, those who have offered up all to His service, been tempted to substitute the dead Body for the living Lord : not on the first Easter Morning only have devout and passionate worshippers sought to make that which is of the earth the centre and type of their service : not on the first Easter Morning only have believers been inclined to claim absolute permanence for their own partial apprehension of truth : not on the first Easter Morning only, but in this later age I will venture to say more than then.

For it is impossible, when we look at the subjects and method of current controversy, not to ask ourselves sadly whether we ourselves are busy in building the tomb of Christ, or really ready to recognise Him if He comes to us in the form of a new life; whether we are fruitlessly moaning over a loss which is, in fact, the condition of a blessing, or waiting trustfully for the transfiguration of the dead past.

It is impossible to open many popular books of devotion, or to read many modern hymns, without feeling that materialism has invaded faith no less than science, and that enervating sentimentalism is corrupting the fresh springs of manly and simple service.

It is impossible not to fear, when in the widespread searching of hearts men cling almost desperately to traditional phrases and customs, that we may forget the call of Christ to occupy new regions of thought, and labour in His name. The dangers are pressing, but the appearance to Mary, while it reveals their essential character, brings to us hope in facing them.

He made Himself known through sympathy. Such is the law of His working. His earliest words to every suffering child of man will always be, "Why weepest thou ? Whom seekest thou ?"

The sorrow which partly veils the Presence quickens the search. And if the voice, when it comes to each one of us, awakens in the silence of our souls the true conviction that we do want a living Friend and Saviour, and not a dead Body, some relic which we can decorate with our offerings or some formula which we can repeat with easy pertinacity, then we in our turn shall be strengthened to bear the discipline by which Christ in His glory leads us to a fuller and truer view of Himself and of His kingdom.

We shall endure gladly the removal of that which for the time would only minister to error: we shall be privileged to announce to others that He whom we have found through tears and left in patient obedience, is moving onwards to loftier scenes of triumph: we shall learn to understand why the Lord's own message of His Resurrection was not "I have risen," or "I live," but, "I ascend:" we shall listen till all experience and all history, all that is in the earth of good and beautiful and true, grows articulate with one command, the familiar words of our Communion Service, *Sursum Corda,* "Lift up your hearts;" and we shall answer in humble devotion, in patient faith, in daily struggles within and without, "We lift them up unto the Lord," to the Lord Risen and Ascended.

The Revelation through Thought—The journey to Emmaus an Allegory of Life

THE journey to Emmaus is, both in its apparent sadness and in its final joy, an allegory of many a life.

We traverse our appointed path with a sense of a void unfilled, of hopes unsatisfied, of promises withdrawn. The words of encouragement which come to us, often from strange sources, are not sufficient to bring back the assurance which we have lost. Yet happy are we if we open our griefs to Him who indeed knows them better than ourselves, if we keep Him by our side, if we constrain Him to abide with us. Happy if at the end, when the day is far spent and darkness is closing round, we are allowed to see for one moment the fulness of the Divine Presence which has been with us all along, half cloud, half light. But happier, and thrice happy if, when our hearts first burn within us, while life is still fresh and the way is still open, as One speaks to us in silent whisperings of reproof and discipline, speaks to us in the ever-living record of the Bible, we recognise the source of the spiritual fire. This we may do,—nay, rather, if our faith be a reality, this we must do,—and so feel that there has dawned upon us from the Easter Day a splendour over which no night can fall.

The Resurrection interprets all Life

THE Resurrection of Christ is no isolated fact. It is not only an answer to the craving of the human heart; it is the key to all history, the interpretation of the growing purpose of life: *Christ hath been raised*, not as some new, strange, unprepared thing, but *Christ hath been raised according to the Scriptures.* So God fulfilled the promises which in many parts and in many fashions lie written in the whole record of the Bible.

The Great Commission

CHRIST comes not to sweep away all the growths of the past, but to carry to its proper consummation every undeveloped germ of right. Even so He sends us to take our stand in the midst of things as they are; to guard with tender thoughtfulness all that has been consecrated to His service, and to open the way for the many powers which work together for His glory.

In Christ's name we take possession of every fact which is established by thought or inquiry. We fail in duty, we fail in faith, if we allow any human interest or endowment or acquisition to lie without the domain of the Cross.

The Priesthood of all Believers

THE greatest danger of the Church at present seems to be not lest we should forget the peculiar functions of the ministerial office, but lest we should allow this to supersede the general power which it concentrates and represents in the economy of life.

Spiritual Sight

WE have not lost more than we have gained by the removal of the events of the Gospel history far from our own times. The last beatitude of the Gospel is the special endowment of the later Church. *Blessed are they that have not seen and yet have believed.* The testimony of sense given to the apostles, like the testimony of word given to us, is but the starting-point of faith.

The substance of faith is not a fact which we cannot explain away, or a conclusion which we cannot escape, but the personal apprehension of a living, loving Friend.

Doubts

WE must notice how tenderly the Lord deals with the doubter who is ready to believe, and with what wise tolerance the Christian society keeps within its pale him whom a ruthless logic might have declared to be a denier of the Gospel.

Doubts are not unbelief, and yet they open the way to unbelief. If they are not resolutely faced, if they are allowed to float about like unsubstantial shadows, if they are alleged as excuses for the neglect of practical duties, if they are cherished as signs of superior intelligence, the history of St. Thomas has no encouragement for those who feel them.

The Lord revealed Himself to Thomas not while he kept himself apart in proud isolation, or in lonely despondency, but when he was joined to the company of his fellow-apostles, though he could not share their confidence.

Doubts are often dallied with: and still worse, they are often affected.

It is strange that the hypocrisy of scepticism should be looked upon as less repulsive than the affectation of belief, yet in the present day it has become almost a fashion for men to repeat doubts on the gravest questions without the least sense of personal responsibility.

Nothing is more common than to be told by easy talkers that this is impossible and that has been disproved, where a very little inquiry will show that these doubters upon trust have never even seriously attempted to examine the conditions of the problems which they presume to decide. For such hope lies in spiritual conversion.

Christ has no promises for dishonest doubt any more than for unreal faith.

Christianity shrinks from no test, but it transcends all.

The Revelation in the Work of Life

WE must work. We must pursue our appointed task till a new command comes. It may seem a poor and dull thing to go back from scenes of great excitement and lofty expectation to simple duties which belonged to an earlier time. But that is the method of God. Perhaps it will be through these that the higher call will come; perhaps no higher call will ever come to us. But our duty is still the same. We cannot tell the value of any particular service either for the society or for our own training. Much must be done to the end of the workman's life which is a preparation only. The Baptist continued to labour as he had first laboured, though he knew and confessed, *I must decrease.*

He does not leave His people desolate, though they do not always or at once recognise their visitation. Not once or twice only, but as often as the cleansed eye is turned to revolutions of society or to revolutions of thought, to the breaking of a new day over the restless waters of life, the believer knows by an access of power, of knowledge, of love, that His words are true: *I come to you.*

The Service of Working.

HE saith to him, Tend—shepherd (not simply feed)—*my sheep* (not lambs). If there are the young and the weak and the ignorant to be fed, there are also the mature and the vigorous to be guided. The shepherd must rule no less than feed. And to do this wisely and well is a harder work than the first.

If we are to do Christ's work we must consider more patiently than we commonly do the requirements of those whom we have to serve. There is not one method, one voice for all. Here there is need of the tenderest simplicity: there of the wisest authority: there of the ripest result of long reflection.

The Service of Waiting

THE comings of the Lord are not such events as we look for. Perhaps they are unregarded by those who witness them; but they are not therefore less real or less momentous.

No one who feels the sorrows of the age would wish to disparage the new earnestness which impels men at present even to undisciplined and self-willed efforts for Christ's sake. We say rather: *Would God that all the Lord's people were prophets.* But there are dangers in this tumult of reawakened life. Patient watching is too often treated at present with suspicion and stigmatised as lukewarmness. Judgments on the deepest mysteries are received without reflection and repeated without inquiry. Humility is interpreted as a confession of weakness, and reserve is condemned as a cloke for doubt. Nothing brings such sad misgivings as this hasty intolerant temper, peculiar to no one party or class, which is characteristic of the age.

St. Peter, St. Paul, and St. John

ST. PETER, St. Paul, and St. John occupy in succession the principal place in the first century, each carrying forward in due measure the work to which he ministered. So, it is said, we may see the likeness of St. Peter in the Church of the Middle Ages, and the likeness of St. Paul in the Churches of the Reformation. There remains, then, such is the conclusion, yet one more type of the Christian society to be realised in the world, which shall bear the likeness of St. John.

Waiting a Martyrdom

WAITING, as we must recognise and remember, is a sacrifice of self, a real martyrdom no less than working.

St. John by his long life, as truly as St. James by his early death, drank of the Lord's Cup and shared in the Lord's Baptism according to His own words.

To win the soul in patience, to bear the trial of delays, to watch for the dawn through the chill hours which precede it, to keep fresh and unsullied the great hope that Christ will come, without presuming to decide the fashion of His Coming, is a witness to the powers of the unseen world, which the Spirit of God alone can make possible.

Christ Present all the Days

Lo I am with you, Christ said, *all the days*—all the days—*unto the end of the world*. And this peculiar phrase in which the promise is expressed in the original turns our thoughts to the manifold vicissitudes of fortune in which the Lord is still present with His people.

He does not say simply "always," as of a uniform duration, but "all the days," as if He would take account of the changing aspects of storm and sunshine, of light and darkness, which chequer our course.

The sense of this abiding Presence of God in Christ both with the Church at large and with individual believers, brings patience, and with patience, peace.

There is something deadening in the strife of words. The silence which follows controversy is very commonly the sign of exhaustion and not of rest. It is not by narrowing our vision or our sympathy, by fixing our eyes simply on that which is congenial to our feelings, by excluding from our interest whole regions of Christendom, that we can gain the repose of faith.

It is a natural but false feeling which leads us to think that at some other time God was nearer to the world than He is now; that His voice was clearer and more intelligible; that His government was more direct and uniform. He is, if only we will look, still among us, speaking to those who listen through the manifold discoveries of the age, guiding even our fierce and selfish conflicts so as to minister to His purpose.

And we ourselves consciously or unconsciously are serving Him. He uses us if we do not bring ourselves to Him a willing sacrifice.

Departure in Blessing

IN ordinary life nothing is treasured up with more sacred affection, nothing is more powerful to move us with silent and abiding persuasiveness, nothing is more able to unite together the seen and the unseen than the last words, the last look of those who have passed away from us, the last revelation of the life which trembles, as it were, on the verge of its transfiguration. The last words of Christ were a promise and a charge. The last act of Christ was an act of blessing. The last revelation of Christ was the elevation of the temporal into the eternal, beyond sight and yet with the assurance of an unbroken fellowship.

That promise, that charge, that blessing, that revelation, are for us, the unchanged and unchangeable bequest of the Risen Lord. His hands are stretched out still. His Spirit is still hovering about us. His work is waiting to be accomplished.

THE

GOSPEL OF THE RESURRECTION

The Resurrection True or False—no Mean

THE power of the Resurrection, as the ground of religious hope, lies in the very circumstance that the event which changed the whole character of the disciples was external to them, independent of them, unexpected by them.

It is a real link between the seen and the unseen worlds, or it is at best the expression of a human instinct. Christ has escaped from the corruption of death; or men, as far as the future is concerned, are exactly where they were before He came.

Whatever may be the civilising power of Christian morality, it can throw no light upon the grave.

If the Resurrection be not true in the same sense in which the Passion is true, then death still remains the great conqueror.

We cannot allow our thoughts to be vague and uncertain upon it with impunity. We must place it in the very front of our confession, with all that it includes, or we must be prepared to lay aside the Christian name.

If the Resurrection be not true, the basis of Christian

morality, no less than the basis of Christian theology, is gone. The issue cannot be stated too broadly. We are not Christians unless we are clear in our confession on this point.

To preach the fact of the Resurrection was the first function of the Evangelists; to embody the doctrine of the Resurrection is the great office of the Church; to learn the meaning of the Resurrection is the task, not of one age only, but of all.

The Value of an Historical Revelation

A SUBJECTIVE religion brings with it no element of progress, and cannot lift man out of himself. A historical revelation alone can present God as an object of personal love.

Pure Theism is unable to form a living religion. Mohammedanism lost all religious power in a few generations. Judaism survived for fifteen centuries every form of assault in virtue of the records of a past deliverance on which it was based, and the hope of a future Deliverer, which it included.

In proportion as the Resurrection is lost sight of in the popular Creed, doctrine is divorced from life, and the broad promises of divine hope are lost in an individual struggle after good.

Like all historical facts, the Resurrection differs from the facts of science as being incapable of direct and present verification. And it differs from all other facts of history because it is necessarily unique. Yet it is not therefore incapable of that kind of verification which is appropriate to its peculiar nature.

Its verification lies in its abiding harmony with all the

progressive developments of man, and with each discovery which casts light upon his destiny.

Completeness, indeed, is but another name for ascertained limitation. The grandest and highest faculties of man are exactly those in which he most feels his weakness and imperfection. They are at present only half-fulfilled prophecies of powers which, as we believe, shall yet find an ample field for unrestricted development.

Special prayer is based upon a fundamental instinct of our nature. And in the fellowship which is established in prayer between man and God, we are brought into personal union with Him in Whom all things have their being.

In this lies the possibility of boundless power; for when the connection is once formed, who can lay down the limits of what man can do in virtue of the communion of his spirit with the Infinite Spirit?

That which on one occasion would be felt to be a personal revelation of God might convey an impression wholly different at another. The miracles of one period or state of society might be morally impossible in another.

Theology and Science

THE requirements of exact science bind the attention of each student to some one small field, and this little fragment almost necessarily becomes for him the measure of the whole, if, indeed, he has ever leisure to lift up his eyes to the whole at all.

For physical students as such, and for those who take their impressions of the universe solely from them, miracles can have no real existence. Nor is this all: not miracles only, and this is commonly forgotten, but every manifestation of will is at the same time removed from the world: all life falls under the power of absolute materialism, a conclusion which is at variance with the fundamental idea of religion, and so with one of the original assumptions on which our argument is based.

Theology deals with the origin and destiny of things: Science with things as they are according to human observation of them. Theology claims to connect this world with the world to come: Science is of this world only. Theology is confessedly partial, provisional, analogical in its expression of truth: Science, that is human science, can be complete, final, and absolute in its enunciation of the laws of phenomena.

Theology accepts without the least reserve the conclusions of Science as such: it only rejects the claim of Science to contain within itself every spring of knowledge and every domain of thought.

This holds true of the lower and more exact forms of Science, which deal with organic bodies; but as soon as account is taken of the Science of organic bodies—of Biology and Sociology—then Science itself becomes a prophet of Theology.

In this broader and truer view of Science, Theology closes a series, "a hierarchy of Sciences," as it has been well called, in which each successive member gains in dignity what it loses in definiteness, and by taking account of a more complex and far-reaching play of powers, opens out nobler views of being.

While we admit that the tendency of a scientific age is adverse to a living belief in miracles, we see that this tendency is due, not to the antagonism of science and miracle, but to the neglect and consequent obscuration by science of that region of thought in which the idea of the miraculous finds scope.

Arrogant physicism is met by superstitious spiritualism; and there is right on both sides.

The Resurrection is either a miracle or it is an illusion. Here there is no alternative: no ambiguity. And it is not an accessory of the apostolic message, but the sum of the message itself.

The same principles which would exclude as impossible a belief in such a miracle as the Resurrection, would equally exclude as impossible a belief in anything beyond ourselves and the range of present physical observation.

Thus the question practically is not simply, Is Christianity true? but, Is all hope, impulse, knowledge, life, absolutely bounded by sense and the world of sense?

The Continuity of Life

ALL creation is progressive. It is a law as well in the moral as in the physical world that nothing is lost. All that has been modifies all that is and all that will be. The present includes all the past, and will itself be contained in the future. Each physical change, each individual will, contributes something to the world to come. The earth on which we live, and the civilisation which fashions our conduct, is the result of immeasurable forces acting through vast periods of time.

There are crises in the history of nature and in the history of man, periods of intense and violent action, and again periods of comparative repose and equilibrium, but still the continuity of life is unbroken. Even when the old order is violently overthrown, the new order is built in part out of its ruins and not only upon them.

The Connection of Christianity with the Past

CHRISTIANITY cannot be regarded alone and isolated from its antecedents. It is part of a whole which reaches back historically from its starting-point on the day of Pentecost for nearly two thousand years. It was new but it was not unprepared. It professed to be itself the fulfilment and not the abolition of that which went before: to reveal outwardly the principle of a Divine Fatherhood by which all the contradictions and disorders of life are made capable of a final resolution; and to possess within it that universal truth which can transfigure without destroying the various characteristics of men and nations.

It is then possible that what we feel to be difficulties in its historic form are removed or lessened if we place it in its due relation to the whole life of mankind; and, on the other hand, the obvious fitness with which it carries on and completes a long series of former teachings will confirm with singular power its divine claims.

There have been attempts in all ages to separate Christianity from Judaism and Hellenism; but to carry out such an attempt is not to interpret Christianity, but to construct a new religion. Christianity has not only affinities with Judaism and Hellenism, but it includes in itself all the permanent truths to which both witness.

It was bound up (so the apostles said) with promises and blessings by which the Jewish people had been moulded through many centuries. It answered to wants of which the Gentiles had become conscious through long periods of noble effort and bitter desolation.

The Victories of Christianity

CHRISTIANITY conquered the Roman Empire, and remained unshaken by its fall. It sustained the shock of the northern nations, and in turn civilised them. It suffered persecution and it wielded sovereignty. It preserved the treasures of ancient thought and turned them to new uses. It inspired science, while it cherished mysteries with which science could not deal. It assumed the most varied forms and it moulded the most discordant characters.

Christianity centred in the Doctrine of the Person of Christ

THERE have been conquerors who, in the course of a lifetime, have overrun half the world and left lasting memorials of their progress in cities and kingdoms founded and overthrown. There have been monarchs who have, by their individual genius, consolidated vast empires and inspired them with a new life. There have been teachers who, through a small circle of devoted hearers, have rapidly changed the modes of thought of a whole generation. There have been religious reformers who, by force or eloquence, have modified or reconstructed the belief of nations. There have been devotees whose lives of superhuman endurance have won for them from posterity a share of divine honour. There have been heroes cut off by a sudden and mysterious fate, for whose return their loyal and oppressed countrymen have looked with untiring patience as the glorious and certain sign of dawning freedom. There have been founders of new creeds who have furnished the ideal of supreme good to later generations in the glorified image of their work. But in all the noble line of the mighty and the wise and the good in the great army of kings and prophets and saints and martyrs, there is not one who has ever claimed for himself or received from his followers the title of having in any way wrought out salvation for men by the virtue of his life and death, as being in themselves, and not only by moral effect of their example, a spring of divine blessings.

The reality of the Resurrection is an adequate explanation of the significance which was attached to the death of Christ. It seems impossible to discover anything else which can be.

The Miracles of the First Age

NOTHING indeed can be more unjust than the common mode of discussing the miracles of the first age. Instead of taking them in connection with a crisis in the religious history of the world, disputants refer them to the standard of a period of settled progress such as that in which we live.

The epoch at which they are said to have been wrought was confessedly creative in thought, and that in a sense in which no other age ever has been, and there seems a positive fitness in the special manifestation of God in the material as in the spiritual world.

The central idea of the time which, dimly apprehended at Rome and Alexandria, found its complete expression in the teaching of the apostles, was the union of earth and heaven, the transfiguration of our whole earthly nature; and the history of ancient speculation seems to show that nothing less than some outward pledge and sign of its truth could have led to the bold enunciation of this dogma as an article of popular belief.

The Progress of Religion and the Progress of Science

It is said that while science is progressive religion is stationary. The modes of advance in the two are certainly not the same, but the advance in science is not more real than the advance in religion. Each proceeds according to its proper law. The advance in religion is not measured by an addition to a former state, which can be regarded in its fulness separately, but by a change: it is represented not by a common difference but by a common ratio.

Viewed in this light, we can trace on a great scale the triple division of post-Christian history as marked by the successive victories of the Faith.

The fact of the Resurrection is its starting-point, the realisation of the Resurrection is its goal.

The fulness of the Truth is once shewn to men, as in old times the awful splendours of the Theocracy, and then they are charged to work out in the slow struggles of life the ideal which they have been permitted to contemplate.

Thus it is that we can look without doubt or misgiving upon the imperfections of the sub-apostolic Church, or the corruptions of the middle ages, or the excesses of the Reformation. Even through these the divine work went forward. The power of the Resurrection was ever carried over a wider field.

At first Christianity moved in the family, hallowing every simplest relation of life. This was the work of the primitive Church. Next it extended its sway to the nation and the community, claiming to be heard in the assemblies of princes and in the halls of counsellors. This was the work of the mediæval Church. Now it has a still wider mission, to assert the common rights and fellowship of men, to rise from the family and the nation to humanity itself.

To accomplish this is the charge which is entrusted to the Church of the Present, and no vision of the purity or grandeur of earlier times should blind us to the supreme majesty of the part which is assigned to us in the economy of faith.

The Reformation an Advance

IT would be easy to point out the weakness of the Reformation in itself as a power of organisation. Its function was to quicken rather than to create, to vivify old forms rather than to establish new.

But however we may grieve over its failure where it arrogated the office not of restoration but of reconstruction, it was a distinct advance in Christian life.

Where it failed, it failed from the neglect of the infirmities of men, and of the provisions which have been divinely made to meet them.

On the other hand, the lessons which it taught are still fruitful throughout Christendom, and destined, as we hope, to bring forth a still more glorious harvest.

What that may be as yet we cannot know, but all past history teaches us that the power of the Gospel is able to meet each crisis of human progress, and we can look forward with trust to the fulfilment of its message to our age.

The fact of the Resurrection the central Point of History

IF the fact of the Resurrection be in itself, as it confessedly is, absolutely unique in all human experience, the point which it occupies in history is absolutely unique also.

To this point all former history converges as to a certain goal: from this point all subsequent history flows as from its life-giving spring.

On a large view of the life of humanity the Resurrection is antecedently likely.

So far from being beset by greater difficulties than any other historical fact, it is the one fact towards which the greatest number of lines of evidence converge.

In one form or other pre-Christian history is a prophecy of it, and post-Christian history an embodiment of it.

The Evangelists' View of the Resurrection

THE Evangelists treat the Resurrection as simply, unaffectedly, inartificially, as everything else which they touch.

The miracle to them seems to form a natural part of the Lord's history. They shew no consciousness that it needs greater or fuller authentication than the other events of His life. Their position and office indeed exclude such a thought. They wrote not to create belief, but to inform those already believing.

The Idea of Sin

IT is evident that the possibility of sin is necessarily included in the creation of a finite, free being; for the simplest idea which we can form of sin is the finite setting itself up against the infinite. Selfishness, which exists potentially as soon as "self" exists, is the ground of all sin. Hence we can see how a perfect, finite being may yet be exposed to temptation, for the sense of limitation brings with it the thought, or the possibility of the thought, of passing the limit.

Evil not the Condition of Good

IT may be said that if moral evil were removed from the world "life would be impoverished." So indeed it appears at first sight to us who are habituated to the startling contrasts of life: for us shadow is a necessity of distinct vision. Yet it would be difficult to shew that the more splendid qualities which are brought out (for instance) by war are better, in any sense, than their correlatives which need no such field for their display: that the heroic forgetfulness or contempt of danger or suffering, which springs from a great passion or a generous impulse in the midst of a fierce conflict or under the sense of a deep wrong, is better than that rational self-control which we have seen can exist in the highest degree without the pressure of evil. We are too apt to think that virtue which is seen on a larger scale is itself magnified.

On the other hand it may be allowed that evil itself serves as a part of our discipline: that it gives occasion for the exercise of special virtues, and by antagonism calls them into play; yet this is only to say that it has been so ordered that evil shall in some degree minister to its own defeat.

Evil, while it may be the occasion of good, is never transmuted into good. Evil remains evil to the last in whatever form it may shew itself. Sin remains sin: pain remains pain: ignorance (so far as it is culpable) remains ignorance: though sin and pain and ignorance may call forth efforts of love and fortitude and patience.

Nor can it be said that sin realised, and not merely

the possibility of sin by the action of a free will, is the necessary condition of human virtue, and consequently of human happiness. For if this were true, then it would follow either that evil in itself will be eternal, or that human life in its true sense will cease to be.

The Resurrection of the Body

OUR present body is as the seed of our future body. The one rises as naturally from the other as the flower from the germ.

We cannot, indeed, form any conception of the change which shall take place, except so far as it is shewn in the Person of the Lord. Its fulfilment is in another state, and our thoughts are bound by this state. But there is nothing against reason in the analogy.

If the analogy were to explain the passage of man from an existence of one kind (limited by a body) to an existence of another kind (unlimited by a body), it would then be false; but as it is, it illustrates by a vivid figure the perpetuity of our bodily life, as proved in the Resurrection of Christ.

The moral significance of such a doctrine as the Resurrection of the body cannot be overrated. Both personally and socially it places the sanctions if not the foundations of morality on a new ground.

Each sin against the body is no longer a stain on that which is itself doomed to perish, but a defilement of that which is consecrated to an eternal life.

In this way the doctrine of the Resurrection turned into a reality the exquisite myth of Plato, in which he represented tyrants and great men waiting for their final sentence from the judges of Hades, with their bodies scarred and wounded by lust and passion and cruelty.

"The Laws of Nature"

WHAT we call "laws of nature" are nothing more than laws of our present observation of nature.

To the Christian the laws of nature are not laws only but prophecies. In the light of the Resurrection they are symbols of something broader and more glorious beyond these. They do not confirm hope but guide it.

The Church a Kingdom

"THE kingdom of God" has been the watchword equally of those who have cast aside the restraints and claims of life and of those who have sought to mould its form by the most merciless fanaticism.

The Church is itself the record of its history: it is a monument and a shrine.

Each race, each nation, each century, nay, each faithful workman, has left some mark upon it. Time gradually harmonises parts which once seemed incongruous.

Christianity and Paganism

THERE is a dark side to the picture which we are apt to forget, but still there is an abiding grace and manliness in classical life as it is seen in history and literature and art.

Unaffected interest in every human feeling, many sided culture, stern and indomitable will, claim our respect and awaken in us responsive efforts.

But so far as we admire Paganism, there is nothing in Christianity antagonistic to it.

Paganism closed its eyes to suffering and death.

Christianity takes account of the whole nature of man, of its good and of its evil, and justifies, in the face of the contradictions of life, the instinct which affirms its dignity. It looks death face to face not as an inevitable necessity but as a final consequence of sin, and yet realises even now more than victory.

Christianity differs from Paganism as a whole differs from a part. It takes up into itself and harmonises with the rest of our experience isolated truths to which Paganism bears witness.

Paganism proclaims the grandeur of man: Judaism the supremacy of God. Christianity accepts the antithesis and vindicates by the message of the Resurrection the grandeur of man in and through God.

The Work of Christianity

THIS then is the work of Christianity, first to establish the common dignity of men as men, and to place on a sure basis all purely human virtues; and next to connect the life of men with its source and consummation, and bring it into fellowship with God.

The Principle of Unity in Christianity

IT may not, indeed, be a mere fancy to regard the manifold appearances of the Lord after His Resurrection as prefiguring in some way the varieties which should exist in after time in His Church.

The unity of His Person was not in any way impaired, and yet He shewed Himself to His disciples in different "forms."

And it may be still that the faithful eye can see a Body of Christ where His Presence is hidden from others. For even in the one body there are many bodies; and as the whole Church is sometimes contemplated in its completeness as distinct from Christ, though most closely bound to Him as His bride; so is the same true of separate Churches. "Ye are a body (*not* the body) of Christ, and members in particular," St. Paul says to the Church of Corinth. The definite article destroys the force of his argument.

And so again in his second epistle: "I espoused you"—the congregation to which he is writing—"to one husband, that I may present you as a chaste virgin to Christ."

Of the life of the Church part is open, part is hidden. We can see divisions, differences, limitations; but all that is eternal and infinite in it, all that controls actions which perplex us and harmonises discords which are unresolved to our senses, is not to be perceived on earth, but is with Christ in heaven.

Essential Unity does not require External Unity

IT follows necessarily that external, visible unity is not required for the essential unity of the Church.

The congregations of Jewish and Gentile Christians were no less One in Christ, though the outward fellowship between them was imperfect or wanting: their common life lay deeper than the controversies which tended to keep them apart. Their isolation was a proof of imperfection, but not of death.

What errors are deadly it does not fall to our part to attempt to determine. It is enough to observe that differences of opinion which were once thought by many to be fatal to unity were really consistent with it. The promise of Christ does not reach to the unity of the outward fold at any time. "Other sheep," He said, "I have, which are not of this fold: them also I must bring, and they shall hear my voice; and they shall become one flock, one shepherd,"—one flock in however many folds it be gathered, because it listens to the voice of the One Shepherd.

The early records of the Church are little more than the records of conflicts which once seemed doubtful; but in each case that which had in it the element of permanence lived on, and Catholicity stood in full strength against the broken forms of partial and erroneous teachings.

No general principles can be laid down to justify a schism or a revolution. The future alone can decide on the sufficiency of the alleged causes from which they arose. And in many cases the issue which is sanctioned by experience may have been occasioned though not caused by selfish motives.

The antagonism of séparate societies of Christians serves not as the best, but as the most appropriate, discipline for bringing out the manifold applications and capacities of the one Gospel.

History has in fact sanctioned divisions of the Christian Church, whatever we may think of the events which first led to them, or of the actors by whom they were made.

On the whole a fictitious unity is more destructive of vital energy than partial dismemberment, for it tends to weaken the striving after essential unity.

The divisions and rivalries and heresies and schisms by which the Church is torn may be means towards the fulfilment of its offices. As we look back we can scarcely doubt that it is so. The storm no less than the sunshine is needed that the rainbow, the visible token of God's covenant with man, may be seen upon the cloud.

There is always a great danger that that which has been found of critical use at one time will be pronounced necessary for all time.

Mistaken gratitude changes the outward means of deliverance into an idol. The organisation through which the spirit once worked is reckoned holy, even when the spirit has left it.

The work of the mediæval Church (for example) required modes of operation which could not be retained now without a faithless neglect of the lesson which God has taught us in the last four centuries.

The spirit of the Resurrection tries and transfigures each transitory embodiment of Truth.

Christ risen the Pledge of the Restitution of all Things

WHEREVER we look the first question which arises is ever: To what purpose is this waste? On all sides we see a prodigal wealth of powers which to us appear to pass away without effect, of germs of life which never fulfil what we think to be their proper destiny, of beauty which gladdens no human eye. In the moral world the same mystery occurs.

All nature teaches the same lesson. We know in part. It is enough. If Christ be risen, in that fact lies the pledge of "the restitution of all things" towards which men are encouraged to work.

Aspects of Positivism in relation to Christianity

NO religion can fail to be a fruitful subject of study: even the rudest reveals something of the natural feelings and wants of man which are awakened by the experience of life.

. And exactly as we believe Christianity to be *the* Truth, we shall confidently expect to find in it all that is true in the manifold expressions of human thought.

Thus it has happened not unfrequently that independent speculations or instinctive aspirations have brought out elements in the Gospel which had been before overlooked or set aside. They were there, and even actively at work, but they were not consciously apprehended.

And so it seems to be now. The religion of Positivism is offered as the final result of a profound analysis of society and man, and its unquestionable attractiveness to pure and vigorous minds indicates that it does meet with some peculiar force-present phases of thought. Are there not then lessons which we may learn from it?

A system is formidable, not by what there is false in it, but by what there is true in it. If then it can be shewn that Christianity assures what Positivism promises —if it can be shewn that it includes in a fact what Positivism symbolises in a conception—if it can be shewn that it carries on to the unseen and eternal the ideas which Positivism limits to the seen and temporal —we may be sure that Positivism will have no lasting religious power except as a transitorial preparation for a fuller faith. Comte will be one more in the long line of witnesses who shew that the soul is naturally Christian.

The Positivist suggests the ideas of continuity, solidarity, and totality; the Christian, going yet further, adds the idea of infinity.

The Living ruled by the Dead

WE can watch how, in old times, the various results of labour and reflection and conflict were gathered up and perpetuated in abiding shapes; but we have no choice but to receive them. It is our privilege to modify, but not to begin. More and more as the ages go on, in Comte's striking phrase, we who live are ruled by the dead.

Comte and Lucretius

COMTE offers a singular parallel to the great poet of the Roman Republic. Both were bitterly hostile to the established faith of their countries. Both sought to lay on the study of nature the firm basis of human life and hope. Both were profoundly impressed with a sense of the unity of the world. But, in spite of the similarity of the moral position of the two teachers, we feel that they are separated by more than eighteen Christian centuries. Lucretius sought in the explanation of the origin of things that confidence which Comte looks for in the observation of their being. The one feels his way towards the intellectual conception of a harmony of nature; the other, towards the moral law of the discipline of life. Both, as it seems, were heralds of a crisis of thought. To both the Resurrection is the complete fulfilment of aspiration and teaching.

Religion Intellectual and Moral

THE sphere of doctrine is thought, and its end is the true; the sphere of discipline is action, and its end is the good; the sphere of worship is feeling, and its end is the beautiful. And, as a whole, religion teaches us to know, to serve, and to love the Great Being, in whom all that falls within the range of our power is summed up.

No Fact to be looked at by itself

EVERY fact in science furnishes new material for religion, and at once enlarges its scope and tends to define its character. But that it may do so, no fact must be looked at by itself. At present, science suffers at least as much as religion from partial and contracted views. The student of physics perpetrates as many solecisms as the student of theology.

Every one would feel the absurdity of a geometrician denying a fact in morals because it is not deducible from his premises; and yet it is not a rare thing to hear some explorer of inorganic nature gravely argue that nothing can be known of God, because his inquiries give no direct results as to His being or His attributes.

THE HISTORIC FAITH

The Idea of Faith

BELIEF deals with that which has been or with that which now is. Faith claims as its own that which is not yet brought within the range of sense.

We live by Faith however we live. Perhaps, it is a sad possibility, we can die without it.

Credulity is not Faith. That indolent abdication of the responsibility of judgment in favour of every pretender, that superficial assent, lightly given and lightly withdrawn, is utterly at variance with the intense clear vision and with the resolute grasp of Faith.

Superstition is not Faith. To choose for ourselves idols, to invest with attributes of the unseen world fragments of this world is to deny Faith, which is active, progressive, being with the infinite.

Conviction is not Faith. We may yield to what we admit to be an inevitable intellectual conclusion. Our opposition may be silenced or vanquished. But the state of mind which is thus produced is very often simply a state of exhaustion or of quickening.

Each generation is able to apprehend something more of that which the word Faith represents. But nevertheless the essential properties of Faith remain the same.

Faith is the harmony of reason and feeling and

purpose. It is, to say all briefly, thought illuminated by emotion and concentrated by will.

Reason stands paralysed by the grave.

Faith a Principle of Power

IF we were to listen to some we might suppose that Faith is the portion of childhood and old age, an infirmity of the weak and the ignorant. And yet, if we will be honest with ourselves, we shall confess that there is nothing which calls forth the admiration and the love of men which is not sealed with the sign of Faith.

Faith not only apprehends the unseen but enters into vital union with it, and so wields, according to its strength, the powers of the world to come.

Faith a Principle of Action

THERE was a time when it was usual to draw a sharp line between religious and worldly things. That time has happily gone by. We all acknowledge more or less that all life is one.

But perhaps our temptation now is to acquiesce in worldly motives for right doing: to stop short of the clear confession both to ourselves and to others that as citizens and workers we take our share in public business, we labour to fulfil our appointed task, because the love of Christ constraineth us.

Faith the Condition and Measure of Blessing

BY faith we lift up the sightless eye and it is opened : by faith we stretch out the withered arm and it is made whole : by faith, bound hand and foot with grave-clothes, we come forth from the tomb of custom which lies upon us *with a weight*
Heavy as frost and deep almost as life.

Every life guided by Faith of some Kind

FAITH in wealth, or in strong battalions, or in refined ease, or in social progress, produces great results before our eyes every day. Even this kind of faith does, in some sense, preoccupy the unseen and realise the future. Thus the man of business and the man of pleasure has a Creed which is the strength of his life.

The Apostles' Creed

THE Apostles' Creed, our sacred heritage only less old than the New Testament, is in its outline as broad as life.

If only a single congregation could enter into full possession of all that lies in this acknowledgment of the divine allegiance which we agree to profess: if we could each feel, and then all act together as feeling, that faith in God as He has revealed Himself is the foundation, the rule, the life of our lives: there would be a force present to move the world.

The history of the Church is indeed sadly chequered, but there is no other history which can be compared with it; and from the first the Apostles' Creed was substantially the symbol of its heroes.

Interpretations, glosses, enlargements were added, but the outline was fixed in the second century at least, fixed unchangeably. And I cannot suppose that any one is insensible to the influence of this testimony of ages.

The Creed is of no one age. As often as we repeat it we are guarded from forgetting the articles which our circumstances do not force upon our notice. All the facts remain, and when a crisis comes that will be ready to our hand which our fathers have delivered to us.

Our Creed Personal

WE want nothing new, but the old rekindled by a fuller light. Our Creed is personal.

We do not say, "I believe that there is a God," that "Jesus Christ came to earth," that "the Holy Ghost was sent to men." In this sense, as St. James says, "the devils believe and tremble." But we say, "I believe in God the Father," "I believe in Jesus Christ," "I believe in the Holy Ghost."

That is, I do not simply acknowledge the existence of these Divine Persons of the One Godhead, but I throw myself wholly upon their power and love. I have gained not a certain conclusion, but an unfailing, an all-powerful Friend. "I believe in Him." He can help me; and He will help me.

Our Creed Historical

OUR Creed is historical.

We believe, not in the Holy Catholic Church, but that there is a Holy Catholic Church.

The Strength of our Creed

OUR Creed is able to guard, to support, to animate us: has strength to fashion our lives in health and sickness, in joy and sorrow, in thought and action, after a Godlike type, strength to correct us with the authority of an inviolable law: strength to fill us with the enthusiasm of a living faith.

Our Creed offers to us a God on whom we can throw ourselves for guidance and support, and not a series of abstract propositions which we must hold as true.

I believe in God the Father All Sovereign

I BELIEVE in God. To say this is to confess that there is, in spite of every unpunished sin, every fruitless sorrow (as we judge), one purpose of victorious righteousness being fulfilled about us and in us.

The idea of God, the idea of One who is described most completely as "Spirit," "Light," "Fire," of absolute righteousness and power and mercy, answers to the maturity of men's growth as light answers to the eye. We were made to recognise Him, and He has made Himself known.

The Hebrew prophets spoke of the Lord as the Father of Israel, but Christ first added the title "my Father" to that of "our Father." It is through the revelation of the Son that we can find each our personal fellowship with a Father in heaven.

We cannot give up the belief that there is a purpose and an order and an end in what often seems the blind tumult of nations. We cannot give it up, and yet here and there perhaps we cannot justify it. Scripture does not veil the darknesses of life while it reveals the light. It speaks most significantly of powers of evil as "world-sovereign," but none the less it proclaims without one note of hesitancy that God is "All-sovereign." The end is not here, and it is not yet.

A Practical Atheism

THERE is, most terrible thought, a practical atheism, orthodox in language and reverent in bearing, which can enter a Christian Church and charm the conscience to rest with shadowy traditions, an atheism which grows insensibly within us if we separate what cannot be separated with impunity, the secular from the divine, the past and the future from the present, earth from heaven, the things of Caesar from the things of God.

God still Waiting to Teach us

LET us thank God that in the silence of our heart's watches, or the distractions of our business, through the temptations which lead us to self-indulgence and self-assertion, which persuade us to appeal to low impulses and to seek easy successes, which embolden us to put aside fresh truths because they will not conveniently fit into the scheme of the world which we have made, He is still waiting to teach us, that we may confess more intelligently and more actively the source from which we came and the end for which we were made.

Through Christ are all Things

HE who has redeemed us by taking our nature to Himself is the Author of every noble thought which has been uttered by unconscious prophets, of every fruitful deed of sacrifice which has been wrought by statesmen and heroes, of every triumph of insight and expression by which students and artists have interpreted the harmonies and the depths of nature.

So we claim for Christ with patient confidence, in spite of every misrepresentation and misunderstanding, "whatsoever is true and noble, and just and pure, and lovely and gracious"; we claim all for Him *through whom are all things*.

It is a truism to say that Christianity is a belief in Christ; but is it not a forgotten truism? We honour with ungrudging admiration those who labour with zeal and patience to shield the weak from injury, the poor from want, and the ignorant from temptation; who hope to elevate the condition of our artisans by giving their opinion the responsibility of power, and to discipline the improvident by ideas of comfort and self-respect: those who investigate the problems of religious thought, and seek to shew how circumstances of time and place call out this and that want, this and that belief, and lay open the manifold elements of truth which give whatever stability and strength they have to the religions of the world: those who in lonely meditation strive to reconnect man's spirit with its source. Such are *not far from the kingdom of God;* but as yet they are not Christians. Christianity is not philanthropy or philosophy or mysticism. It realises, guides, chastens, each noblest energy of man, but it is not identified with any one of them. It gives permanence and power, it gives light and support, to the many activities of body, soul, and spirit, but no one of these richest activities can take its place.

For us there is—and the confession is able to give its true majesty, its proper joy, its lofty meaning to every office of our daily duties—*one Lord, Jesus Christ, through whom are all things, and we through Him.*

All Human Goodness gathered up in Christ

AGAIN and again even in our own experience some new flush of courage or wisdom or patience or tenderness goes to brighten the picture of man's completed and real self. But in Christ there are no broken or imperfect lights. In Him everything which is shewn to us of right and good and lovely in the history of the whole world is gathered up once for all.

The Fall a Condition of Hope

THE idea of Christ's sufferings, the idea of redemption, presupposes the idea of a fall. Such an idea is, I will venture to say, a necessary condition of human hope. No view of life can be so inexpressibly sad as that which denies the fall. If evil belongs to man as man, there appears to be no prospect of relief here or hereafter. There can be nothing in us to drive out that which is part of ourselves.

Imagery only Imagery

WHILE we are constrained to use words of time and space, and to speak of going up and coming down, of present and future, in regard to the spirit world and Christ's glorified life, we must remember that such language belongs to our imperfect conceptions as we now are, and not to the realities themselves : that we must not be startled if it leads us to difficulties and contradictions : that we must allow no conclusions to be drawn as to the eternal from the phenomena of time.

This is no doubt a difficult demand to make; and it may seem to deprive us of much which brings joy and strength in the trials and sorrows of earthly life. But indeed the gain is worth the effort. If once we can feel that the imagery in which the glories of the world to come are described is only imagery, we can dwell upon it with ever-increasing intelligence and without distraction.

There is then no monotony in eternal praise, no weariness in unbroken day, when praise is the symbol of a heart conscious of God's infinite goodness, and day of the manifestation of His unclouded truth. The gates of pearl and the streets of gold cease to suggest thoughts of costly display and transitory splendour.

The soul uses the figures as helps to spiritual aspiration, and welcomes their irreconcilable contrasts as warnings against treating them as literal descriptions of that which it has not entered into the mind of men to conceive.

Lessons from the Creed

THIS at least we can see in our Confession, that Christ *descended into Hell, rose again, ascended into Heaven, sitteth on the right hand of God:* perfectness of Divine sympathy in every phase of our existence, absolute ennobling for every human power, access to the Divine Presence beyond every confinement of sensible being, assurance of final victory in every conflict with evil.

The Lesson of the Resurrection

WE believe that Christ bore from the grave the issues, the fruits, not only of His open ministry and of His final Passion, but also of the unnoticed, silent years of obscure discipline and duty, and shewed these in their spiritual meaning.

We believe, and come to feel as we look to Christ risen, that we have a motive for work prevailing through all disappointment and failure.

Christ has taught us not to turn away from earth that we may find heaven, but to behold in earth the scene of a veiled glory. We believe, and come to feel as we look to Christ risen, that here and now we *live and have our being* in God.

The Lesson of the Ascension

WE are not to think of the Ascension of Christ as of a change of position, of a going immeasurably far from us. It is rather a change of the mode of existence, a passing to God, of whom we cannot say He is "there" rather than "here."

When we declare our belief in Christ's Ascension, we declare that He has entered upon the completeness of spiritual being without lessening in any degree the completeness of His humanity.

We cannot indeed unite the two sides of it in one conception, but we can hold both firmly without allowing the one truth to infringe upon the other.

Christ sitteth on the Right Hand of God the Father

THESE words express, under a natural image, the three ideas of an accomplished work, of a Divine sovereignty, and, by consequence, of an efficacious intercession.

Christ's Return

WE cannot but notice that in the teaching of Scripture the earth where we suffer and toil is presented as the scene of a universal revelation of Christ's sovereignty; that He enters again into the conditions of human life; that all men are affected by His coming; that His coming is something infinitely more, though it includes this, than the just retribution of individuals.

Comings of Christ

THE apostles looked for Christ, and Christ came in the lifetime of St. John. He founded His immovable kingdom. He gathered before Him the nations of the earth, old and new, and passed sentence upon them. He judged, in that shaking of earth and heaven, most truly and most decisively the living and the dead. He established fresh foundations for society and a fresh standard of worth.

The fall of Jerusalem was for the religious history of the world an end as complete as death. The establishment of a spiritual Church was a beginning as glorious as the Resurrection.

At the foundation of the Byzantine Empire in the fourth century, at the conversion of the Northern nations in the eighth century, at the birth of Modern Europe in the thirteenth century, at the rebirth of the old civilisation in the sixteenth century, Christ came as King and Judge.

He came, and we can see that He came, at the time when Athanasius, the champion of the East, vindicated the supreme independence of the Faith, and Augustine, the champion of the West, affirmed the world-wide embrace of the Church.

He came, and we can see that He came, at the time when the Irish saint Columban offered to the barbarian warriors the virtues of an unseen power stronger than the arm of flesh, and our own English Boniface sealed by a fearless death a life of victorious sacrifice.

He came, and we can see that He came, at the time when the Italian Francis of Assisi claimed once more for the poor their place in the Church beside emperors and popes and nobles, and taught the love of God and the love of men in the universal language of his age.

He came, and we can see that He came, at the time when men as far apart as Loyola and Philip Neri,

Luther and Calvin, Colet and Cranmer, shewed in many parts and with many failures that Christ claims and satisfies the individual power of every man.

On each of these occasions new thoughts, new principles, new estimates of things, entered into the world, and remain still to witness to their divine origin.

The successive spiritual revolutions were not at once recognised or understood. Christ moved among men and they did not know Him. But, meanwhile, believers were confessing their faith, as we do, that He should come again to judge the quick and the dead; and we now rejoice to acknowledge that their faith was not in vain, though it was confirmed in ways which had not been foreseen.

A Present Coming

THE wider range of our vision enables us now to recognise these manifold comings of Christ already accomplished, and we may be most thankful for such teaching of experience, but we do not rest in them.

We take the great thought that this world in which we work, with all its sorrows and sins, with all its baffled hopes and unworthy ambitions, is the scene of a divine government. We take the thought, and therefore we believe that Christ has not yet revealed the fulness of His power or uttered the last voice of His judgment.

We still say, as we look often with sad hearts on what man has made of man, upon the terrible disproportion between human capacities and human achievements, that He who lived for us and died for us and ascended for us, shall come again to judge the quick and the dead; and the confession, if we enter into its meaning, is sufficient to bring back trust.

There are abundant signs of change about us now. New truths are spreading widely as to the methods of God's working, as to our connections one with another, and with the past and with the future.

Through these, as I believe, Christ is coming to us, coming to judge us, and His coming must bring with it trials and (as we think) losses.

Every revelation of Christ is through fire, the fire which refines by consuming all that is perishable.

None but believers saw the risen Christ during the forty days: none but believers see Christ in the great changes of human affairs.

The Final Coming

BUT beyond all these preparatory comings there is a day when "every eye shall see Him, and they also which pierced Him."

In that Coming, that Manifestation, that Presence, the first coming on earth and the later comings in history shall be shewn in their full import.

Then all things, our actions and ourselves, shall be seen as they are, seen by ourselves and seen by others.

Then the whole course of life, the life of creation, of humanity, of men, will be laid open, and that vision will be a judgment beyond controversy and beyond appeal.

The Judgment Personal

THE judgment of God is the perfect manifestation of truth. The punishment of God is the necessary action of the awakened conscience. The judgment is pronounced by the sinner himself, and he inflicts inexorably his own sentence.

We judge of others by what we see in them: and, what is more perilous still, we are tempted to judge of ourselves by what others can see in us.

But in the perfect light of Christ's Presence everything will be made clear in its essential nature: the opportunity which we threw away, and knew that we threw away, with its uncalculated potency of blessing; the temptation which we courted in the waywardness of selfish strength, the stream of consequence which has flowed from our example, the harvest which others have gathered from our sowing.

Ours the Dispensation of the Spirit

WE are all now living under that dispensation which is essentially the dispensation of the Spirit. Our whole attitude towards the facts of life is determined by the devout conviction with which we hold it.

The Book of the Acts is the Gospel of the Holy Spirit, the typical record of His action.

The Spirit is ever fashioning for our use, as we gain power to use them, new forms of thought, new modes of worship, new spheres of action. There can be no stationariness where He is present.

I believe in the Holy Ghost.—He who is able to make the confession stands as a listener to a Divine message. In the confidence of his faith he will not close the least avenue through which one word of God may come to him. In the vigour of his hope he will bear the season of silence when searching finds no answer. In the breadth of his love he will welcome as fellow-helpers them who serve unconsciously the Creed which they deny.

The Unity of the Church

THERE never was an epoch since the Church spread beyond Jerusalem when the "one body of Christ" was one in visible uniformity or even one in perfect sympathy.

It is possible to trace already to the apostolic age the essential features of those divisions over which we grieve. And if we look forward to the fulfilment of the great promise which gladdens the future, it is not that there shall ever be, as we wrongly read, "one fold," one outward society of Christians gathered in one outward form, but, what answers more truly to present experience and reasonable hope, "one flock and one shepherd."

And, in the meantime, let us rate the differences of Christians as highly as we will, there yet remains a common faith in the presence of which they are almost as nothing.

The Power of the belief in the Communion of Saints

TO belong to a great family, to a great society, to a great nation is, if rightly viewed, a man's noblest birthright. He whose name is a memorial of past honours, and whose earliest years are spent, as it were, in the light of illustrious deeds: he who has learnt to feel that there is a history in which he has a part, and who has rejoiced in the triumphs of a people whose hopes and impulses he shares: must from time to time be raised above all that is selfish and even personal; he must become conscious of the accumulated power with which he is endowed, and of the social destiny to which he is called.

Let the name be that name which is above every name: let the history be written in every splendid achievement by which the kingdom of God has been advanced: let the triumphs be those by which faith through the ages subdues all things to herself: let the fellowship be that of saints and confessors; and then we shall understand, dimly it may be, but yet so that effort will be kindled with fresh enthusiasm, what our fathers meant when they handed down to us truths which they had proved: then we shall say with livelier imagination and fuller heart, each in the prospect of our little work and with the sense of our peculiar trials, acknowledging that that work is transfigured by a divine consecration, and that these trials are conquered by a spiritual sympathy: I believe in the Holy Catholic Church: I believe in the Communion of Saints.

The Forgiveness of Sins

NOTHING superficially seems simpler or easier than forgiveness. Nothing, if we look deeply, is more mysterious or more difficult. With men, perhaps, forgiveness is impossible.

For forgiveness is not the careless indifference to wrong by which we seek impunity for our own faults while we lightly regard the faults of others. It is not the complacent bounty of a superior who has a proud satisfaction in giving to others release from small debts. It is not the perfunctory remission of a present penalty which leaves behind unremoved the sense and the contagion of evil.

True forgiveness involves two things, a perfect knowledge of the offence and a perfect restoration of love. In this sense we believe in the forgiveness of sins.

Nature knows no Forgiveness

NATURE knows no forgiveness. With her there is no return of opportunity, no obliteration of the past. The deed done remains while the world lasts. The deed left undone is a blank for ever.

There is no exaggeration in the startling thought of a recent writer that it would be possible with powers not different in kind from our own to read backwards in the succession of physical changes the history of our earth, to hear again the last cry of the murdered slave cast into the sea, and to look again on the last ripple of the water that closed over him.

Each act of man obviously goes on working, and working after its kind, in the doer and in his children's children.

So it is with thought and with feeling. The bad thought once admitted avenges itself by rising again unbidden and unwelcome.

The bad feeling once indulged in spreads through the whole character and gives birth to other like passions.

Sin in every form is the violation of law, and law inexorably requires its penalty to the uttermost.

We need not discuss whether the penalty is retributive or reformatory: it is in the nature of things that it must be paid. That is enough for us. To reason, if we are honest with ourselves, the great mystery of the future is not punishment but forgiveness.

This being so we can understand how the forgiveness of sins was the essential message of the Gospel.

The Resurrection of the Body

I BELIEVE in *the resurrection of the body*, or, as it is in the original without variation, *the resurrection of the flesh*. I believe, that is, that all that belongs to the essence of my person, manifested at present in weakness, marred by the results of many failures, limited by the circumstances of earth, will remain through a change which the imagination cannot realise.

The "flesh" of which we speak as destined to a resurrection is not that substance which we can see and handle, measured by properties of sense. It represents, as far as we now see, ourselves in our actual weakness, but essentially ourselves. We in our whole being, this is our belief, shall rise again. And we are not those changing bodies which we bear. They alter, as we know, with every step we take and every breath we draw. We make them, if I may so speak, make them naturally, necessarily, under the laws of our present existence. They are to ourselves, to use a bold figure, as the spoken word to the thought, the expression of the invisible.

> *For of the soul the body form doth take,*
> *For soul is form and doth the body make.*

When therefore the laws of our existence are hereafter modified, then we, because we are unchanged, shall find some other expression, truly the "same" in relation to that new order, because it is not the same as that to which it corresponds in this.

All imagery fails in some part or other to present a truth like this. But we should have been spared many sad perplexities, many grievous misrepresentations, if we had clung to St. Paul's figure of the seed in looking to our future resurrection. *We sow not*, he tells us, *that body which shall be.*

The Body a Seed

THERE is then no question here of the regathering of material particles, no encouragement for unsatisfying appeals to God's omnipotence, what St. Paul teaches us to expect is the manifestation of a power of life according to law under new conditions. *God giveth to every seed a body of its own:* not arbitrarily, but according to His most righteous will.

The seed determines what the plant shall be, but it does not contain the plant. The golden ears with which we trust again to see the fields waving are not the bare grains which were committed to the earth. The reconstruction of the seed when the season has come round would not give us the flower or the fruit for which we hope. Nay, rather, the seed dies, is dissolved that the life may clothe itself in a nobler form.

True it is that we cannot in this way escape from a physical continuity; but it is a continuity of life, and not of simple reconstruction.

Such a faith as this, even in its necessary vagueness, is sufficient to fill the heart of man. It substitutes for the monotony of continuance the vision of being infinitely ennobled.

An Antithesis in Nature and in Scripture

THE reserve of the prophetic and apostolic writings as to the unseen world is as remarkable as the boldness with which uninspired teachers have presumed to deal with it. But two thoughts bearing upon the future find clear expression in the New Testament. The one is of the consequences of unrepented sin as answering to the sin; the other of a final unity in which God shall be all in all. We read of an "eternal sin," of "a sin which has no forgiveness in this world nor in the world to come," of a debt incurred of which the payment, to be rigidly exacted, exceeds all imaginable resources of the debtor, of "eternal destruction," of "the worm that dieth not and the fire that is not quenched."

And on the other side we read of the purpose, the good pleasure of God "to sum up all things in Christ," and "through Him to reconcile all things unto Himself, whether things upon the earth or things in the heavens," of the bringing to naught of the last enemy death, and the final subjection of all things to God.

Moreover, it must be added, these apparently antithetical statements correspond with two modes of regarding the subject from the side of reason.

If we approach it from the side of man, we see that in themselves the consequences of actions appear to be for the doer, like the deed, indelible; and also that the finite freedom of the individual appears to include the possibility of final resistance to God.

And again, if we approach it from the Divine side, it seems to be an inadmissible limitation of the infinite love of God that a human will should for ever refuse to yield to it in complete self-surrender when it is known as love.

A final Divine Unity

IF we are called upon to decide which of these two lines of reasoning, which of these two thoughts of Scripture must be held to prevail, we can hardly doubt that that which is the most comprehensive, that which reaches farthest, contains the ruling idea; and that is the idea of a final divine unity.

How it will be reached we are wholly unable to say; but we are sure that the manner, which has not been revealed, will be in perfect harmony with the justice of God and the obligations of man's responsibility.

More than this we dare not lay down. But that end —"the end"—rises before us as the strongest motive and the most certain encouragement in all the labours of the life of faith.

To the last we see little, and we see dimly. When the vision seems to grow clearer, we are forced by our earthly infirmity to bow the head and veil the face before the exceeding glory.

But in the person of the Lord Jesus Christ we can see the Father. That is enough.

Of Him and through Him and unto Him are all things.

The Duty of Spiritual Thought

THE life of man is the knowledge of God, the contemplation of Him who is the Truth. That is the message of Christ.

But this knowledge lives and moves. It is not a dead thing embalmed once for all in phrases of the school which can be committed to memory. It is offered ever fresh as time advances for reverent study in the person of the Word Incarnate.

The surest knowledge once gained cannot supersede the necessity of unwearied, unceasing inquiry. No one can absolve himself from the duty of spiritual thought.

The mother of the Lord had received that direct, personal, living revelation of the purpose and the working of God which none other could have: she had acknowledged in the familiar strain of the *Magnificat* the salvation which He had prepared through her for His people: she might well seem to have been lifted far above the necessity of any later teaching; but when the simple shepherds told their story, a faint echo as we might think of what she knew, she *kept all these things, pondering them in her heart*, if haply they might shew a little more of the great mystery of which she was the minister: she kept them waiting and learning during that long thirty years of silence, waiting and learning during that brief time of open labour, from the first words at the marriage feast to the last words from the Cross.

And shall we, when we think on such an example—we with our restless and distracted lives, with our feeble and imperfect grasp on truth—be contented to repeat with indolent assent a traditional confession? Can we suppose that the highest knowledge, and the highest knowledge alone, is to be gained without effort, without preparation, without discipline, and by a simple act of memory? Must the eye and the hand of the artist be trained through long years to discern and to portray subtle harmonies of form and colour while this spiritual faculty by which we enter on the unseen may be safely left unexercised till some sudden emergency calls it into play? Is it credible that the law of our nature, which adds capacity to experience and joy to quest, is suddenly suspended when we reach the loftiest field of man's activity?

The sum of human experience grows visibly from age to age; the sum of personal experience grows visibly from year to year; and the truth ought to find fresh fulfilment in every fact of life.

Unreconciled Antitheses are Prophecies and Promises of a Larger Future

UNRECONCILED antitheses are prophecies and promises of a larger future: "our failure is but a triumph's evidence for the fulness of the days."

If our faith could find a complete and consistent

expression here it would be condemned. It would not cover all the facts of life. The forms of thought belong to this world only.

The truth of life, like man, like Christ, who is Himself the Truth, belongs to two worlds. It is not simply the determination of physical phenomena, but the interpretation of the relation of man to nature and to God. The heart has its own office in the search for it.

Outlines a Necessity, but a Symbol of Man's Weakness

WE acknowledge that outlines are a necessity for man's representation of the truth of things; but they are a concession to his weakness and a symbol of it. There is no outline in nature, and no form of words can adequately express a spiritual reality.

The soul uses the outline, the formula, as an occasion, an impulse, a help; but it brings for its own treasure that which quickens them. And in this work the soul of the simplest, the most untutored, is at no disadvantage. Its chief instrument of spiritual progress is not knowledge but love.

Reflection on the Incarnation

SO we shall look upon the Incarnation, the greatest conceivable thought, the greatest conceivable fact, not that we may bring it within the range of our present powers, not that we may measure it by standards of this world, but that we may learn from it a little more of the awful grandeur of life, that by its help we may behold once again that halo of infinity about common things which seems to have vanished away, that thinking on the phrase *the Word became flesh*, we may feel that in, beneath, beyond the objects which we see and taste and handle, is a Divine Presence, that lifting up our eyes to the Lord in glory we may know that phenomena are not ends, but signs only of that which is spiritually discerned.

And while we confess that clearness of vision cannot be gained when we turn towards such an object except by the loss of that which is characteristic of it, as we look at the sun shorn of its glory through a darkened glass or through the thick mists of earth, it will be our joy to place ourselves in that atmosphere of light which transfigures all that falls upon it.

We are on the point of losing the sense of the spiritual, the eternal, as a present reality, as the only reality. Thought is not all: conduct is not all: life is unspeakably impoverished if it is unhallowed by the sanctities of reverence and worship.

The Blessing of the Contemplation of Christ Born, Crucified, Ascended for us

AND, if we have felt one touch of the spirit which should animate our contemplation of Christ Born, Crucified, Ascended for us; if we have realised one least fragment of the end to which our work is directed, we shall know what the blessing is: know what it is to see with faint and trembling eyes depth below depth opening in the poor and dull surface of the earth; to see flashes of great hope shoot across the weary trivialities of business and pleasure; to see active about us, in the face of every scheme of selfish ambition, *powers of the life to come ;* to see in the struggles of the forlorn and distressed fragments of the life which "the poor man" Christ Jesus lived; to see over all the inequalities of the world, its terrible contrasts, its desolating crimes, its pride, its lust, its cruelty, one overarching sign of God's purpose of redemption, broad as the sky and bright as the sunshine; to see in the Gospel a revelation of love powerful even now to give a foretaste of the unity of creation, powerful hereafter to realise it.

It is when the physical order is held to be all, that life appears and must appear to be hopeless.

The Ennobling Faculty of Wonder

AS years go on there is great danger lest we should lose the ennobling faculty of wonder.

If it be true that great duties and little souls do not go well together, it is no less true that little thoughts do not suit little duties. It is in the fulfilment of simple routine that we need more than anywhere the quickening influence of the highest thought.

Commemoration of Saints

WE are learning, by the help of many teachers, the extent and the authority of the dominion which the dead exercise over us, and which we ourselves are shaping for our descendants.

We feel, as perhaps it was impossible to feel before, how at every moment influences from the past enter our souls, and how we in turn scatter abroad that which will be fruitful in the distant future. It is becoming clear to us that we are literally parts of others and they of us.

The communion of saints in the largest sense, the communion of angels and men, of men already perfected, and of men struggling towards the crown which is prepared for them, is a present reality.

No one can fail to have felt how imperfectly our Kalendar reflects the divine history of the Church.

As a necessary consequence of this narrow range of the commemoration of saints among us, our type of saintship has been dwarfed and impoverished; it has been removed far from the stir and conflicts of ordinary action.

The kingly type and the prophetic type, the type of the artist and of the poet and of the scholar, have been put aside. We do not turn to those by whom these characters have been fulfilled in Christ's strength as the peers of martyrs and apostles. We do not seek in their examples the pledge of the consecration of gifts similar, however small, among ourselves.

And yet we cannot afford to dispense with the widest teaching of consecrated lives. We daily lose much by not placing these in their right position in the open teaching of the Church.

It is true, indeed, that every type of essential human excellence coexists in Christ, the Son of man; but we, "who are but parts, can see but part—now this, now that." We have no power to apprehend directly elements which are combined with others in an absolute ideal.

It is only through Christ's servants each realising, according to his nature, his endowments, his age, his country, some feature in the Christly life that we come to have a real sense of the fulness of His humanity.

The many typical characters who foreshadowed Him find their counterpart in the many saints who offer for our welcome and our study the riches of His manhood. Nor do they in the least degree trench upon His inviolable honour. Their saintliness is wholly from Him. They are what they are, so far as we call them to mind and seek their fellowship, by His presence, He in them and they in Him. They have made His power visible; and for this we are bound to commemorate them, and their Lord through them.

The Need of continuous Commemoration

THE neglect or the indifference of centuries, no less than the discordances which are found in every life, involves such commemoration in great difficulties. Yet our faith encourages us to face them; and in many cases the solution will come through obvious channels.

There are few parishes which do not include in their annals some names fitted to recall memories of Christ's manifold victories through believers.

A dedication festival may not unfrequently lay open a fruitful page of Christian work.

Our Cathedrals, Monuments of Sacrifice and Service

OUR cathedrals are monuments of sacrifice and service which constrain us to recall Christ's working through those whose benefactions we inherit. Most of us have been deeply stirred by the commemoration services of college and university.

We have wondered, perhaps, that the use is not universal.

At Peterborough, in old time, to take one instance, almost every abbot had his memorial day, and four times in the year, in the Ember weeks, all were commemorated together.

There is surely here something for us to embody under new forms of thought.

I should be the last to forget or disparage the services of unknown benefactors. These have in a large degree made life for us what it is. These have their own commemoration when we recall the progress of the ages.

But there are others who stand out as leaders, as representatives. Gifts, labours, thoughts of distinguishable ancestors go to swell our spiritual patrimony. It may have been by some conspicuous work which was nobly spread over a lifetime; it may have been by some sweet trait which was just seen in a crisis of trial; but "here and here" they have helped us, and if we are to enjoy the fulness of their service, we must solemnly recall it.

In doing this we arrogate to ourselves no authority of final judgment by grateful celebration. We recognise a blessing; and, so far, we acknowledge God's love in him by whose ministry it was shown to us. Nor would it be difficult, I think, to make a list of names from our own Church which all would accept as worthy of memory,— names of rulers and scholars, of men who taught by their words and by their lives, who spread the faith and deepened our knowledge of it.

Recognition of the Powers of the Unseen World

SUCH commemoration of men, such peopling with familiar forms of the vacancies of All Saints' Day, such filling up the noble but blank outlines of the *Te Deum*, would help us to understand better, as a society, the vastness of the Christian life; but we require also the commemoration of ideas (if I may so speak), in order that we may bear in mind the new conditions of the spiritual life, which are suggested by the belief in the communion of saints.

The Festival of the Transfiguration

ONE festival still survives by name in our Kalendar which completely expresses part of what I mean, the Festival of the Transfiguration.

The Transfiguration is the revelation of the potential spirituality of the earthly life in its highest outward form.

In the Transfiguration the present and the past are seen in a fellowship of glory; and the future in its great features lies open for consideration.

Such an event, distinct in its teaching from the Resurrection, and yet closely akin to it, calls for more religious recognition than it receives. It is able, if we enter into its meaning, to bring vividly before us the reality of a communion of the living and the dead.

Here, as elsewhere, the Lord, as the Son of man, gives the measure of the capacity of humanity, and shews that to which He leads those who are united with Him.

The Festival of the Transfiguration furnishes an opportunity for bringing out the idea of the widest fellowship of men.

The Festival of St. Michael and All Angels

THE Festival of St. Michael and All Angels furnishes an opportunity for bringing out the complementary idea of the interpenetration of human life by life of another order.

And if it be true (and who has not felt it?) that "the world."—the world of sense—"is too much with us," then a remedy is here offered for our use.

The reserve and the revelations of Scripture are equally eloquent.

We commonly limit our notion of angelic service to personal ministration. No doubt Scripture dwells specially on this kind of office; but it indicates yet more,—a ministration of angels in nature, which brings both them and the world closer to men.

Perhaps one effect of the growing clearness with which we apprehend the laws of physical phenomena is to bring out into prominence the thought of the powers which work according to them.

The sense of action by law places the agent very near to us. "I can see," writes one who was himself a distinguished physiologist, "nothing in all nature but the loving acts of spiritual beings."

However strange the conception may be, it contains, I believe, truths which we have not yet mastered. And in this respect we commonly embarrass ourselves by mentally presenting all action under the forms of human action.

Spirit, it is obvious, may act in other ways; and our festival of the heavenly order remains to help us little by little to apprehend in this larger sense the revelation of the communion of saints.

Commemoration made effective by Meditation

To our great loss, the faculty and the habit of meditation have not as yet been cultivated among us.

Our national character, and, at present, the prevailing spirit of realism, are alien from it.

Yet the praise to God's glory, which comes through the devout consideration of His action in men, is true work.

We are apt to dwell on the littlenesses of men, or, if not, upon the picturesque aspects of their lives,—to bring them down in some measure to our level, and not aspire to their highest.

It is, however, through such aspiration alone, quickened by the thoughtful study of that which the Spirit wrought in them, that we can enter into fellowship with their true life.

Weaknesses, faults, errors, accidents of time and place, fall away. We learn to look upon the love, the courage, the faith, the self-sacrifice, the simplicity of truth which they embodied, and so become invigorated by vital contact with the eternal manifested through men.

The fellowship of spirit with spirit is closer, and may be more powerful than the precious fellowship which we can hold with books.

And there is no limit to this inspiring communion. It embraces the living and the dead. It acknowledges no saddest necessity of outward separation as reaching to the region in which it is. It does not even seek for the confirmation of any visible pledge.

By saints we understand all who welcome and appropriate and show forth, in whatever way, the gifts of the Spirit.

If we are ready to follow, Christ, through the Spirit sent in His name, will guide us to some one in whom we may study the virtue of His presence.

Christian names are, and they can be treated as, the dedication names of each believer.

Importance of Dwelling on the Highest Ideals

MEDITATION on the saintliness of saintly men must be supplemented by meditation on angels, as the representatives of the unseen world, if we are to feel the full extent of the communion of saints.

We cannot, it is true, presume to press such meditations into detail. It is enough if we recognise the service, the sympathy, of the host of heaven.

We must, as far as we may be able, both in public service and in private thought, present and dwell upon the greatest facts, the greatest aspects of things, the greatest truths, refusing to rest upon the transitory and temporal, if we are to realise, as we can do, the communion of saints, the fulness of the manifestation of the spiritual life, and its eternal power.

A hymn-book is a confession of the communion of saints.

There is, indeed, a danger as well as a use in the contemplation of great ideals. If they lift us for a while above the strife of details, they may unfit us for dealing with the concrete questions which arise in daily work.

But this ideal of our spiritual life, seen in its many parts, through the ages and everywhere around us, made our own by the communion of saints, seems to me to be most practical in its influence.

The one ground of union is the possession of a common life, and not any nicely calculated scheme of compromise. To see the life even from afar, to look towards it, is in some degree to reach a serener atmosphere, to feel the true proportion of things, to gain the earnest of an interpretation of the mysteries by which we are perplexed.

The thought of a life eternal, underlying, so to speak, the fleeting phenomena of sense, not future so much as shrouded, is characteristic of Christianity; it is included in the fact of the Incarnation, and it meets our present distress and disharmony with a message of hope.

Most of us will remember the magnificent myth in the *Phædrus*, in which Plato seeks to explain the origin of the highest forces in our earthly being. On stated days human souls, he says, follow in the train of the gods, and rising above the world, gaze on the eternal and absolute. It is only by strenuous and painful endeavour that they can gain for a brief space the vision, which is the appointed food of diviner natures. Then they fall to earth, and their bodily life corresponds with the range and clearness of the celestial impressions which they retain. So they recognise about them during their earthly sojourn the images of higher things, and again strive upwards.

For us the revelation of Christ has made this dream a truth. In Him we see perfect sacrifice, perfect truth, perfect wisdom, perfect love; and having seen it, we can discern signs of His presence in them who shew His gifts. He gives unity, and they reveal to us His fulness. In our kinsmanship with them we welcome the pledge of a life which is beyond time.

Christianity meets the Needs of Man

CHRISTIANITY claims to be a Gospel; to offer to men that which answers to their needs; to disclose in a form available for life eternal truths which we are so constituted as to recognise, though we could not of ourselves discover them. Its verification, therefore, will lie in its essential character; in its fitness to fulfil this work, which is as broad as the world.

The religion which is able to bring peace at one stage of human development may be wholly ineffective at another.

When, therefore, we look for a religion which shall perfectly satisfy the needs of men, we look for one which is essentially fitted for the support of man as man.

Such a religion must have a vital energy commensurate with all conceivable human progress.

And yet again: the perfect religion must not only

have the power of dealing with man and men throughout the course of their manifold development; it must have the power of dealing with the complete fulness of life at any moment. It must have the present power of dealing with the problems of our being and of our destiny in relation to thought and to action and to feeling.

A perfect religion—a religion which offers a complete satisfaction to the religious wants of man—must be able to meet the religious wants of the individual, the society, the race, in the complete course of their development and in the manifold intensity of each separate human faculty.

This being so, I contend that the faith in Christ, born, crucified, risen, ascended, forms the basis of this perfect religion; that it is able, in virtue of its essential character, to bring peace in view of the problems of life under every variety of circumstance and character—to illuminate, to develop, and to inspire every human faculty.

My contention rests upon the recognition of the two marks by which Christianity is distinguished from every other religion. It is absolute and it is historical.

Christianity is not a theory, a splendid guess, but a proclamation of facts.

Nothing in the whole realm of nature can be alien from man, who gathers to himself an epitome of nature; nothing, therefore, is incapable of sharing in the consecration and transfiguration by which he is ennobled.

The Incarnation and the Resurrection reconcile the two characteristics of our faith; they establish the right of Christianity to be called historical, they establish its right to be called absolute.

Our Need of Light satisfied by Christ

THERE is not, I think, a more impressive image in literature than that in which Dr. Newman describes the first effect of the world upon the man who looks there for tokens of the presence of God. "It is," he says, "as if I looked in a mirror and saw no reflection of my own face." This is the first, the natural effect.

But the record of the life of Christ, the thought of the presence of Christ, changes all. Christ, as He lived and lives, justifies our highest hope. He opens depths of vision below the surface of things. He transforms suffering; He shews us the highest aspirations of our being satisfied through a way of sorrow. He redresses the superficial inequalities of life by revealing its eternal glory. He enables us to understand how, being what we are, every grief and every strain of sensibility can be made in Him contributory to the working out of our common destiny.

Let us once feel that the anguish of creation is indeed the travail-pain of a new birth, as Scripture teaches, and we shall be strengthened to bear and to wait.

Our Need of an Ideal satisfied by Christ

AS men—as men in our essential constitution, and not only as fallen men—we need an ideal which may move us to effort.

It is generally agreed that the type of character presented to us in the Gospels is the highest which we can fashion. The person of the Lord meets us at every point in our strivings, and discloses something to call out in us loftier endeavour.

In Him we discover in the most complete harmony

all the excellencies which are divided, not unequally, between man and woman.

In Him we can recognise the gift which has been entrusted to each one of us severally, used in its true relation to the other endowments of humanity. He enters into the fulness of life, and makes known the value of each detail of life.

Christ offers an Ideal for us, for all Men and for all Time

AND what He does for us He does for all men and for all time. There is nothing in the ideal which He offers which belongs to any particular age or class or nation.

He stands above all and unites all. That which was local or transitory in the circumstances under which He lived, in the controversies of rival sects, in the struggles of patriotism, in the isolation of religious pride, leaves no colour in His character. All that is abiding, all that is human, is there without admixture, in that eternal energy which man's heart can recognise in its time of trial.

So it is that the person of the Lord satisfies the requirement of growth which belongs to the religious nature of man. Our sense of His perfections grows with our own moral advance. We see more of His beauty as our power of vision is disciplined and purified. The slow unfolding of life enables us to discern new meaning in His presence. In His humanity is included whatever belongs to the consummation of the individual and of the race not only in one stage, but in all stages of progress, not only in regard to some endowments, but in regard to the whole inheritance of our nature, enlarged by the most vigorous use while the world lasts.

We in our weakness and littleness, confine our

thoughts from generation to generation, now to this fragment of His fulness and now to that; but it is, I believe, true without exception in every realm of man's activity, true in action, true in literature, true in art, that the works which receive the most lasting homage of the soul are those which are most Christian; and that it is in each the Christian element, the element which answers to the fact of the Incarnation, to the fellowship of God with man as an accomplished reality of the present order, which attracts and holds our reverence. In the essence of things it cannot be otherwise. Our infirmity alone enfeebles the effect of the truth which we have to embody.

Our Need of Power satisfied by Christ

NO accumulation of failures can destroy the sense of our destiny. But alone in ourselves, as we look back sadly, we confess that we have no new resource of strength for the future, as we have no ability to undo the past. The loftiest souls, apart from Christ, recognise that they were made for an end which "naturally" is unattainable.

This need brings into prominence the supreme characteristic of the Faith. Christ meets the acknowledgment of individual helplessness with the offer of fellowship. He reveals union with Himself, union with God, and union with man in Him, as the spring of power, and the inspiration of effort.

The Solution of the Problem of Essence

IT has been excellently laid down by one who was not of us that "the solution of the problem of essence, of the questions, Whence? What? and Whither? must be in a life and not in a book."

He who said, "I came forth from the Father, and am

come into the world; again, I leave the world, and go to the Father," illuminated the words by actions which made known the divine original and the divine destiny of man.

The Happiness of the whole the Happiness of all

POLITICIANS aim at "the greatest happiness of the greatest number," but we have a surer and wider principle for our guidance, that the happiness of the whole is the happiness of all.

Christians Believers in a living, a speaking God

WE are, we must be, as believers in Christ, in the presence of a living, that is, of a speaking God. Nothing, indeed, can be added to the facts of the Gospel, but all history and all nature is the commentary upon them. And the loftiest conceptions of human destiny and human duty cannot but be quickened and raised by the message which reaches through the finite to the infinite, through time to eternity: "In the beginning was the Word, and the Word was with God, and the Word was God. . . . And the Word became flesh, and tabernacled among us."

The Canon of Scripture

THE question of the Canon of Holy Scripture has assumed at the present day a new position in Theology. The Bible can no longer be regarded merely as a common storehouse of controversial weapons, or an acknowledged exception to the rules of literary criticism. Modern scholars, from various motives, have distinguished its constituent parts, and shewn in what way each was related to the peculiar circumstances of its origin.

Christianity has gained by the issue; for it is an unspeakable advantage that the Books of the New Testament are now seen to be organically united with the lives of the Apostles: that they are recognised as living monuments, reared in the midst of struggles within and without by men who had seen Christ, stamped with the character of their age, and inscribed with the dialect which they spoke: that they are felt to be a *product* as well as a *source* of spiritual life.

Their true harmony can only be realised after a perception of their distinct peculiarities.

It cannot be too often repeated that the history of the formation of the whole Canon involves little less than the history of the building of the Catholic Church.

The Bible is for us the sum of prophetic and Apostolic literature, but that is not its essential characteristic. It contains "all that concerns Christ" in the same sense in which the Gospel contains all the teaching of Christ. The completeness in each case is not absolute but relative to the work which is to be accomplished.

The Bible justifies our loftiest Aspirations

NO one who regards with calm, open eyes the superficial prospect of the world can fail to feel its sadness. That which we hold to be the highest truth is to a great extent unknown, or defaced by corruptions, or discredited by divisions. We are met on every side by signs of what appears to be inevitable waste, incompleteness, suffering. We look within, and find in our own souls the fruits and the elements of a conflict which make the attainment of peace by our own power impossible except at the price of insensibility. We look without upon society, and we find there reproduced upon a large scale the passions, the selfishness, the ambitions, the pains, by which we ourselves are distracted. We look on nature, and as we look we learn to recognise that in "meadow, grove, and stream" there is beneath the smiling surface a fierce and unending struggle for existence which in some sense makes the whole earth a tomb. If what we see with our feeble powers, our transitory experience, were all, we might well despair. To man, using his own faculties only, the present, as far as I can judge, offers no prospect of a future more bright than the chequered past. The certainty of change brings no assurance of progress.

But in spite of every discouragement we cling to the trust with which we were born. Even when the last conclusions of despondency are forced upon us by the facts of life, the heart will not surrender its loftiest aspirations.

And the Bible justifies them. The Bible, in which we can see human life, the simplest and the loftiest, penetrated by a Divine life, gives us as an abiding possession that which nature and the soul shew only far off for a brief moment, to withdraw it again from the gaze of the inquirer—the vision of a Divine Presence.

The Bible discloses to us behind the veil of phenomena something more than sovereign law, something more than absolute being.

It may for long ages be silent as to the future, but from the beginning to the end it is inspired by the eternal.

It places man face to face with God from the first symbolic scene in the Garden of Eden to the last symbolic scene in the New Jerusalem.

It enables us to discern with spiritual perception One who is not loving only but Love, One from Whose will all creation flows, and to Whose purpose it answers, *of Whom and through Whom and unto Whom are all things.*

In a word, the Bible writes hope over the darkest fields of life. Man needs hope above all things; and the Bible is the charter of hope, the message of the God of revelation, Who alone is *the God of hope*.

For us it is the view which the Bible gives of His forbearance and long-suffering; of His compassionate and gentle dealing with the rude, the ignorant, and the erring; of His large counsels, whereby all faithful though imperfect labour is made to minister to His service, which keeps our hope freshest in the face of our own trials.

We are for the most part busily occupied with the cares, the problems, the lessons of our own place and time.

The range of our activity tends to limit the range of our interest. We yield to the temptation of forgetting the great deserts of barbarism which are spread over the face of the earth—the long ages of dull monotony which represent the life of many peoples. But those dreary spaces also belong to the history of that one body of mankind in which we are members, of that planet which was the scene of the Incarnation.

Each period of silence, the most unbroken in its awful stillness, is part of the education of the world. As we look upon the spectacle—the long discipline, fruitful in its manifold complexity; the glorious issue, prevailing in its infinite sorrows—there comes to us a joy proportioned to the vast blanks which we have felt.

The Biblical interpretation of pre-Christian history reveals to us the law of God's dealing with men in the present.

And so we in our day of trial gain strength to wait in the presence of ends unattained, and as yet unattainable.

Humanity is not a splendid ruin, deserted by the great King Who once dwelt within its shrine, but a living body, racked, maimed, diseased, it may be, but stirred by noble thoughts which cannot for ever be in vain.

Hope is the child of sympathy and faith, born not without pain.

That we might have hope—hope for the single soul, hope for the body to which we inseparably belong; hope for the creation committed to our care—fair under conditions of decay; hope for honest thought in the contemplation of solemn problems; hope for courageous action in the presence of aggressive evil; the infinite hope which we need, and which, as far as I see, we cannot find elsewhere.

Every fragment of human life will illuminate the teaching of the Bible, and no single race can exhaust it.

That which the light of language and the monuments of antiquity did in the sixteenth century to illuminate the sacred writings and shew their power on the individual conscience, the light of science in its widest sense, and the broader apprehension of history, promise to do now.

Symptoms converge from every side to shew that our own race and our own country is being called to fulfil the evangelic charge for which material prosperity, wide dominion, social freedom, unbroken national development, have been only the preparation.

PART II

The Christian Society: its Office
and Growth

THE CHRISTIAN SOCIETY: ITS OFFICE AND GROWTH

The two Empires—the Church and the World

THE coincidence of the establishment of the Roman Empire with the rise of Christianity has always attracted the attention of modern historians.

Christianity was destined by its very nature not to save but to destroy the Empire: at the same time their outward correspondence was not less full of meaning. All that was progressive in the old world was united under one supreme head at the time when the new faith was revealed which should bind the universe together in a sovereign unity.

Peace won by arms ushered in Him who revealed the peace of life in God.

The Failure of the Empire and the Victory of the Church

SO it was that the only two powers which have claimed absolute dominion over mankind appeared together. For three centuries each followed the necessary law of its development. Then at last the Empire was seen to have failed; and the Church was seen to contain the forces which could regenerate and rule the world. Diocletian, when he finally organised the old power of the State with the greatest political genius, gave the occasion for the concentration of the power of the Church, and prepared the way for its victory.

The Gospel essentially the Proclamation of a Kingdom

THE message of the Gospel was essentially the proclamation of a Kingdom, "a Kingdom of heaven," "a Kingdom of God," "a Kingdom of the Son of Man."

The coming of a Kingdom was the keynote of the preaching of John the Baptist and of Christ Himself.

The disciples were "the sons of the Kingdom." As a King Christ died. During the great forty days He spoke of "the things pertaining to the Kingdom." When the faith was first carried beyond the limits of Judæa, Philip announced to Samaria "the Gospel of the Kingdom of God." The burden of St. Paul's first teaching in Europe was that there was "another King than Cæsar, even Jesus." The same Apostle, when he sums up his work, describes himself as having gone about "preaching the Kingdom of God"; and the last glimpse which is given of his labours at Rome shews him there still preaching the Kingdom.

Everywhere the same idea is prominent in the history of the Acts and in the Apostolic letters. At one time it excites the hostility of unbelievers; at another time it gives occasion to mistaken hopes in Christians. But however the truth was misrepresented and misunderstood, however much it gave occasion to unjust attacks and visionary expectations, it was still held firmly. The idea may have grown somewhat unfamiliar to us now, but it is clearly impressed upon the New Testament.

The two Empires compared

IT is quite true to say that two Empires, two social organisations, designed to embrace the whole world, started together in the first century. The one appeared in the completeness of its form: the other only in the first embodiment of the vital principle which included all after-growth. But the two Empires had nothing in common except their point of departure and their claim to universality. In principle, in mode of action, in sanctions, in scope, in history, they offer an absolute contrast. The Roman Empire was essentially based on positive law; it was maintained by force; it appealed to outward well-doing; it aimed at producing external co-operation or conformity. The Christian Empire was no less essentially based on faith: it was propagated and upheld by conviction: it lifted the thoughts and working of men to that which was spiritual and eternal: it strove towards the manifold exhibition of one common life. The history of the Roman Empire is from the first the history of a decline and fall, checked by many noble efforts and many wise counsels, but still inevitable. The history of the Christian Empire is from the first the history of a victorious progress, stayed and saddened by frequent faithlessness and self-seeking, but still certain and assured though never completed.

The necessary Collision between Christianity and Roman Law

IF a distinct conception be formed of what Christianity is, it will be evident that a sincere and zealous pagan could not but persecute it.

Christianity came forward as a universal religion. It could not take a place as one among many; and this was the utmost which ancient modes of thought could concede to it.

The idea of toleration as expressing a respect for personal conviction was utterly unknown to the statesmen of the old world. It found no clear expression in the new world till the seventeenth century. The toleration of the Empire was in effect not unlike toleration in Russia now: it accepted diversities which had established themselves by actual existence, but it allowed no change away from the national faith.

The national religion was a part of the historical development and habits of the nation, a mode of expressing certain thoughts and convictions which could no more be changed than language.

Nothing struck the apologists with more amazement than the first natural consequence which followed from this difference between the Christian and heathen conceptions of religion. They saw the popular gods held up to mockery upon the stage, degraded in the works of poets, ridiculed by philosophers, and they could not reconcile such license and sarcasm with resolute devotion. But to the polytheist of the empire—and to all later polytheists—the offices of worship were an act of public duty and not of private confession. Outward conformity in act was owed to the State, complete freedom in opinion and word was allowed to the worshipper. There was no complete and necessary correspondence between the form and the thought.

With the Christian it was otherwise. His religion was the expression of his soul. So it was that the Christian confessor would make no compromise. This phenomenon was a novel one; and we can see in the records of the martyrdoms how utterly the magistrates were incapable of understanding the difficulty which Christians felt in official conformity. In their judgment it was perfectly consistent with religious faith to drop the morsel of incense on the fire, and still retain allegiance to Christ.

All that they required was the appearance of obedience and not the distinct expression of conviction. "Have regard for thy gray hairs" or "for thy tender youth" was the common appeal of a merciful judge, who failed to apprehend that the faith of the Christian like his own being was one.

"What harm is it to say, 'O Lord Cæsar,' and to sacrifice and be saved?" was the well-meant expostulation which was addressed to Polycarp on his way to trial.

The Early Christians' Position one of continued Protest

THE pagan temples were to Christians like unclean sepulchres, of which they were tempted to shew their loathing openly. Though *Origen* condemns such conduct as lawless and rude, it is easy to see that zeal would often be carried beyond the limits of reason and good order.

Heathenism, indeed, was so mixed up with the ordinary routine of society and home, that the believer would be forced to stand in the position of continued protest. The proceedings of the courts, the public ceremonies, the ordinary amusements, were more or less connected with idolatrous forms or observances. The smoking altar constantly called for some sign of abhorrence. The universal presence of the images of the gods made watchful caution a necessity for the believer. The common language of familiar conversation often required a disclaimer of the superstition on which it was framed.

The History of Nations and the History of the Church

THE history of nations is but an episode in the history of the Church. They perish, but she lives on. They furnish the materials, and she constructs with them fresh sanctuaries for the service of her Lord. They fulfil their special office in developing the powers of man, and she gathers into her stores the abiding fruits of their experience.

The material magnificence of power and conquest bears in itself the seeds of its decay; it is exhaustible because it is earthly: but the spiritual progress of which it is the occasion is an eternal force.

There may be times of storm and times of sunshine, but the Christian society still grows with a growth which man is equally unable to originate and to destroy. The Gospel continues to leaven, however slowly in our eyes, the whole mass of life.

I will not leave you comfortless; I come to you. The words have been fulfilled at each crisis in the progress of the Church, and we believe they are being fulfilled still. Christ came to His own aforetime, now in this form and now in that, when His Presence seemed to be most sorely needed. And as we read the marvellous history, we *know* that He will not leave us bereaved of His love.

Faithlessness can exist only if we seek to measure the might of Christianity by our ability to use it.

The larger teaching of the past, which we too commonly forget, has promises of unfailing power.

Roughly speaking, the history of Christendom, up to the Reformation, falls into four periods of nearly equal length. The close of each period was followed by a time of danger and progress, of suffering and new-birth, and each reveals to us a presence of Christ.

The first crisis was the conquest of the Empire. Three centuries of conflict and persecution had disciplined the growing vigour of the Church, and the moment of anticipated freedom was the moment of peril. The Church was in danger of being imperialised. An unbaptized Emperor preached to his courtiers, and presided at the council which he called. If his policy had prevailed, Christianity might have become mainly an instrument of government, or even a modified adaptation of polytheism.

Athanasius

ATHANASIUS, a greater hero than Constantine, arose. His life was one long battle. Cast down, betrayed, exiled, he fought on. For forty-six years he knew no peace, and to human judgment the conflict was unequal. "Athanasius was against the world, and the world against him."

But Athanasius triumphed. He triumphed over the court with the policy of a statesman; he triumphed over his persecutors with the endurance of a martyr. He lived for the truth, and it is scarcely too much to say that the truth lived through him. He vindicated the inheritance of Faith. He maintained the independence of the Church. He vanquished the spirit as well as the form of Paganism. He handed down to us, in the Nicene Creed, the words which shape our earliest thoughts by the measure of Divine Faith.

But imperialism was not the only danger of the time.

There was the opposite peril of isolation. Recoiling from the semblance of worldly compliance, some sought to establish an exclusive society of saints. They soon found occasion for their efforts, and an adversary to defeat them.

Augustine

WHEN Athanasius died at Alexandria, Augustine was still a brilliant student in the schools of Carthage. For fourteen years afterwards he laboured for the knowledge which seemed to fly from him, and he gathered unconsciously that rich harvest of manifold experience which gave him in his later age his depth of sensibility and his energy of command.

Athanasius, with the subtle wisdom of a Greek philosopher, had marked out the true conception of Redemption in relation to God.

Augustine, with the moral sagacity of a Roman jurist, determined its relation to man.

Athanasius had shewn that the Church was no function or creature of the State. Augustine shewed that potentially the Church was co-extensive with the world. The one laid open the principles of its life; the other the conditions of its existence.

And so the Christian society was prepared to meet the storms which were already gathering around it.

Columban and Boniface

At the end of three centuries of barbarian desolation in the West, the Church found herself face to face with a new world.

The arms of her former warfare were powerless now. There was need of sterner, ruder champions to bear her standard into the camp and the forest, of heralds cast in the mould of Elijah or John the Baptist; and they were not wanting. A fresh field was open, and fresh labourers were ready to enter it: men not tutored in the wisdom of Alexandria or the policy of Rome, but unwearied in the devotion of enterprise, and fearless in the consciousness of self-conquest.

It is perhaps the worthiest of our boasts that our own islands supplied them; and even to the present day we 'can see, in the libraries of Germany and Switzerland and Italy, the Bibles which those great missionaries carried with them on their holy work.

Two stand out as the representatives of their class—Columban the witness and Boniface the preacher.

Trained in the peaceful stillness of an Irish cloister, Columban felt, at last, after years of silent study, "a fire kindled in his breast." "It was wrong," he said, "to look to his own good rather than seek the welfare of others." And with twelve companions he crossed over to the wildernesses of Gaul.

A legendary miracle may serve as the symbol of his life.

As he walked one day through a wood in prayer, suddenly, it is said, a pack of wolves appeared on his right hand and on his left. He stood undismayed and cried, "O Lord, be Thou my shield: O Lord, haste Thee to help me."

The hungry beasts still rushed on, and already touched his dress; and then, as if stricken by his presence, swept by and returned to the depths of the forest.

Such, in fact, was Columban's position always, and almost such his power. The savage chiefs were awed by the grandeur of his supreme self-sacrifice. Kings sought his presence and trembled at his reproof.

He stood among wild and lawless warriors, a witness to an unseen power greater than that of earth; an apostle of a spiritual service harder than their own; speaking with a stern majesty of acts which appealed to their senses, and awakening hopes not quenched by the battle or the feast. He was himself his message, and that message of a life found many to welcome it. Before he died, though baffled and exiled, he knew the truth of his own words: "Whoever overcomes himself treads the world under foot."

Boniface was a man of broader activity. To the victorious asceticism of the Irish Columban he added the earnest laboriousness of a Saxon nature. There was even in him something of that adventurous daring which made the worthies of his native Devon famous in after times. But all he had, and all he was, he offered to God; and the sacrifice was turned to the noblest uses.

Near Geismar, in Hesse-Cassel, there was a giant oak, sacred to Thor, and hallowed by ancient superstition. Boniface determined to overthrow it, and with it the dread of the ancient idols which lingered among his converts. In the presence of a trembling crowd he smote the trunk, and a sudden blast from heaven completed the work which he had begun. Thereupon he gathered the shattered fragments, and with them built a Chapel to St. Peter. In that act of pious transformation lay the secret of his successful work. He used what he found for God.

And his death shewed the secret of his devoted life. On an appointed day his converts were to come together to him from all quarters for confirmation. In their stead a host of armed heathen appeared, sworn to take vengeance on the enemy of their gods. The friends of Boniface prepared resistance, but he forbade them. "For a long time," he said, "I have earnestly desired this day. Be strong in the Lord, and bear with thankful endurance whatever His grace sends. Hope in Him, and He will save your souls." And having so said, he received the crown of martyrdom, about twenty years after Charles Martel had driven back for ever the hosts of Saracens upon the plain of Tours.

Francis of Assisi

THUS the West was won to Christianity, and through four centuries was moulded by its sovereign power. The

Empire and the Papacy grew side by side; the strength of feudalism was matched with the strength of the Church; and again it seemed as if the Gospel would be lost in the triumph of its messengers.

At the beginning of the thirteenth century Innocent III., the greatest of the Popes, dispensed the crowns of Europe at his will. Bishops vied in state with the loftiest nobles. Churchmen marked out the channels within which thought was directed for four centuries. On every side those cathedrals were rising which it is the highest ambition of later art to imitate. But the poor —the truest representatives of Christ—were forgotten.

With the peril came also the remedy. In the crisis of popular desolation Francis of Assisi claimed Poverty as his bride, "whom none," he said, "had chosen for his own since Christ Himself." And in the assurance of his choice he carried glad tidings to the neglected and the outcast. A vision had revealed to him that he should be a soldier, and he found that his post was in Christ's army. A heavenly voice had charged him to repair the falling Church, and he knew at last that his labour was with the spiritual fabric.

His character united the opposite traits of intense idealism and intense realism. He was a rigid ascetic, and at the same time he cherished the deepest sense of the beauty of all that God had made. He had the truest loathing of sin, and yet his soul melted with tenderness towards the most abject and the most fallen. He felt the fulness of actual communion with Heaven, and yet he would take to himself no title but that of a servant.

He translated, in a word, the practical Christian virtues into visible facts. He was in every act a type of poverty and obedience, of purity and love. He offered to the simplicity of the Middle Ages a sensible image of the two commandments—the love to God and the love to our neighbour—which they could not fail to understand.

He spoke to his own age, and his voice was the voice of blessing.

Loyola, Luther, Calvin, Cranmer

TIME went on, and in the sixteenth century the conditions of life were changed. The tutelage of the nations came to an end. The Church had lived through the crises of imperialism, of barbarism, of supremacy. It had to face the crisis of freedom. The revival of learning had enlarged and multiplied the domains of thought. The invention of printing had extended the circle of students and scholars. The development of industry and the accumulation of wealth had consolidated states, and impressed them with peculiar characters. The outward unity of the Empire was finally broken, and with it the outward unity of the Church.

But men were not wanting to carry forward in every direction the manifold applications of the one Faith. Loyola, Luther, Calvin, and wisest, perhaps, of all, our own Cranmer, saw the wants of their age and of their countries, and in various ways, and with frequent failures, laboured to satisfy them.

We may shrink from many of their conclusions: we may condemn many of their acts: we may deplore the bitterness of their controversies, and grieve over the inheritance of division which they have bequeathed to us, but still no one can deny that we owe to them, to the vehement expression of their convictions, to the startling individuality of their faith, a larger view of the capacities of Christianity, a truer sense of its adaptation to every variety of thought, a more absolute confidence in its vital energy, than was ever granted to any earlier age. Even in the day of apparent humiliation and failure Christ did not *leave His people desolate*, but *came to them*, not in one form but in many, as their eyes were opened to see Him.

A Crisis at Hand

IF we may trust the cycles of the past, it would seem that we are, in this our day, close upon another crisis, and that even now our Lord is waiting to reveal Himself to us.

In what shape He will reveal Himself we cannot tell, but yet we feel dimly that the revelation will be more glorious than any yet made known. This confidence lies in the conditions under which we live.

It is the characteristic of our time that it offers an epitome of all history in the present varieties of national life.

Thus there is no past age to which we can look back for the one type of our labour. There is no past age which we can neglect as wholly obsolete in its teaching.

There is room among us now for the vital dogmatism of Athanasius and Augustine; for the stern and fearless zeal of Columban and Boniface; for the imperial soul of Innocent; for the loving asceticism of Francis; for the varied energy of the Reformers.

The work of to-day is not for one nation, but for all; and therefore it is that the exclusive passion of patriotism is tempered with a wider sympathy among peoples.

The Gospel of to-day is addressed to men not of one form of civilisation only, but of many; and therefore it is that the manifold grace of God has now the widest application.

The Church of Christ calls all to active service, and

welcomes all with each power they bring. Every variety of intellect may find its scope. Every diversity of gift may find its consecration.

Samuel a type of the Teacher of our Day

SPEAK, Lord, for thy servant heareth.

He who was a child and yet a prophet is a true figure of the priest of God in every age. He who was called to stand between the old and new is in an especial sense a figure of those who are sent forth to labour now, when we seem once again to draw near to a crisis in the history of the world.

The words sum up the true relation of the teacher to the One Source of wisdom. They are an expression of Faith, of Reverence, of Self-devotion.

They describe the spirit in which it becomes us as Christians to regard the speculative and civil movements through which articulate voices of the Lord come to us.

They will be to us a sure voice of encouragement in the chill darkness which precedes the dawn; a sure test of truth in the concourse of many cries.

Happy, thrice happy, will that teacher be who can gather himself up in each season of oppressive doubt with the assurance that God does speak; who can listen heedfully in the strength of that conviction to the wild strains of earthly music, to see if it may be that in them also there is mingled some melody from heaven.

The last utterance of God is not yet spoken to the world. We can look without misgiving upon the darkness which rests here and there upon the field of life, and acknowledge with grateful faith that the facts by which we live, the facts by which the world lives, like the heaven from which they come, overarch our farthest prospect and, as we advance, crown some remote region with a fulness of glory.

From century to century, terms, phrases, whole passages of the written Revelation gain in breadth of meaning as men grow in largeness of experience and in capacity of vision.

It is not that the sense of the Scriptures is changed, but that they are felt to be more luminous as we gain fresh power to bear the light.

Nothing is lost of that which has been once found in them, but partial interpretations are taken up, absorbed, transfigured, in others which embrace a little wider range.

The Substance of our Historic Belief Inexhaustible

THE Christian teacher should from the first keep alive in himself, that he may keep it alive in others, the sense of the indefeasible vitality of his creed.

He must think and speak as one who is charged with the interpretation of a life to which every other form of being ministers, and not with the mere reiteration of stereotyped clauses.

He must watch and listen as knowing that every word which he has received has force within it to draw to itself new vigour from each conquest of inquiry.

The experience of our own personal progress shews how it is so. Christ is always the same, eternal, unchangeable. We confess Him in the same words from childhood to youth, from youth to manhood, from manhood to age, and yet do we not all know that the Holy Spirit which the Father sends in His name—*in His name*, let us treasure up the marvellous promise—enables us to apprehend better what the confession of those truths signifies as we gain worthier notions of ourselves and of the world and of God?

Thus the course of our brief lives helps us to see that we must hold fast alike the absolute immutability of the principle of life in the Church, and the manifold progress of the manifestations of life.

Just as that which we each call "I" remains unchanged through all the vicissitudes of our material and moral being, so is it with the presence of Christ by the Spirit in that vaster body which He quickens through all its growth.

The truth was perceived when as yet it had gained but little illustration. Every one is familiar with the famous description of catholic belief: "quod semper, quod ubique, quod ab omnibus." And there is another passage of the book from which this sentence is taken which, though it is less known, is far more fruitful in its application.

In answer to the question whether there is any progress in the Christian religion, Vincent replies :—

"There is, and that enormous. . . . For who would wish men so ill . . . as to seek to hinder it? But it is a true progress and not a change. . . . The understanding, the scientific knowledge, the wisdom alike of individual Christians and of the whole Church, must grow and advance greatly from age to age, though the truth which they maintain does not lose its identity. . . . The ancient doctrines of the heavenly philosophy cannot without profanation be altered or mutilated, but they may in process of time be shaped with greater care and delicacy. They may gain clearness, light, definiteness, while they necessarily retain their fulness, their integrity, their essential character."

The words thus briefly paraphrased are remarkable words, and the events of fourteen hundred years have witnessed to their truth. The sixth, the ninth, the thirteenth, and sixteenth centuries have seen Christianity draw strength from what seemed to be danger. So will it be, if we are faithful, in the nineteenth.

How, indeed, can it be otherwise? For it is the glory of our historic Faith to have reunited in a sacramental bond the visible and the invisible, and, therefore, every advance in the knowledge of Nature, every lesson in the course of human affairs, must add something to our power of realising the things which we most certainly believe.

Progress not a Development but an Illumination

THE progress which we desire, as being permanent and fruitful, comes from bringing our creed, as we are encouraged to do, into the bracing air and bright sunshine of life.

The result is not so much a development as an illumination.

It is not that anything new is added to the original treasures of revelation, but that which was latent is realised.

Each great word, even the greatest, as man, and world, and God, and sin, and grace, becomes charged with new associations, enriched with new wealth of thought, tested by new trials of labour and suffering, and so fitted to carry on one degree farther the victories of Faith.

In the confidence that this great law will be realised through his ministry, the Christian teacher will approach his work. Strange and startling voices may sound about him. Once and again he may be tempted to believe that they are only of the earth, earthy. But in the end, if he give heed to the lessons of the past, he will take heart to stand, though it be alone and in the gloom, and answer without impatience and without distrust, *Speak, Lord, for Thy servant heareth.*

God Speaking to us

I BELIEVE that God is speaking to us as He has not spoken to men for four centuries; and I believe that there is great danger lest we neglect His voice.

We are absorbed in our own interests and perils, and we fail to see that there is being accomplished around us a revolution in the conditions of thought, a revolution in the conditions of action, which, if unheeded now, will sooner or later shake our Faith to its foundations.

But I believe no less surely that we can shew that even here Christianity is in advance of the latest generalisations of science, and able, in virtue of what we know, to shape to noble issues the latent aspirations and tendencies of men.

All that is required of us is that we should turn once again to the first records of the Gospel and read there lessons which, in the order of God's providence, could not be read till this generation.

Let me endeavour to illustrate my meaning by two examples, one from speculation and the other from life.

There is, I suppose, no more characteristic result of physical research than the growing sense of the intimate

THE FAITH ONE AND PROGRESSIVE

connection of all forms of being one with another, of the continuity and solidarity of existence, of the dependence of man upon man and upon the world.

As these facts are put forward they are often made to appear antagonistic to the Faith; and the over-hasty zeal of believers accepts the false interpretation.

But what is the case? From the beginning of the Bible to the end, from the record of the making of the heavens and the earth in Genesis to the vision of the new heaven and the new earth in the Apocalypse, the mysterious unity of creation is shadowed forth.

Every political student, whether in hope, or fear, or simple acquiescence, points to the fact that the whole current of affairs is setting towards democracy.

I accept the conclusion without discussing it; and what then? If it be true, I see in it an opportunity for the greatest work which the Church of Christ has ever been summoned to do.

No other power can deal efficiently with the problems which will arise out of democratic society, because no other power can take account of man as man, in all his strength and in all his weakness, as one who is heir of time and heir of eternity.

In the Middle Ages Christianity was the effectual protector of the poor, and it has not yet lost the virtue by which it can interpret and fulfil their wants.

Even now our Faith alone can give an intelligible meaning to the triple watchword which for three generations has charmed them with vain hopes.

Liberty, Equality, Fraternity

FOR us Christians, if only we have strength given us to learn and to teach the lesson, Liberty is the power of complete obedience to the true law of our nature: Equality is the recognition of one life in which we all share, and to the perfection of which each owes all: Fraternity is the devout acknowledgment of a common Father.

No dream of civil reorganisation can go beyond the life which would follow naturally from the acceptance of the Gospel which we are charged to proclaim. And no motives to stir men to sacrifice, to love, to faith, can be found elsewhere equal to those which flow from the thoughts of Bethlehem and of Calvary and of Olivet.

Even Fragments of Truth to be Embraced

THE foremost leaders of change use language which is for the most part repellent by its one-sidedness and want of sympathy. But let no fastidiousness rob you of their instruction, and no prejudice blind you to their contributions to the sum of knowledge.

Watch for the smallest fragment of truth wherever you can discover it, and embrace it as your own.

"Let posterity welcome as understood that which antiquity reverenced when not understood. Still teach the same that you have learnt, and avoid novelty of essence when you adopt novelty of form" (Vincent of Lerins).

Be sure that the voices of God are not yet withdrawn from the world; and be prepared to interrogate His messengers importunately, even if they come to you in strange disguises.

The fashion of the world changes: forms of thought and language and polity come and go: but He in Whom we live binds all together.

Neither we nor our Fathers have Exhausted the Treasury of God

IT has been hitherto the Divine purpose to bring men to a knowledge of the one infinite, eternal, unchanging truth little by little in manifold ways.

So it was that under the Old Testament the faithful were led to regard the unity of God not as the basis of a petrified monotheism, like that of Islam, but as the pledge of a supreme Fatherhood which, starting from the reality of a personal covenant, could find its consummation and crown only in the Incarnation.

So it has been that under the New Testament the Church has been guided by the Spirit, which came in Christ's name, to larger and deeper conceptions of the significance of the revelation of the Son, which grows more luminous with each fresh access of knowledge, because it corresponds with the fulness of all life and with the results of all history.

Age after age has seen the dawn brighten; but we dare not think that we gaze even now upon the perfect day.

Much has been made clear already; but much—how much we do not know—remains to be made clear. And when we thank God most devoutly that He has been pleased to endow us in our island home with all the gathered wealth of the past, we cannot but pray in the very outpouring of our gratitude that He will accomplish through others that which we are unable to achieve.

We with our history, our position, our faculties, cannot arrogate to ourselves to be the measure of the truth. What we have received and experienced is, as it ought to be, inexpressibly precious to us; by that we live and work; but neither we nor our fathers have exhausted the treasury of God.

We may see distinctly, but we do not see all; and we are not constituted to see all.

Greek and Roman and Teuton have been enabled to interpret each some fragment of the unchanging Gospel; but the interpretation will not be complete till every race has done its part, and the witness of the nations gives universality to the confession of the Church.

The Present Crisis

NEVER has there been a crisis when there was greater need of a vital apprehension of an ever-present, and yet ever-coming Advocate; never has there been a crisis when the temptation to deny His efficient energy was stronger; never has there been a crisis when the conflict between will and law has seemed to issue in more hopeless darkness; never has there been a crisis when faith clinging to the sacred past has faltered with more trembling steps upon the threshold of a new age.

The Mission of the East

AND while we doubt and shrink, the East is calling us with a million voices; and, as it calls, it promises in turn to bless.

For if we can in any way read the Eastern character, the peoples which have found in Brahminism, in Buddhism, in Mohammedanism, the natural satisfaction of their religious instincts, are fitted to seize and to enforce those lessons of the Incarnation which now ask for a preacher.

They have an intensity of feeling to meet our sternness of thought; they have a calm sense of dependence and community to meet our individualism; they have an instinct of self-surrender to meet our self-assertion, an intuition of totality to meet our fragmentary isolation.

Only let us extend to them our historic Gospel, embodied in the life of the Christian society, and in a brief space our Creed will grow radiant with a fresh glory by the light which they are fitted to cast upon it.

The Catholic Sovereignty of Christianity

WE have too often, perhaps, made ourselves and our own Church the one test of the fulness of the Gospel; we have imperilled the acceptance of Christ's message by substituting the partial for the universal; we have tried to fence round the definitions which correspond with our own spiritual apprehension beyond the possibility of growth.

But the experience of the Mission-field tends to correct, and has already corrected these dangerous limitations. In the face of new conditions of thought and life Christianity is seen to assert its catholic sovereignty.

Missions no Failure

NO one will venture any more to speak of the failure of Missions. Whether we look to India or to Newfoundland, to China or to the Southern Seas, we see that Christianity can still count her new martyrs, can still ennoble degraded races, can still make articulate, and satisfy, the deepest wants of souls.

And, as we look upon the world-wide field we shall learn to know better than we have yet known what is the magnificent sum of energies and instincts, of histories and actions, of services and sacrifices, which go to make up the unity of the Church.

When we look abroad we can see how forces which

are perilous in the close conflict and pressure of our own life may find elsewhere free scope for beneficent action.

There is, for example, no austerity of self-sacrifice which may not become fruitful service in India.

There is no simplicity of faith which may not be blessed to win the childlike races of Africa.

There is no wealth of thought and learning which may not be consecrated for the conviction of the Moslem.

In one place the Christian family best fulfils the work of the Evangelist; in another the lone brethren who are ready to go, bound to Christ only, whenever an opening can be made by heroic effort.

As the range of our vision is extended, we shall not only become more tolerant of variety, but we shall feel that variety is necessary.

Our Universities may inspire Missionary Effort

OUR universities are the proper homes of the loftiest aspirations, the meeting places of every power.

In them the past and the future are united in a life at once reverent and intense. Their very notes are continuity, catholicity, and progress. They cherish a contagiousness of enthusiasm to which all things are possible. They are prolific of opportunities for splendid achievement.

They can inspire our Missionaries with that power of a corporate life which gives to one man the strength of a thousand.

The Cambridge Missions at Delhi

THOSE who love Cambridge and are free to choose their field of labour, can serve her, I believe, better in

India than in England. Many dare to tell us that the religious character of the place is gone for ever. Whatever other answers may be given to the sentence, one will be beyond cavil, if men are ready at every call to accept work for Christ, however difficult, and however perilous, as the natural outcome of their University teaching. This we confidently ask; and in asking we bid those who hear us remember that they are sent not to hold a beleaguered fort but to win a kingdom.

We do wrong to the promise on which the Church rests when we interpret it of successful resistance, and not of irresistible advance. It is comparatively a poor thought that the power of Hades will not prevail over us: but the true thought of the promise is a thought of which we have not as yet appropriated the invigorating inspiration, even that the strongest citadel of evil shall not for ever keep out the triumphant hosts of the Cross.

"They shall bring the Glory and the Honour of the Nations into it"

WHEN the Prophet of the Apocalypse looked upon the Holy City of the new creation, he saw that there was no longer any temple there—that was the symbol at once of religious fellowship and religious separation—*for the Lord God Almighty is the Temple of it, and the Lamb:* he saw that it had no need of the sun—that was the symbol of the quickening energy of nature and the measure of time—*for the glory of God did lighten it, and the lamp thereof was the Lamb:* he saw *the nations* (not *the nations of them which are saved,* according to the gloss of the common texts) *walking in the light of it,* and so revealed in their true abiding power: he saw *the kings of the earth bring their glory into it,* offering, that is, each his peculiar treasures to complete the full measure of the manifested sovereignty of the Lord. This is the end; in this magnificent vision of faith the Church and the nations are at last revealed as one in the open presence of God. And meanwhile the promise is for our encouragement and for our guidance, as we strive to win for Christ the manifold homage of men.

The promise is characteristic of the Gospel.

Alone of all religions, Christianity deals with peoples no less than with individuals. The history of kingdoms no less than the history of souls contributes to our knowledge of its power.

If, as we believe, the dispensation of the Spirit is the revelation of Christ, then humanity in all its breadth and in all its diversity is the element through which the Spirit reveals Him; and nothing less than every different gift of every different race, the slowly-gathered thoughts of all the kindreds of the earth, tried, purified, hallowed, can represent to us adequately what He is as the Son of man, and enable us to feel what He has done *by whom and for whom all things were created.*

Mission-work, the Condition, the Sign, the Support of our Christian Growth

IN this aspect we can perhaps see most truly the meaning and the grandeur of mission-work. It is not simply a duty of Christian obedience; it is not simply the spontaneous energy of love. It is the condition, the sign, the support of our Christian growth. It is the power whereby we may hope to see our faith advance to ampler proportions and more perfect beauty. It is the ministry by which God directs us to make the natural endowments of alien races contributory to a deeper understanding of His counsels.

As it was in past time, so is it still. The Christians of the West had something to tell their Greek teachers. The Saxon Christians had something to tell the Roman missionaries. The Christians of India will, I cannot doubt, have something to tell us.

The Spiritual Problems of the East brought together in India

INDIA has been manifestly given to England. It is there that all the spiritual problems of the East are brought together.

The religious history of India is an epitome of the religious history of heathendom. The religions of India are the religions of the world. Every great aspiration of mankind has found an embodiment there, and with the same issue. Fragmentary truths have been made absolute, and in each case have become degraded.

The patriarchal faith of Zarathustra was arrested at its splendid dawn, and then sank into a lifeless ritual.

The simple Nature worship of the earliest Vedic hymns degenerated through progressive stages into gross polytheism.

The noble moral system of Buddhism was either extinguished on the scene of its earliest triumphs or supplemented by a service of demons.

Even the pure monotheism of Islam has now come to be known popularly among the Hindus as "saint-worship."

The ethnic religions have established, on a vast scale, that neither morality without a God nor a God without a mediator can finally satisfy the heart or the mind of man.

The Meaning of Mission-work in India

THROUGH corruptions and excesses Hinduism witnesses in different ways to the ideas of revelation, of sin, of retribution, of atonement, of fellowship. It offers, in an exaggerated shape, the controversies which have agitated Christendom on faith and works, on freewill and fate.

It witnesses to the fact that men are impelled to struggle heavenwards by self-sacrifice, and yet are no less driven to bring the gods down to earth to redress the evils of life.

In all these ways it enables us to feel how Christianity deals with enigmas which it does not create; how it answers to wants which we have not realised; how *the Holy Spirit, sent in Christ's name*, is still waiting to make known, in some new fashion, that the strangely-varied strivings of humanity after unity and peace, the unceasing endeavour to combine the idea of personality with the recognition of dependence, the invincible effort to embody the thought that in God *we live and move and have our being*, without destroying the sense of responsibility, are satisfied in the one fact of the Incarnation; that the conflict of action and worship, of the service of God and the service of men, of "the way of devotion" and "the way of works," are reconciled in the one grace of holiness.

For these problems of our own theology find a bold and even startling expression in the sacred books of Hinduism. Their presence gives vitality to the system; and not once or twice only efforts have been made to purify the old faiths from within, and to bring out of them satisfaction for the contrasted wants to which they witness.

But the great reformers have laboured to no purpose. If they clung to the idea of a historic connection of God

INDIAN MISSIONS 133

and man, their followers have been swept back into the excesses of superstition. If, as in the last movement of the kind, this idea is sacrificed, that is sacrificed by which Hinduism has triumphed; for Hinduism has had its triumphs. Twice it has been overpowered, and twice it has risen from defeat. It remains, then, for Christianity to reveal its sovereignty where Buddhism and Islam have failed.

This is the meaning of mission-work in India, and the charge is given to England, and to the English Church, to direct the conflict.

No charge—it is simple truth to say so—no charge was ever given to nation or to Church more momentous or more difficult.

The evangelisation of India is practically the evangelisation of Asia, the conquest of the world for Christ.

We need sympathy with castes which despise us as well as with castes which honour us; sympathy with untiring if undisciplined strivings after truth; sympathy with passionate if wild longings after a conformity to the likeness of God.

The Battle of our Faith to be fought and won in India

THE coming battle of our faith is, I believe, to be fought and won rather in India than in Europe. The manifestation of life is the one true answer to scepticism. Let it be seen, on that great and fresh field, that our historic Gospel meets, interprets, fulfils aspirations which are written in the records of untold generations; that it is able to reconcile order and progress; that it gives an intelligible meaning to the Hindu prayer—"To see God in all things and all things in God;" that it is not exhausted by our interpretation, or limited by our embodiment of its vital power; and we shall be enabled to bear our own temptations and difficulties with more trustful submission.

Foreign missions help us to rise to a worthier apprehension of the truth which we hold, so simple that it comes home to the rudest savage, so vast that it requires the experience of every race to unfold its mysteries in the language of men.

We each have our own theory, our own ideal of action.

We dare not dissemble our convictions even when we submit to the practical necessity of co-operation.

Christianity alone is able to preserve and hallow and combine all that is noblest in the endowments of every nation, pervading with a new energy and consecrating to a new use the manifold gifts of that humanity which God has taken to Himself.

India was saved by the soldiers and statesmen who did not shrink from saying that the province which saved the Empire was "conspicuous for two things,—the most successful government, and the most open acknowledgment of Christianity."

Successes leave us with the burden of responsibility. Each blessing comes as a promise, and is as it is used. It ceases to be real when it is made an occasion for rest.

The conquest of India for Christ is the conquest of Asia for Christ. And the conquest of Asia seems to offer the near vision of the consummation of the kingdom of God.

We must be a missionary people. So far we cannot change our destiny. We cannot abdicate our position or alter our heritage. The choice which we have is simply what shall be the message which we bear through the world.

A School of Indian Students

IF we are ourselves to draw from India fresh instruction in the mysteries of the divine counsels; if we are to contribute to the establishment of an organisation of the Faith which shall preserve and not destroy all that is precious in the past experience of the native peoples; if we are to proclaim in its fulness a Gospel which is universal and not western; we must keep ourselves and our modes of thought in the background. We must aim at 'something far greater than collecting scattered congregations round English clergy who may reflect to our eye faint and imperfect images of ourselves.

We must adopt every mode of influence which can be hallowed to the service of the Faith,—the asceticism, the endurance, the learning which are indigenous to the country.

We can in some degree, as the Spirit helps us, teach the teachers, but we cannot teach the people. The hope of a Christian India lies in the gathering together of men who shall be, to quote the words of a native journal, "as thoroughly Hindu as they are Christian, and more intensely national than those who are not Christian."

There is nothing that I should more earnestly desire for Cambridge than that some school of Indian students should be formed and sustained to witness to her devotion and to represent her spirit in the East.

We should gain by being brought into closer connection with men among whom the "struggling, hard-working, hard-living scholar" is the noble ideal of the race: they would gain by feeling that they were called into actual fellowship with a centre of the religious thought of England.

To organise such a school appears to me to be the true University Mission. For it is, in some degree, to offer to God the firstfruits of the best which He has given us. There is other work to be done abroad, but the Universities should aspire to that which is most difficult; to that which calls for their peculiar gifts; to that which may consecrate, so to speak, their proper work at home. And is it too much to hope that we may yet see on the Indus, or the Ganges, some new Alexandria?

England and her Colonies

IF we say that in the providence of God England has been appointed to be the mother of nations, it is with the feeling of overwhelming responsibility, and not of indolent pride.

We shrink from bringing our deepest personal conviction to bear upon questions of state till we unconsciously forget the divine element in the nation.

We fall under the temptation of seeking material solutions for spiritual problems; material remedies for spiritual maladies. The thought of spiritual poverty, of spiritual destitution, is crowded out. We treat the symptoms and neglect the disease itself.

The experience of Australia, as rich in resources as in enterprise, dissipates the illusion which animates such efforts. Vice and squalor find a place in Sydney no less than in London.

THE COLONIAL CHURCH

Boundless opportunities for industry and the independence of democratic equality have not brought universal competence or true freedom.

If the greatest present dangers of rich and poor are, as they surely are, moral in their origin, they must be removed by a moral cure.

For more than three centuries we have been led to develop individualism in religion, and to regard religion simply as a matter for the soul and God.

And now once again we are beginning to understand the language and the spirit of the Jewish prophets; to feel how the highest privilege of Israel was to be a Messianic people; to see that the message of the Incarnation is social no less than personal; to see that it reveals to us the destiny not of individuals only, but of humanity.

That which can regenerate a man, can regenerate a nation. This, nothing less than this, is the meaning and power of the announcement which still rings in our ears, *The Word became flesh*.

All around us we can discern the promise of creation, the unspoken expectation which changes the agonies of nature into the travail-pains of a more glorious birth (Rom. viii. 20 ff.) So the great announcement passes into life, and comes forth from life a living faith.

In our English Church seems to lie the best hope of the social Christianity of the future.

It must at least rest in a large measure with the English Church whether the civilisation of the Southern world shall be penetrated by Christianity as a social force.

To this end it must, we readily allow, vindicate to itself more fully than heretofore every force of truth and right and beauty—of spirit and soul and body—by which men are moved.

We grow so timorous about details, so anxious to meet every objection to the faith, that we are in danger of forgetting that we are commissioned to proclaim a message of glad tidings, to which the world and life and the soul of man bear spontaneously the witness of welcome: of forgetting that our creed rests upon a fact by which man is bound so closely to man and earth to heaven that, while we hold it, love can never fail and hope can never be desolate. We grow content to interpret Christ's promise to His Church (Matt. xvi. 18) as if it assured to us survival and not victory. We accept the position of a beleaguered garrison, holding some last stronghold at desperate odds, when Christ would have us move forward in His name with a great tide of conquest, before which the last barriers of death and sin shall fall and set free their captives. We think of ourselves and not of God, of our feebleness and not of His might, of our temporal isolation and not of His eternal fellowship.

Yes, *faithful is He that calleth*. In that assurance we rejoice in our brother's work,[1] for the sake of Australia and for the sake of England. He will take with him the wealth of the old life which he has made his own: he will give back to us the energy of the new life which he quickens and guides: he will help us to see the continuity of the old with the new by a vital progress. The prayers of this loved Abbey, closely connected from the first with our Colonial episcopate, will blend with the prayers and prophecies of the distant Cathedral: thoughts stirred here by memories of princes and statesmen with

---

[1] The Consecration of Dr. Barry to the See of Sydney.

THE GOSPEL OF CREATION

thoughts stirred there by names of founder-bishops blazoned on the piers. But here and there one call will be addressed to him and to us, fresh from day to day, bidding each in his place occupy new realms for Christ—one call welcomed by one prayer, the inspiration and the stay of faith.

The Incarnation Independent of the Fall

FROM the beginning of the thirteenth century the question "whether Christ would have been incarnate if Adam had not sinned," became one of the recognised questions of the schools.

The belief that the Incarnation was in essence independent of the Fall, has been held by men of the most different schools, in different ways and on different grounds. All, however, in the main agree in this, that they find in the belief a crowning promise of the unity of the divine order; a fulfilment, a consummation, of the original purpose of creation; a more complete and harmonious view of the relation of finite being to God than can be gained otherwise.

It is impossible for us now to understand a formula which deals with man and the world in the sense in which it was understood when the earth was regarded as the centre of the system of material creation, and the human race as having existed for five or six thousand years.

The effect upon the mind of the words in which it is expressed must be different even if we use the same words. And the sovereign preeminence of Scripture as the vehicle of spiritual knowledge lies in this, that it finds fuller interpretation from growing experience.

The Scripture does not change, but our power of entering into its meaning changes.

If man had fulfilled the law of his being, he would still, so far as we can see, have stood in need of a Mediator, through whom the relation of fellowship with God might have been sustained and deepened and perfected. Nor is it easy to suppose that this fellowship could have been made stable and permanent in any other way than by the union in due time of man with God, accomplished by the union of man with Him who was the Mediator between God and man, and in whose image man was made.

The argument which was drawn from Ephesians v. 31 f. by several early writers, deserves more consideration than we are at first inclined to give it. The main idea in the passage seems to be that the Church, the representative of perfected humanity, of that which the race would in the end have been if sin had not intervened, is related to a Head, just as in the typical record of Creation woman is related to man. The Church and woman are severally regarded as derived, and yet belonging to the completeness of that from which they are derived, and so destined finally to be restored to perfect fellowship with it.

Man ideally is not man only but man and woman; Christ, such appears to be the thought, however unfamiliar it may be to us, unites with the Godhead the idea of perfected humanity, and that not accidentally but essentially. The personal relation of sex regarded in typical individuals represents, as we should express the view, beyond itself a corporate relation which exists in respect to the race.

Just as the individual union is necessary for the fulfilment of the idea of woman, so the corporate union is necessary for the fulfilment of the idea of humanity. Christ is the true Adam: the Church is the true Eve. And both these relations, the individual relation and the corporate relation, are independent of the Fall.

The Fall has disturbed and disordered each, but it was not the occasion for the first existence of either.

"Ye are the Salt of the Earth: ye are the Light of the World"

THE salt, because in Me is the promise of incorruption: *the light,* because in Me is the fulness of truth.

For it is not of ourselves we must think, but of that which is entrusted to us, of that which works through us, of that which rises serene and clear above our tumults and our doubts.

We need a spiritual power which shall cherish the sense of the loftiest ideals while it enters sympathetically into the wants of the individual; a spiritual power which shall labour to express in our language, in our thoughts, the fact of the Incarnation.

Our whole existence is in danger of being broken into fragments. There is among us a growing isolation of studies, which tends to create intellectual misunderstanding, to harden prejudices, to dehumanise toil.

The result is discordant dogmatism and materialised standards of well-being.

When we look round we are forced to confess sadly that there is no body among us whose work it is by organisation and training to remind the isolated student of the fragmentariness of his labours; to quicken and temper his devotion by the prospect of the whole; to plead for progress in the name of loyal devotion to the past; to unfold doctrines with an undoubting faith that all experience makes truth clearer, though it cannot change it; to welcome every accession to human knowledge as a fresh revelation of Him who has made Himself known to us in His Son, Son of man and Son of God.

Here and there solitary voices are raised to bear witness to these spiritual axioms, and in their loneliness they are not without power. There are also wide spiritual influences among us, without which society would perish; but they are either repressive or dispersive.

The imposing organisation of Romanism is framed so as to keep down, rather than to bring out, the fulness of individual and growing life: the strivings of Protestantism after personal development are made at the cost of the sense of social unity, and tend to further separation.

We have not, in other words, the organisation of the spiritual powers which answers to our circumstances, and ignorance becomes more perilous even than wickedness.

But the experience of earlier ages furnishes us with instructive precedents. Again and again in past times, societies of clergy separated from the main body have formed a centre round which the intellectual forces of the age have gathered for the hallowing of noble thoughts. So it was when the society of Benedict saved the precious remains of Roman civilisation in the isolated security of their secluded homes. So it was when the societies of Francis and Dominic bore the Gospel into the thickest turmoil of common life, and unconsciously prepared the way for the Reformation. So it was when, with an imperfect and self-willed devotion, the society of Loyola strove to bring again the scattered forces of quickened intelligence to the unity of one service.

Work for a Society of Clergy

THERE is still a way open by which a society of clergy in our own Church may find an office for the Faith, more comprehensively human than that of the monks, more simply natural than that of the mendicants, more loyally truthful than that of the Jesuits. We require brotherhoods of fellow-workers.

No single scholar can any longer command the sum of human learning.

The most encyclopædic student of life must supplement his own experience by the experience of others; and while no man can make another's learning or another's experience his own, still those who meet in sympathetic intercourse can apprehend the lessons of the different methods of study and of different social influences. In this way even a small college of clergy living for truth, if I may be allowed the phrase, rather than for action, will perceive spontaneously the direction and the conditions of human movement.

Disappointment the Fuel of Hope

THERE is danger in the very intensity of zeal; there is a restless anxiety for measurable results in our eager enthusiasm.

We think that our labour is lost if the frosts of winter bind the field in which our seed lies buried.

But we must not accept the surface of things as the revelations of their essence.

We shall, by trust in Christ, make disappointment the fuel of hope. For surely our discontent is a witness to our destiny.

The Consecration of all Powers

IF it be true that "labour is prayer," it is no less true that "prayer is labour." If when the knee is bent in toil the soul does not rise to the Source of all strength, that effort perishes with the earth.

The soul acts through the body; and the body lives by the soul. On earth there can be no divorce of the spiritual and the material.

There is a figure in the unparalleled gallery of Saints which surrounds the chapel of Henry VII. at Westminster, which serves to express in a parable the truth which I desire to realise. A bearded man in armour wears over the armour a chasuble, and over the chasuble a hood and scapular. With one hand he leads a dragon bound by his stole, in the other he holds a book. Warrior, priest, monk, doctor, he keeps evil in subjection by his spiritual force. The statue is a true emblem of Allhallows; and it looks upon the most touching monument in the Abbey, through which Mary and Elizabeth tell us from their common grave that they sleep together in the hope of the resurrection. The difference of function is reconciled in the one service. The difference of opinion is reconciled in the one life. The unity of consecration meets the unity of glory.

We are the Heirs of the Past

TRUE nobility is clothed in many dresses; and he is blessed in his measure who can recognise the soul touched by a Divine love which still speaks to us through the past. Our fathers were different from ourselves; different and therefore we can learn from them.

We cast away the invigorating obligation of a noble patrimony. We are contented to stand as if we were the creation of to-day or yesterday,—we who are the heirs of immeasurable purposes, aspirations, hopes, treasures, fashioned and brought together through twelve centuries, and entrusted to our keeping and to our use.

Materially, socially, intellectually, morally, in all we do and think and feel, we owe a debt to those who have gone before us which we can only acknowledge and not pay. In such a case payment must simply be the use of the blessings which have been given; and to be thankless, to be thoughtless, is to lose that which makes the blessing a living power.

We count up with a jealous minuteness the efforts which we have ourselves made without any obvious result, our unlooked-for failures, our disappointments, our discomfitures, our painful sowings, which have been followed by no harvest.

But while we do so, we forget to reckon how incalculably small all these are compared with the accumulated treasures won by our fathers which are fruitful for our service.

The wealth which we all enjoy in various ways, rich and poor alike, is the stored-up labour of earlier generations. And, further, the possibility of enjoying it, of drawing from it, on the one side, the opportunity of thoughtful and cultivated leisure, and on the other the support of vigorous and efficient industry, was won even more hardly than the wealth itself.

The Patrimony of Language

MORE precious than the resources of material prosperity, more precious even than the environment of liberty and order, is the patrimony of language and art with which the past has enriched us.

Few among us ever pause to consider what periods of conflict, what long strivings after truth, what manifold trials of experience, what concurrences and combinations of different elements, are epitomised in a language. Words are monuments of thoughts grappled with and overcome. They are not the production of any one man, but rather partial revelations by which "the Word" interprets the mind of a nation. They place within the reach of all of us, and so that we can use them, the results which the greatest intellects have been able to reach. The use of a noble language, and no language is nobler than our own, is, if we regard it rightly, a perpetual lesson. The thought cannot be clear till the word has symbolised it: the word cannot be current without stirring speaker and hearer to fix its meaning for themselves. We can understand what this implies when we remember that there are still people who have no words for "faith" and "hope" and "charity." And if that seems strange, it is scarcely less strange from another point of view that for us these three words represent our connection with Rome and Germany and France.

"Sermons in Stones"

IT is by their buildings and by their sculpture that the men of the middle ages hold converse with us now.

They wrote on parchment in a foreign language, but they wrote also in a universal language on stone, as men cannot write now.

When men build out of the fulness of their hearts, they put their deepest thoughts into their buildings.

Sometimes they expressed things just and lovely, sometimes things false and hateful. But with whatever message, they do still speak to us for encouragement and for warning. The great churches are the sermons of the middle ages, and we shall do well to study them.

We too are Ancestors

WE take account of the gifts of our unknown benefactors—wealth, order, language, art; and at length perhaps the words come home to us: *Other men have laboured, and ye are entered into their labour.* At the same time the words turn our thoughts forwards as well as backwards. We too are ancestors; and we are constrained to ask what is the inheritance which we are preparing for future generations? For what will our descendants bless us? Will they be able to say when they look back at the work which we have wrought in our brief time of toil, at the words which we have coined or brought into currency, at the spirit which we have cherished: "They gave us their best, their best in execution, and their best in thought: they embodied splendid truths in simple forms and made them accessible to all: they kept down the hasty and tumultuous passions which an age of change is too apt to engender: thus they have made sacrifice easier for us; they have made wisdom more prevailing: they have made holiness more supreme: and for all this, and for the innumerable pains of which we know not, we bless their memory." Or will the voice of blessing be silent? Will they say as they look on what we have done, "That crumbling heap, that desolate iron furnace, tells of work performed only for the moment, which has cumbered the earth with ruins: those coarse and mean phrases which have corrupted our language, tell of men who had no reverence and no dignity: that class antagonism which torments us, tells of the selfishness of our fathers, who, when there was yet time, failed to bind man to man as fellow-labourers in the cause of God." For we must remember, there is a harvest of sorrow and desolation, a harvest of the whirlwind and the storm, such as has been once and again sown and reaped in the world's history, children helplessly gathering the fruits of their parents' sins. And they have not read the prophets well who persuade themselves that they can do their work for God without looking to the future which they are preparing for the earth.

The Unknown Heirs of our Toil

IF we give less than our best to that which we have to do, be it a small thing or a great, we are sowing to corruption. We shall reap, and sadder still, others will reap of its growth.

Even in the humblest place, even with the feeblest powers, there is an infinite, an unending capacity for influence.

The joy of life, the strength of life, is then assured when we come to see how the Gospel of the Word Incarnate has blessed the necessary bonds by which we are united to all the past and all the future, as well as to all the present: how it consecrates true effort and gives, what nothing else can give, efficacy to sincere repentance; how it enables us to enter on our daily tasks stirred with gratitude towards those who through many failures prepared the way for our success, and stirred with love towards those who shall hereafter add what we have been unable to accomplish. *Other men laboured and ye are entered into their labour.*

Let us look back with pious regard to our unknown benefactors, that we may also in the power of that life which Christ has made one, look forward with loving joy to the unknown heirs of our toil.

The Benedictine Rule

EARLIER ascetics have shewn the foundation of individual freedom in self-conquest. Benedict shewed the foundation of social freedom in self-surrender. It may seem to be a paradox, but all experience teaches us that perfect obedience to a perfect law coincides with perfect liberty, and that he is strongest in action who seeks "not to do his own will, but the will of Him that sent him."

Thus Benedict literally transferred to life the command of St. Paul, "Submit yourselves one to another in the fear of God;" and on this solid basis he reared a permanent society in which for the first time equality and brotherhood were practically realised. It was his glory, so far as his Rule reached, to abolish slavery, to devote property to a common use, to combine differences of character and power for the perfecting of Christian fellowship.

Within the walls of the monastery the noble and the bondman were equal. No one was allowed to say that anything was his own, except his sins. The ties of family were lost in the larger bond of spiritual kinsmanship. "A monk," in the striking language of one of themselves, "was a kind of Melchizedek, without father, without mother, without genealogy." Handicraft and study were enjoined as the complement of religious exercises, with no rivalry and with no preference. For him who ruled, and for him who served, there was one absolute law—to prefer his brother's good to his own. It was made plain that all true human action was for God, and through God. No one might determine his own occupation or take upon himself without permission self-chosen obligations and austerities. If any one was called to an office, however humble, he was directed to fall at the knees of the brethren and beg their prayers; and when the work was done he closed it with the thanksgiving: "Blessed art Thou, O Lord God, who hast holpen me and comforted me."

At the same time the most unsparing demands on devotion are combined with singular tenderness, and love of souls. It was enjoined that public prayer should be short in order to secure easily concentrated attention. Readers were chosen likely to attract by their skill. Offences were strictly punished; but room was offered for repentance even to the third time to a brother who had been expelled from the society. "There was always," in Benedict's own words, "something to which the strong might aspire, and something from which the weak might not shrink."

Disciplined on these principles, each Benedictine Society became, as it were, a little garrison, holding a citadel of peace, in the midst of a turbulent people. It was independent, and in the main unmolested.

The Benedictine Monasteries

THE monastery included within its walls all that was requisite for the support of the inmates; the fish-pond and the barn, the bakehouse and the brewery; and monks were privileged to be neutral in the fiercest conflicts.

Sometimes a group of monasteries united themselves together for mutual encouragement and support, as when, in 1075, "the seven monasteries of Worcester, Evesham, Chertsey, Bath, Pershore, Winchcomb, and Gloucester agreed to be as one minster, with one heart and one soul."

It is no wonder, then, that young boys were dedicated to a monastic life at the altar of the monastery church. Henceforward, the monastery was the home of these new Samuels, who became the nucleus of a monastic school, and at the same time a spring of perpetual freshness in the house itself.

Bec

THE birthplace of the mediæval monasticism of England was Bec; and I doubt if any single fragment of antiquity can appeal more touchingly to an Englishman than the solitary tower, built on the verge of the Renaissance, which now alone witnesses to the glory of the Norman monastery. Rising high above the battlements, on the crest of the staircase-turret, stands the figure of the Lord, as on the pinnacle of the Temple: below, wrought in the stonework of the wall, are the words, *Noli temptare Deum.* It seems like a voice; a monument of Divine judgment.

The Continuity of English Institutions

WE are bound to ask, What is this Benedictine life to us now—this effort after systematic service of man and God, this aspiration after complete self-surrender, this which was at least for a time a fertile source of learning, of art, of personal religion, of social feeling? What is it? I reply, without a moment's hesitation, the very staple of our inheritance.

There is no end in human things which is not a beginning also, and it is the peculiar glory of English institutions that they preserve continuity through change. In this respect the cathedrals of the New Foundation are the appointed representatives of the ancient monasteries.

On those who are called to work in them is laid the charge to study under new conditions the law of responsibility, work, and worship which was the inspiration of the Order of Benedict; and is there not a growing need of that power of a corporate life which it may yet quicken and rule?

King's College, Cambridge

SOCIETIES, like men, have their ancestry, their treasures of accumulated experience and enthusiasm, their traditional spirit, their nobility which makes service an obligation, their ruling thought.

They have, in other words, a life richer and more complex than that of the individual, but no less real.

This life they who for the time represent them have to cherish and advance with loyal and enlightened reverence; and no one can take his part, however humble, in the great labour who does not strive to learn the characteristics of the body to which he is called to minister, and faithfully subordinate self in the acknowledgment of a common work.

The connexion of the college with Eton may be less close, or rather, I should say, less exclusive in the time to come than it has been; but the significance of that connexion remains for ever.

It is blazoned on the two shields which for more than two hundred and fifty years have stood upon our Chapel screen. These declare simply and impressively what is the change, what is the unity in education. As time goes on the white lily is replaced by the white rose, the purity of simple innocence by the grace of a maturer growth, but all else is unaltered.

The symbol of courageous energy and the symbol of divine service, the symbol, that is, of true kingship taken from the royal coat, are for the boy and for the man alike; and no less for the man and for the boy alike is the dark background which sadly fills the field of life.

So it is set before us in intelligible figures, in the very badges of our Foundation, that our whole training from first to last must be one, if it is perfect, the fulfilment of one thought, in one spirit, under one supreme influence. And therefore, as many will have noticed, to complete this conception, as I must think, the lily and the rose are placed together on our western door under the glory of the Sacred Name.

Whatever changes, whatever revolutions may take place in the society itself, this Chapel will abide to witness to the Founder's main idea, the consecration of learning.

It is, and must always be, disproportionate to any direct use which can be made of it; but that is because it embodies a master thought of life. Crowd it with worshippers from end to end, and they will be felt to be accessory to the building. More impressive than any voice of music or of prayer is the grand stateliness of the temple itself. The silent monumental teaching of the past is here more eloquent than the numbers of living men.

We are slow to understand what was instinctively apprehended as long as architecture was the outcome of national character. It is no affectation to say that the thoughts of the middle ages found expression more often on stone than on parchment.

No one can study our great Cathedrals without recognising that they are the spontaneous expression of noble imaginings.

Their designers wished to give form to feelings by which they were intensely moved. They were poets rather than students. They cared for their thoughts and not for their names.

In this sense King's College Chapel is the last complete utterance of pure mediæval art. Already when the plan was formed "the Book," to apply memorable words, "was on the point of killing the Building." Before it was finished architecture had ceased to live.

It is the last characteristic voice of the middle age in England. On the verge of a new era, heralded by ominous shakings of nations and churches, the Founder willed that over all work and over all study should be inscribed in a universal language, "To the Glory of God." This is, he saw, the end of life and this is the strength of life.

No one can doubt the Founder's meaning. At Cambridge, as at Eton, the Chapel was the centre and the crown of his design.

Therefore it was that when the great storm came and unsympathetic fanaticism destroyed elsewhere the memorials of a faith which it took no pains to understand, the Chapel remained absolutely untouched. Even the soldiery who were quartered in it were enabled—as I must believe—to see that it did bear written upon its stately form, though in strange characters, "To the Glory of God."

Successive generations have been enabled to guard with reverent care what they have held to be a sacred heritage, to repress the influence of present taste in dealing with the past.

The Need for an open Confession of our Faith

THE ordinary circumstances of life tempt us to disguise our faith. We are surrounded by an atmosphere of irony.

There is indeed a tender reverence which guards what it holds dearest from unsympathising eyes. But even so the power of a great affection will naturally make itself felt.

Strangers will perceive that he who is possessed by it is stirred by some secret force unless he labours to conceal the master spirit of his life.

But with us too often the case is far otherwise.

We repeat the articles of our Creed, and then we allow it to be supposed that they are inoperative, that they are a burden rather than an inspiration, a tradition rather than a revelation of life, a law at the most and not glad tidings of great joy.

There may be a joy of private possession in other things, but the value of spiritual truth—the value of the truth to the possessor—is increased by diffusion. It grows by scattering. To hold it back from others is to cast doubt upon its reality.

Sooner or later we feel the doubts which we occasion: the disguising, the dissembling, of our highest principles reacts upon ourselves. We come to accept the estimate of our motives which our conduct leads others to form.

A Faith unacknowledged is ready to vanish away. For this reason we find that Holy Scripture lays singular stress upon the open confession of our Faith. Faith indeed, if it is real, must declare itself.

The crown of life is not reached till the life has revealed its energy.

We know what strength, what resolution, what scattering of idle doubts, what concentration of aim, come when we once have avowed our choice. Numberless temptations are removed by the mere fact that our part is taken. The obligation of our cause is upon us.

We are tempted in the vigour of our fresh convictions to isolate ourselves: to confine our sympathies to those who see the Truth as it appears to us: to measure the message of the Gospel by our own power of apprehending it: to surrender the inspiring sense of that Divine life which embraces, harmonises, transfigures the fragmentariness of human schemes, and the varieties of human service.

We dare not disparage or neglect the least truth which we have gained. We dare not affect to hold that which we have not made our own.

Our narrow vision will, if we allow the soul to dwell upon it, suggest far more than it defines.

In order to meet the temptation to reserve and the temptation to narrowness, we need the courage of confession and the inspiration of sympathy.

The Courage of Confession natural to Youth

YOUTH without the love which believes all things, hopes all things, endures all things; youth without the enthusiasm which thinks all things possible and without the bold frankness which declares its confidence, is a strange and stunted growth, or rather it is as some heir who has not learnt the grandeur of his heritage.

Trust, therefore, the widest, noblest, loftiest, thoughts which the Holy Spirit stirs in your hearts. Trust them, obey them, embody them now in their fresh fulness, and they will remain with you as the soul of your soul, a sure solace and encouragement in later days when the promise of the Lord's coming seems to linger, and the cold dark evening closes over a field to men's eyes not yet won.

Let it be seen that you approach every task, and study every problem of life, as those who have a Gospel to announce as wide as the needs of men and as lofty as their hopes.

It is enough that we should tell what we have known.

It is treason to keep to ourselves the least truth with which we have been entrusted.

Combination in Diversity, the Secret of England's Power and the Tenour of her Mission

"COMBINATION in diversity" is, if I read aright, the lesson of the Bible, the lesson of Church History, the lesson of human nature.

In many parts, and in many fashions, the divine revelation has been given to man and preserved for man's guidance.

Each part, each fashion abides with us for ever: no one mode of instruction can ever lose its significance: no one fragment of recorded truth can ever cease to be fruitful.

From age to age the life of the Church has manifested in an organic growth the action of the Divine Spirit by which it is quickened; and when we look back over its magnificent course, fretted, checked, sullied as it has been, we feel that we could not dispense with any one, even the least, of the tributary forces which have been taken into its fulness.

Man who is but part can only see by parts; and if he aspires, as he must do, to approximate completeness even in his present conception of Truth, the blessing cannot be gained otherwise than by the co-ordination of the thoughts of many minds.

The law is true everywhere; and if we rise to the loftiest subjects, nothing short of the whole experience of all men can answer to the fulness of the Gospel.

"Combination in diversity" thus understood is in a peculiar sense, as I am constrained to think, the truth which England and the English Church can teach; it is the comprehensive and abiding correlative to the fragmentary systems which by their negative forms are fitted only to meet temporary or partial wants: it is the master power capable of overcoming finally the indifferentism which endangers the vigour and vitality of personal conviction.

All life will leave its significance unexhausted to the end.

But when we regard the position and the history of England, which necessarily correspond to one another in a great degree, I do not suppose that we can mistake the part which she has to play in the future of the world.

Unexampled national prosperity has hitherto tended to hide from us the signs of her nobler office as yet unfulfilled.

It may be that times of trial and disaster will come, and will be necessary, before the nation can enter upon her apostleship. It may be that wealth and power will be made instruments of divine service. But nothing can deprive us of the endowments by which God has fitted us, as a people, to be the missionaries of the world, the common interpreters of the East to the West and of the West to the East, the depositaries of truth recognised as manifold.

The physical isolation of England has secured for it a development of institutions, feelings, thoughts absolutely unique.

Progress may have been often slow among us, but it has been essentially spontaneous. Foreign elements have been successively introduced into the stream of popular movement, but they have been forced to act in channels already determined.

When the rest of European Christendom was embraced in the Holy Roman Empire, England stood outside it, and yet sympathising with it: when the Reformation desolated the Continent with civil wars, the change in England was made by the people and not by a party: when the French Revolution rudely severed elsewhere the ties by which the middle age was bound to later times, England was enabled to reconcile progress with continuity.

England, in a word, has never broken with the past.

How much is included in this we have perhaps hardly yet understood; but it is something to know that the fulness of our national life includes vital sympathy with every age; that for us what has been is yet; that we can set aside the uniform schemes of impatient speculators in the strength of varied experience.

And present obligations impose on us the duty of keeping alive, in the fullest intensity, all that has been assimilated in the manifold growth of the past.

We are bound, as no other nation can be bound, to

the most extreme types of human history and human feeling.

India on the one side, and America on the other, claim from us the lessons of Wisdom and Truth, which can only find expression through sympathetic powers.

Whether we look at what England has been, or at what England is, the secret of her power and the tenour of her mission are the same—combination in diversity.

But while this is true generally, it is most true of our English Church. Our inheritance does not begin with the Reformation. We claim as our own, not only the Church of Alban, but the Church of Augustine, the Church of Anselm, the Church of Becket, the Church of Wykeham.

The one life in which they all shared, may have been often checked, hidden, disguised, but their life is still ours, and we abandon a priceless blessing if we abridge the amplitude of our descent.

We can never want the form of any past time, but we always want the spirit of the past.

Experience tends to shew that the evils with which we have to contend will be best met, not by a recurrence to the examples of the primitive Church, not by a revival of the divided energies of the sixteenth century, but by that which the middle age offered in rude and transitional shapes, by a personal discipline, by a system of religious co-operation, by an organised spiritual power.

If we retain at least potentially whatever there was of permanent value in Roman organisation, on the other hand we maintain the pure and simple outlines of dogmatic faith which the genius of the Greek Church above all others was providentially fitted to draw, and at the same time acknowledge the sovereign duty of personal inquiry and personal conviction which was brought into prominence by the religious awakening of the Teutonic spirit.

It would be vain to look elsewhere for any Church which can shew within it the concurrence of these three distinct tendencies to abstract truth, to social authority, to individual freedom, co-ordinated in one life.

If we strive to guard faithfully our whole religious inheritance from the past; if we strive to make it fruitful for the actual service of Christendom, it will be by obeying the principle which the Providence of God has made clear to us—combination in diversity.

The Peril of Partial Views

WHEN we pass into the active business of life, it cannot but be that our thoughts grow narrower.

It is the very condition of successful energy—whether we deplore or rejoice in the law—that it should be so.

Our experience, our powers, our interests are concentrated within a smaller circle. And this concentration brings great perils with it. Little by little we are tempted to think that perfect which we know to be true: to bend our efforts towards making others see with our own eyes: to regard our work as unaccomplished if we cannot persuade those who are looking for truth to occupy the position from which it has been unfolded to ourselves: to cut ourselves off from the fellowship of those who will not be content to gaze on the prospect in which we delight: to treat as essential whatever we have found to be salutary: to attribute to that which answers to our own experience, or, as we think, to the experience of our own age, or of our own country, a completeness which would be real only if we were omniscient, or were absolute epitomes of humanity.

Partial views grow perilous, not when they are held firmly, but when they are held as if they were universal.

Since the value of words must change with widened or contracted thought, no formula expressed in words can be exhaustive.

Truth is one because it is infinite, and no authority therefore can define beforehand the limits within which inquiry shall be found.

True unity—the unity of life and not of form—can, or rather must, spring out of the free and simultaneous maintenance of different portions of the one Truth as they are made known to us severally.

Words which at one time sum up earlier experience become at another time centres, as it were, round which new and foreign thoughts crystalise.

The Fundamental Differences of the two Universities

THE two great ancient Universities are, and have always been, marked by special characteristics.

The intellectual spirit of Cambridge is grave, sober, patient, self-questioning. There is amongst us a certain reserve, a lingering caution, perhaps an unfitness for action.

But out of these qualities springs something of an unbroken sympathy underlying our differences.

If we miss the energy of decision, we are spared the divisions of party.

At Oxford, if I may for one moment criticise what I revere, the case seems to be otherwise.

There the tendency to action with the capacity for action appears to dominate. And as I look from without, I cannot but feel, that a society broken up into parties is the price paid for the swift conversion of thought into practice.

At Cambridge, in a word, if I may so presume to sum up what I mean, the Teutonic element of our national life prevails, in which thought as thought is supreme; at Oxford the Romanic element, in which thought is regarded as the basis of organisation.

A single illustration may be added. For it cannot be an accident that Cambridge has been fertile beyond all proportion in great poets.

It cannot be an accident that he who among Oxford men of this generation was endowed with the greatest poetic genius turned aside from his poetic calling to place himself at the head of a great party which he was at last constrained to abandon.

It would not be difficult to point out that the two last great religious movements in England—the Evangelic movement which belongs peculiarly to Cambridge, and the Tractarian movement which belongs peculiarly to Oxford—reflect these fundamental differences of the two Universities.

Combination in Diversity rests on a frank Acknowledgment of our Differences

WE are so eager for agreement that we are often ready to sacrifice the very element which it is our part to contribute to the final harmony.

But it is nothing short of treason to Truth to surrender as trivial that which we have ourselves been allowed to see or to feel.

It is exactly this personal revelation, this personal intuition, to which we must cling most devoutly.

If the man who thinks he can grasp the whole truth dishonours it, he is not less guilty who is willing to treat any fragment of it as of little moment.

In Truth there can be no degrees.

In spiritual Truth whatever we know is infinitely precious, and we are bound at all costs to uphold the convictions which are borne in upon us.

At the same time, we are not bound by any equal obligation to force them upon others.

An opinion will always be a resultant of the outward fact and the individual constitution, if not in expression, certainly in conception.

Thus the very intensity of assurance with which we hold some particular view, will be to us a sign that it is personal, and therefore incomplete.

Completeness in that which is visible would shut out all higher aspirations.

The complexity of modern life demands the use of

all that has been gradually and separately evolved in former times.

In our missions we have not relied on the simplicity of the historic Gospel, but have endeavoured to create in every people, however different, some exact and feeble copy of ourselves, transplanting a system where we should have been content to sow the Word.

In public questions we have hardly ventured to find a place for distinctively Christian thoughts, though it is through them alone that a solid basis can be found for determining the relative duties of nations, the claims of labour, and the regulations of common life.

We can be content to rejoice in the sense of co-operation without restlessly seeking to reconcile differences in service rendered in absolute devotion to a common Saviour.

Striving together for Christ as the End of all effort, *through Christ* as the Mediator of all action, *in Christ* as the Centre of all life, we shall come to a fuller sense of the breadth, the power, the unity of the Gospel.

Thoughts from the Ordinal—The Call

CHRIST finds us and calls us through the circumstances of our life, which represent for each one of us the expression of the Divine Will.

Christ finds us and calls us, touching our souls with desires and encouragements which are not of the earth.

The Due Order of the Realm

THERE is a depth of thought in that phrase "the due order of the realm" which we shall do well to consider. It brings the whole fabric of society into immediate relation with the will of God. As we ponder the words we see how it is that He speaks to us through the institutions, the opportunities, the trials, the gifts, the discipline of civil life. He speaks to us through these, and as soon as we feel that it is so, the past becomes a school for gratitude, and therefore a school of strength.

Signs of a Divine Guidance

LET us summon before us in thanksgiving the many leadings by which God has been pleased to bring us to our present choice; the many silent whisperings by which He has made us feel His will: the many signs by which we know that He has found us. Face to face with Him in the Person of Jesus Christ, let us confess His constraining call and in absolute faith let us follow as He guides.

He will call us to the end of our days: call us in the word read and in the work done: call us in the great questions of social life: call us in the experience of our own souls.

The Rule

WE require nothing as of necessity to eternal salvation but what the Scriptures sufficiently contain. We exclude no variety in the apprehension of infinite Truth which they hallow.

The Scriptures are set before us as the central object of our personal study, the treasury of our public teaching, the final standard of all necessary doctrine.

The Vast Range of the Bible

LET us look at the vast range of the Bible: let us realise in the sacred history of the discipline of the world the largeness of the mode of God's action : let us ponder the manifestations of His love, of His patience, of His long-suffering, sometimes even startling to our eyes : let us trace, if with aching sight, how He makes man minister to man, and race to race, and generation to generation : let us notice how He accepts in compassion varieties of service according to the state and means of those who render it : how He turns to a source of blessing what appears to our eyes simple misery and ruin : and a hope will rise upon us which we often sorely want : a hope which will not cover with a dull, colourless cloud of indifference the religious positions of men, but on the contrary make us feel, since we have received a priceless heritage, what is perilled in our energy, what we owe and what we render to others who are heirs with us of a common salvation.

Our Creed translated into Action in the Bible

THE Bible teaches us by shewing how God dealt with men one by one, and how He dealt with nations. It lifts the veil, so to speak, from His hidden movements; and at the same time we hear the voice of innumerable witnesses telling of victories of faith.

In the Bible our Creed is translated into action ; or rather we see there in the intercourse of God and man, broken and restored, the Truth which our Creed expresses.

The Book itself forces us to go beyond the Book to a Person. It constrains us to find the only rest of the soul in Him Whom it reveals. *Tu fecisti nos ad Te, Domine, et inquietum est cor nostrum donec requiescat in Te.*

The Scriptures a Message of the Living God to struggling Men

WE do not think that we *have life in them* but in Him of Whom they witness.

In each act we catch some vision of the Divine Worker. In each word we listen for some accent of the Divine Speaker. As He wrought in old times He works still: as He spoke in old times He speaks still.

The Bible is not merely the Charter of our Faith written in a language obsolete and only half-intelligible, but a message of the Living God to struggling men.

Through this—through this illuminated by every ray of truth which can be gathered from every source—He shews Himself to us.

The Work

WE work for others; since our aim in every effort of self-culture is social and not personal.

The Christian minister has the strongest motive which a man can have for cultivating, according to his opportunity, every power which he possesses, because he has the noblest object.

We are tempted to measure ourselves by others, to acquiesce in an average standard and an average attainment. We forget that while we are not required to judge our neighbours, we are required to judge ourselves.

As Messengers we have a gospel to proclaim, always the same and always new. As Watchmen we have foes to keep off.

As Stewards we have treasures to increase by wise forethought, and to dispense with just counsel.

That others may "wax riper and stronger" through our service, we must wax riper and stronger ourselves. And far beyond every success which can crown our labours, is the issue towards which we are bidden to strive when "no place shall be left among us, either for error in religion or viciousness in life."

The Witness

UNDER one aspect our Work is our Witness; and under another aspect our Witness is our Work.

What we are seen to be is in many ways the measure of what we can do. We are, we must be, regarded by men as tests and types of our teaching. They will judge our words by our acts.

So far as we appear to acquiesce in falling short of our precepts they will hold that we speak for form's sake.

The Warning against occasioning Offence to others

WE can recall occasions in which we have been impatient, inconsiderate, self-willed, self-asserting. We have sharply resented some want of good taste: we have made light of a scruple or of a difficulty which weighed heavily on another: we have yielded ungraciously a service which may have been claimed inopportunely: we have been exact in requiring conventional deference to our judgment: we have not checked the keen word, or the smile which might be interpreted to assert a proud superiority.

In all this we may have been justifiable according to common rules of conduct; but we have given offence. We have not, that is, shewn when we might have shewn that Christian sympathy, devotion, fellowship, come down to little things; that the generosity of love looks tenderly, if by any means it may find the soul which has not revealed itself.

The recognition of duty is the surest protection of rights. We can, indeed, never for one moment lower our reverence for that which we hold to be the truth, or pay respect to that which we hold to be error; but we can patiently keep within the present limits of our actual experience, hastening neither to affirm nor to condemn, waiting till a fuller knowledge shall enlighten our darkness.

We shall not, indeed, by such forbearance escape enmity, and we shall not win over our adversaries. This (most mysterious of all mysteries of sin) the Lord Himself did not do on earth. But we shall be seen to love the Truth: and we shall not offend by seeming to care only for victory or for favour.

The Witness we pledge ourselves to Give

WE cannot dare to say with the Gospels before us that a witness however wise and bold, a life however pure and loving, will prevail at once: but we can say that it kindles a flame which will not be extinguished.

The witness of the martyr is the witness of the believer. The witness of Christian life and the witness of Christian death are one in their scope and in their persuasiveness, the witness to the powers of an unseen world about us and in us.

Reverence in Feeling and Obedience in Action

WE are tempted by the current modes of thought to refuse, in a sense different from that of Christ, to call any man master.

The temper of the time is equally indisposed to recognise authority and to incur responsibility.

The infinite details, the infinite disguises, by which our attention is diverted, make us for the most part incapable of taking a fair estimate of the spiritual forces and of the spiritual issues in the midst of which we move.

Reverence for the great brings that trustful confidence which leads to calm peace: reverence for the weak brings that tender considerateness which is pure joy.

Reverence in feeling corresponds in part with obedience in action. The foundation of reverence is the conviction that beneath that which we see there is something concealed or only half-revealed to which we are bound to do homage.

Obedience springs out of the same conviction. To obey is to bow to a power which we acknowledge as having authority without passing judgment upon its separate orders.

Obedience implies some sacrifice, some faith.

To do at another's bidding that which falls in with our pleasure or with our judgment is not to obey.

He who obeys enters by faith on the unseen: he recognises more than man in the ordinance of society.

We cannot each of us arrange everything, test everything.

The spirit of reverence, and the spirit of obedience, one spirit in two shapes, is the true spirit of the Christian ministry.

The End of the Christian Ministry

WE promote God's glory not by adding to it, which is impossible, but by acknowledging it, by displaying it, by reflecting it.

It may be that multiplied services, forms and the like,

really tend to hide God's glory from us, to keep us from seeking it by occupying and satisfying our thoughts.

It has been finely said that "wicked men bury their souls in their bodies." Something of the same kind, I fear, happens also as to things without us. Our want of sensibility, our deadness, turns creation into the tomb of God's glory, when it is truly the living shrine through which His glory is brought near to us.

We are poor judges of what is done even to the last. Nothing is more eloquent to us in this respect than the long silence of the Lord's Life.

Looking back upon that long silence followed by a short ministry of active service, He said: *Father . . . I glorified Thee upon earth, having perfected the work which Thou hast given me to do*. The flight of the disciples, and the Cross, might have seemed to shew failure: the unbelief of Israel, and the corruption of the Church, might have seemed to seal it. But the work was done: the glory was shewn. Without haste and without rest Christ won for men, and now brings home to them, the fulness of divine sonship. That is the message which we on our part have to bear and to shew in ourselves, glorifying God.

Man is born for fellowship. He is strong only so far as he can go out of himself. The experience of every one shews that isolation of thought and spirit brings weakness and pain.

Work is dissatisfying when we think of it only in relation to ourselves. Life itself is a sad mystery if our own pleasure or gain forms the measure of its worth.

But if the end of life is the reflection of the glory of God: if the strength of life is a living union with Him, a life in Him, then our estimate of things is wholly changed.

What we need is to strive to give a present meaning to the fact of the Incarnation which is too apt to pass away into the region of speculation: to ask ourselves what, indeed, Christ would have us understand now by His "little ones" and by the "childly mind."

The result of seeking after the true nature and proportion of the ways and aims of life will be to lead us to forget ourselves that we may find ourselves. Such forgetfulness is not the loss of our special faculties, but the consecration of them.

First we bring ourselves "body, soul, and spirit" to God: *we* are *in Him;* and then the fire of His love kindles the offering in a new energy: *He* is *in us.*

Growth

FAITH, in as much as it is living, must be in movement. That which is stationary is dead. If we rest in what we have already gained, our treasure perishes in our hands. Each new victory which we win must be so used that it may furnish the vantage-ground for further conquests.

We are busy and we are inclined to think that all is well with us.

We are led to discuss and to commend noble truths, and we take it for granted that they are influencing ourselves.

We come to forget that intellectual and spiritual privileges are talents lent to us for use, and not fruits of our own husbandry on which we can pride ourselves.

They increase our obligations: they do not compensate for our failures.

Do we keep before our minds as a fact that every endowment of sense and reason and intuition belongs to the undying fulness of our nature, and that we shall carry all these with their fruits of use and misuse before the judgment-seat of God?

We to whom large opportunities of study are given, we to whom the office of teachers is given, are bound to strive to gain the widest prospects of the Truth. We dishonour no less than endanger our deposit when we limit its application to the narrow wants which we can see or feel.

We cannot, perhaps, determine from our own limited experience why this is written, or that, why we must believe this or that. The whole experience of humanity will be required before that can be clear.

But of this we can be sure, that as long as we guard scrupulously the unproved wealth of the Gospel, we shall find ourselves prepared for any revolution of science or history.

It needs but little reflection to find that this is so in the crisis of our own age.

Christ and the teaching of Physicists

PHYSICISTS tell us, with an air of triumph, that man's highest powers are dependent upon his material frame: that he cannot truly exist apart from it.

Christ told us so long ago, and guarded the truth from exaggeration, though we may not before have felt the full significance of His Message, when He raised His Body from the grave to the right hand of God in token of His victory over Death.

Physicists tell us that the dead rule the living, that man is bound to man by an inexorable law.

Christ told us so long ago, when He presented the relation of Himself to His disciples as that of the Vine and Branches, of which each part is energetic and fruitful by the ministry of all according to the operation of one life.

Physicists tell us that we are but fragments of a vast whole which, though we may seek to isolate ourselves from it with a vain pride, yet cannot be separated from our destiny.

Christ told us so long ago, when by the mouth of His Apostle He spoke of the summing up, the reconciliation of all things in Himself as the Divine purpose before the foundation of the world and, as it seems to me, essentially independently of the Fall.

From Strength to Strength (84th Psalm)

IT is not necessary to attempt to fix the exact circumstances under which these words were written. The Psalter in its spiritual fulness belongs to no special time; and this Psalm is the hymn of the Divine life in all ages. It brings before us *the grace and the glory* of sacrifice, of service, of progress, where God alone, the Lord of Hosts, is the source and the strength and the end of effort. It is true now, and it is true always, that the voice of faith repeats, as in old time, through loneliness, through labour, through sorrow, its unchanging strain *from strength to strength*. A Northumbrian saint, it is said, carried up into Heaven in a trance, heard the same thanksgiving rendered by a choir of angels before the Throne of God. It must be so. *The Lord God is a sun* to illuminate, *and a shield* to protect. In the pilgrimage of worship that which is personal becomes social. The trust of the believer passes into the trust of the Church. The expectation of one is fulfilled in the joy of all. If the travellers grow weary on their way, it is that they may find unexpected refreshment; if they faint, it is that they may feel the new power which requickens them. *They go from strength to strength ; every one of them appeareth before God in Zion.*

The law of life, personal and universal, as God has willed, is summed up in this—*from strength to strength.* It is not true of men, and it is not true of humanity, that their sad journey is ever farther from the East. If they move westward, it is with the light, and again towards the light. Without dissembling or extenuating the effects of sin, without forgetting the dark mysteries and open sorrows which hang over generations, centuries, continents, we dare to repeat the sentence—not, indeed, in exultation, and yet without doubt, as the lesson of the past—*from strength to strength.*

A great Society needs great Ideas

A GREAT society cannot exist without great ideas; and great ideas perish unless they find worthy utterance. To organise is not to rule: merely to repeat a formula is not to instruct. The ruler must grasp the just proportion of the objects and duties of government; he must measure the wants and capacities of all his subjects; he must develop vital powers and not simply marshal them ;. he must never lose sight of his ideal while he does the little which is within his reach.

The teacher must be ready to bring out of his treasure things new as well as old; he must never be weary of translating into the current idiom the thoughts which his ancestors have mastered, and never backward to welcome the fresh voices of later wisdom.

The growing Complexity of Life unfavourable to great Ideas

IT is a natural consequence of our restless and busy life that we are turned by multitudinous details from the steady contemplation of the broad aspects of things. It is easier to crowd the day with little duties than to spend it in the silent study of enigmas which yield no immediate answer. But the issue is already seen to be disastrous. We hear it said that "a large part of the business of the wise is to counteract the efforts of the good." And meanwhile the growing complexity of life brings widespread hesitancy and doubt and moral relaxation. We feel ourselves, if it be but for rare moments, that there are whole regions of life on which we have not looked; and we tremble at the phantoms with which we unconsciously people them.

Our Universities discipline the Spiritual Counsellor

OUR ancient universities supply with singular fulness the discipline which may train the spiritual counsellor. Nowhere else, I believe, is a generous sympathy with every form of thought and study more natural or more effective; nowhere else is it equally easy to gauge the rising tide of opinion and feeling which will prevail after us; nowhere else is there in equal measure that loyal enthusiasm which brings the highest triumphs of faith within the reach of labour. He who has striven there towards the ideal of student and teacher will have gained powers fitted for a larger use. He who has lived in communion with the greatest minds of all ages will not be hasty to make his own thoughts the measure of truth.

He who has watched the specious transformation of assertion into fact will not withdraw anything from rigorous inquiry. Not one acquisition of toilsome research will be unfruitful in lessons of patient endurance. Not one rule of exact criticism will be unserviceable in fixing the limits of possible knowledge.

The character of a scholar has in its direct force infinitely greater power than any product of his skill. Literary work, however perfect, reflects in some degree the passing temper of the age; but character enters into the very depths of life, quickening, moulding, inspiring: the one is a fair building, the other is a tree *whose seed is in itself.*

The Church and Social Problems

NOTHING but our Faith can deal finally with the problems of democracy. I know no problem of society which the Gospel is not able to illuminate. It proclaims the true basis of fellowship in the Incarnation; it ennobles and concentrates the many offices which are united in one body; it reveals the abiding supremacy of character, which is independent of the accidental circumstances of life. Nor may we stop here; for I will not shrink from adding that the English Church seems to me to be marked out by its history, by its inheritance, by its constitution, reaching through all classes, in contact with all religions, in sympathy with all truth, able in St. Paul's sense to become *all things to all men*, as destined by God to give expression to the social Gospel for which we are waiting. Such a Gospel lies in Christianity; such an office appears to be committed to our Church; and as yet we have not acknowledged it.

Can we then wonder that we are met by sad doubts and suspicions, that we are charged with insincerity, that we are disheartened by the sense of a mission unrecognised? To gain quietness and confidence we must look for the manifestation of a power of life which shall vindicate for Christ every interest and every faculty of man.

An Episcopal Work

To provide for this, to call it out, to cherish it, is above all things an Episcopal work. Here lies for our age that care for the weak which is characteristically committed to our Bishops. They who bless all for life's work in the name of God must claim for God as a harmonious service every energy of personal and social power. A Bishop is not the father of the clergy only, but of the Church—the head not of an order only, but of a people. Let us not doubt that when our Bishops have measured the problems of the age by the spirit of counsel, they will receive the spirit of prophecy in answer to the prayer of faith. This spirit comes through the old channels. Therefore it is that the Bible is delivered again into the Bishop's hands, but with a new charge. It is not enough that he should 'preach the Word of God.' He must 'think upon the things contained in that book' with resolute meditation. He must be 'diligent in them, that the increase coming thereby may be manifest unto all men.' On him rests the responsibility of mastering the latest meaning of the written Word, and commending it practically to the world.

For the Scriptures, like the human character of Christ, are of no age and of no country. Their last utterance will not be spoken while the world lasts. To each generation it is given to see something more of their wealth. Already, I will venture to say, the facts which have been established in our time as to the relations of man to man and of man to nature have filled with a new meaning mysterious passages of St. Paul, and revealed fresh depths in the historic message of the Gospel. It is hard indeed to realise that in these ways God is speaking to us. For many, as of old, the Divine voice is but a thunderpeal. We want then the disciplined guidance of the prophet; but we can feel that the whole significance of life will be changed when we have learnt to listen for tidings of the will of our God and Saviour from every investigator of His works; when the enthusiasm of discovery is no longer met by the cry, 'No further,' but hallowed by the petition, *Speak, Lord, for thy servant heareth.* To refuse to welcome any truths, however fragmentary they may be, to dissemble them, to force them to the model of our prepossessions, is to dishonour the Spirit which is sent in Christ's name. Little by little He is unfolding now that Name on which all being is a commentary. Theology, Christian Theology, cannot be stationary. Every fact which is added to our knowledge of man or of the world illuminates our knowledge of God. Here, also, the Psalmist's words are true—*from strength to strength.*

The loftiest Functions of the Episcopate

WE must look to our Episcopate for the expression of the spirit of counsel and of the spirit of prophecy. It may seem chimerical to seek from those who are overburdened by routine duties the fulfilment of these loftiest functions, which can only be fulfilled in spaces of calm thought. Something, no doubt, must be sacrificed if the end is to be gained. But if the end appears to be attainable, every needful sacrifice will be cheerfully made.

Men are growing weary of the restless activity which makes reflection impossible where it is most necessary. Let it but be seen that the whole life is given to the office, and they will be content to postpone their own wants.

A Choice of Work necessary

IN the highest places there must be a choice of work. Much must be left undone that that which is most needful may be done. To determine what is most needful is the supreme responsibility of leadership; and he will best fulfil the office of spiritual government who has courage to regard the proportion between the manifold demands which are made upon his care; who has patience to labour in silence for the distant harvest which he will not reap; who has sympathy to win and to use that devotion of others by which great leaders are strong; who can follow the movements of science, of philanthropy, of legislation, from the vantage-ground of Faith; who can recognise the Divine call which bids him offer no conventional service, but that which the past has given him in practical experience and intellectual wealth.

A life spent in dealing with the young may bias my own judgment; but I feel that there are untold victories for Christ within the reach of him to whom it may be given to keep alive and strengthen the simple devotion and the high desires of early manhood when entering on the active business of life.

There is often a rude contrast between our first ideals and our first practical efforts. In the shock many let Faith slip, many try to support it by artificial stays. On all sides we banish to some distant time the immediate action of God. We treasure as dead relics the forces which we should recognise as living powers. Because the fashion of the world changes, we think that Heaven is farther off now than in the childhood of the Church.

But let our Fathers in God make it clear that every righteous activity is a Divine service, that every aspiration after truth is, consciously or unconsciously, a looking to Christ, that every Article of the Creed is a motive and a help to holiness.

Let them proclaim again the words of Apostles and Evangelists without disparaging the partial formulas in which men of old time have translated them, and without accepting any one formula as final and exhaustive.

Let them offer as the scene of human labour a world not left fatherless, echoing with spiritual voices, and bound together through all its parts with underlying harmonies of love.

Let them keep steadily before the eyes of men *the weightier matters of the law, judgment, mercy, and faith,* which bring into their true place deep and doubtful questionings, framed of necessity in imperfect language.

Let them gather round them, as Bede bade Egbert, such a companionship as may shew by a simple life the power of that Presence on which they look.

Let them hold forth in all its splendour to eager souls the ideal of that Kingdom in which each earthly achievement finds its consummation, and each earthly effort its hallowing; and I can well believe that a revolution will be effected, even in a single generation, more beneficent than that of the Fourth Century in social influence; more disciplined than that of the Thirteenth in personal self-sacrifice; more comprehensive than that of the Sixteenth in the co-ordination of truth.

Who is Sufficient for these Things?

As the vision rises before us, as we feel that it answers to the inherent power of our Faith, as we confess that it lingers far off, dim and fleeting, through our great fault, we cry again, bowed down with past failures, disheartened by our present divisions, paralysed by the measures of our hopes, *Who is sufficient for these things?*

There can be but one answer—He who wholly forgets himself in God Who called him.

The Ministerial Office

THE welfare of the Church is, indeed, always perilled in the ministers of the Church; and if we dare interpret by earlier precedents the signs of this immediate crisis, it rests in a degree with the English clergy of this generation, under the Divine providence, to determine the part which Christianity shall play hereafter in the national life of our empire—I had almost said, in the civilisation of the world. Every circumstance combines to stir us to something of heroic effort; and it is well that we should pause from time to time, teachers alike and taught, to gain inspiration, so to speak, from the grandeur of our cause.

The work cannot be fashioned on one traditional type, but grows with the growth of nations, and corresponds to the fulness of the life of man.

It does not deal with any fragmentary section of human interests or feelings, but claims to consecrate everything which we are and have in due order to an eternal destiny. It may find a readier acceptance when sorrow or sickness dulls our sense of present joy and power and hope; but in itself it is the ministry of strength and not of weakness, of life and not of death,— of strength made perfect through weakness, of life rising out of death.

It is progressive in form; it is comprehensive in range; it is universal in application.

The Work of the Christian Ministry progressive in Form

THE work of the Christian ministry is progressive in form.

What Luther said of the Christian is most true of the minister. He who *is* a minister is no minister.

Becoming, not being, movement, not repose, effort, not acquiescence, is the rule of the ministerial character. Because truth is one and infinite while men are ever changing, the expression of truth in order to be adequate —complete it cannot be—must vary ceaselessly. And those to whose care the ministry of Truth is committed must labour with absolute devotion to fashion their message according to the exigencies of their hearers.

Experience shews that no adequate expression of truth can ever lose its spiritual value, when taken in connection with the circumstances under which it gained currency; but if dissevered from them it may, in new relations, become misleading, or even false.

It results from the constitution of our minds, and the conditions under which opinion is formed and expressed, that no infallible teaching can ever relieve us from the obligation to thought,—that no paramount authority can ever deprive us of the prerogative of judgment.

The very simplest words necessarily change their value as we or the world grow older.

"Man" and "heaven" and "God" mean something very different to us now from the acceptation in which we used them when we were children: something very different to the Englishmen of our generation from the thoughts which they stirred in the minds of the Saxon converts of Augustine.

The Work of the Christian Ministry comprehensive in its Range

OF all men the Christian minister is enabled to cherish the widest sympathies, the most varied interests, the most passionate devotion to truth.

He has reached the central idea of all life, and therefore he welcomes without jealousy everything, from whatever source, which contributes to the greater completeness of its realisation.

He rejoices in every discovery which helps him to feel more distinctly the unity of our complex powers, the dependence of man on man, the connection of men with nature, and to see in all, with a faith which reaches forth to its true goal, one order embodying, as it were, one thought.

He may not be endowed with original genius, but he has a power of recognising the due proportion of things from the constant use of a Divine standard.

He may not be a scholar, but he knows that no documents, however sacred, are exempted from the general laws which rule the transmission and interpretation of written memorials.

He may not be a physicist, but he perceives clearly what can be determined by observation and experiment, and adjusts at once without an effort the complementary revelations of the seen and of the unseen.

And, according to his ability, he turns his convictions into practice. He accepts it as a sacred duty to strive to understand the forms and methods of each typical section of inquiry in which he has no independent part.

A theologian who studies theology only is like a man who is master but of one language.

The student of theology who is also, however humbly, if honestly, a student of history and a student of nature, will have gained a universe in service to his faith.

He will feel that his royal science is indeed the sum and crown of all sciences, sharing in the amplitude of their growth, and harmonising the variety of their issues.

The Application of the Office of the Christian Ministry universal

UNDOUBTEDLY the Gospel has a characteristic message for the poor, the sick, the sorrowful, the outcast; but that message rests upon the essential human nature which it recognises in them in common with the wealthy, the vigorous, the powerful.

The Christian minister abandons the hardest portion of his work if he shrinks from claiming for his Lord, in virtue of his faith, "the high things of the world." He is commissioned to conquer as well as to receive: to bring into subjection the strong who claim to stand by themselves, as well as the weak who rejoice in the prospect of shelter.

He may fail, but at least he must not derogate from the extent of his charge.

The facts of the Incarnation and the Resurrection have a peculiar lesson for every state and every character and every age.

Our greatest privilege is not to suppress what belongs to sense, but to see all transformed; not to regard time as a tedious parenthesis, but as the veil of eternity, half-hiding, half-revealing what *is* for ever: not to divert the interests of men from that which their hands find to do, but to invest every fragment of work with a potential divinity, and point out its necessary permanence.

The Discipline of Expectancy

IT is not for us to fix the duration of our proving. Nothing is more fatal to the cause of truth than the premature zeal which anticipates the divine hour for action.

We may be sure, as the apostles were sure, of our mission, but there are perhaps good reasons why silent delays should follow our call.

We may think that something already lies within our power, but, if God so orders, we shall find in the sore trial of inaction that quiet heavenward watching is the very condition of lasting success.

Over the whole Bible, over the whole history of the Church, over the record of each soul's life, the words are written: *Not by might, nor by power, but by My Spirit, saith the Lord of Hosts.*

Sit still until ye be clothed with power.—Again and again it has seemed that the world has been on the point of conquering when the time of waiting has been crowned by spiritual triumph.

It was so when the old Roman Empire in one last struggle attempted first to crush and then to absorb the Church.

It was so when about four centuries later the pagan northmen on the one side, and the Mohammedan armies on the other, threatened to desolate and unchristianise all Europe.

It was so again when, after another like period, the Church itself had become an imperial tyranny, and the spiritual aspects of the Gospel seemed to be in danger of being effaced by its material splendour.

It was so yet again when the treasures of ancient thought were reopened in the sixteenth century, and in the boldness of reawakened life nations were eager to cast off the restraints of religious discipline, and scholars were not careful to reverence the domains of faith.

But in every case the Lord vindicated the majesty of His word. The promise of the Father never failed in its accomplishment, though it was accomplished in unexpected ways. After the earthquake and the fire came the still small voice; and the disciples of Christ, as they caught its accents, were clothed with power, and claimed —claimed in triumph—for their King the very forces which had been arrayed against Him.

Christ's Words not exhausted by past Fulfilments

THE words of the Risen Christ suffer no change. They were not exhausted by past fulfilments. Past fulfilments, if we regard them rightly, serve mainly to enlarge our hopes and to confirm our courage. They shew us where we may advance and not where we may rest. The promise looks forward as long as one fragment of Truth remains to be realised. The power is given to be used as long as one enemy of God remains to be overcome.

There is a stirring eloquence in the shaking of states and the restlessness of society which our hearts, if they heed, cannot mistake. They are, I believe, a prelude to some new victory of Faith to be won after patient waiting.

A Social Revolution to be faced

IF I may venture to forecast what the future will be with which you will have to deal, I ask you while hope is still fresh and enthusiasm unchilled to gain some conception of the solemnity, the vastness, the unity, the purpose of life; to pause in the street or on the riverbank and ask yourselves what that strange stream of pleasure and frivolity and sorrow and vice means, and means to you: to reflect that you are bound by intelligible bonds to every suffering, sinning man and woman: to learn, while the lesson is comparatively easy, the secret of human sympathy: to search after some of the essential relationships of man to man : to interpret a little of the worth of even trivial labour : to grow sensitive to the feelings of the poor : to grow considerate to the claims of the weak.

You will have to face, I believe, the forces of a social revolution ; and you will face them with a transforming energy, if you offer yourselves now as expectants of the promise of Christ.

The Spiritual Office of the Universities

IT is just fifty years since De Maistre, in reviewing the future of Europe, said (*Du Pape*, p. 374, ed. 1860. The whole passage is worthy of study) that England was "destined to give the impulse to the religious movement then in preparation which should be a sacred epoch in the annals of the world ;" and these fifty years have gone far to confirm his assertion.

To fulfil it rests now, I believe, in no small degree with our ancient universities.

These magnificent societies, which are themselves the monuments of the ancient spiritual power of England, contain within them the elements of a new spiritual power fitted to deal with the problems of our own age.

The meaning of the phrase "spiritual power" has

been unduly narrowed in these later times. Yet it is evident that there are two main functions of the spiritual power. It has a ministerial office and it has an intellectual office. It is charged to perform sacred duties, and it is charged also to guide opinion.

For a time, during periods of transition or preparation, both functions may be discharged by the same organ; but in this, as in every case, the highest development is marked by the specialisation of action.

As thoughts widen a regular clergy, so to speak, rises beside the secular clergy; and men who devote their energies to the pious duties of divine ministration are fain to look to others with ampler leisure and wider opportunities for the fulfilment of an intellectual work of which they may receive the fruits.

It has been so in past time; and yet for the present we seem to be abandoned to anarchy. As a necessary consequence energy is misdirected, faith is shaken, and individualism cramps the highest natures.

Action, even with the leaders of opinion, outruns thought. Administration is mistaken for government. Those who might be great teachers are content to be indifferent practicians. The vivifying and progressive power of counsel is postponed to the constraining force of command. Political remedies are proposed as adequate for spiritual evils. An empirical system is substituted for a disciplined life.

Now it is not too much to say that the Universities, and the Universities alone, can remedy these evils. And for this end no change is needed in their constitution: no revolution in their studies: no modification of their essentially religious character. We ask only that they interpret to our own age their history, their scope, their spirit.

The "Relativity" of all Human Development to be taught

WE ask that they teach the relativity of all human developments, as opposed to finality, and thus guide action.

We ask that they teach the catholicity of study, as opposed to dispersiveness, and thus guide thought.

We ask that they teach the spiritual destination of every personal effort, and of every fragmentary inquiry, as opposed to selfish isolation, and thus, not indeed consecrate being, but reveal to all the fulness of its divine grandeur.

We ask first that the Universities as a spiritual power teach the "relativity" of all human development.

The position which ancient languages and literature have always occupied in them is a pledge that they recognise what has been called by a profound instinct "humanity" as the basis of their teaching.

But the exigencies of direct education have a tendency to narrow the limits of this vast subject; and we have suffered, suffered grievously, from the undue contraction of the rich field of historical labour.

We have lost, or are on the point of losing, that encyclopædic conception of the life and monuments of antiquity which is alone sufficient here.

For purposes of elementary discipline it may be, it must be, well to concentrate attention on the details of language, and on the highest models of style. Grammatical precision and cultivated taste are unquestionably the essential foundation, but these are nothing more than the foundation of classical learning.

If the University exercises upon these studies her spiritual prerogative, she will shew that the subtlest delicacies of expression, the noblest masterpieces of literature, belong to and spring out of a slow national growth, and pass away in a slow national decay.

Two Great Dangers

AT present we are exposed to two great dangers which this spiritual interpretation of earlier times may avert.
 On the one hand a powerful school of politicians aims at reconstructing society independently of history.
 On the other hand a powerful school of churchmen aims at regenerating society by reproducing the past.
 Both efforts may be disastrous, though in the end they must be alike futile.
 In life there is no fresh beginning. In life there is no possibility of repetition.

Antiquity should be to us as our own youth, rich in hope, in vigour, in aspiration, which mature age is called upon not to contemn or depreciate, not to vainly regret, or still more vainly rival, but to fulfil with sober progress and to crown with ripe achievement.

The Catholicity of Study to be taught

THE first work of the University as a spiritual power is to connect its literary teaching both in form and purpose with the whole progress of humanity. But it has also to co-ordinate the various departments of science. For we ask again that the University should openly recognise and teach the catholicity of study.

To speak of the imaginary conflicts between
"science" and "religion" may be humiliating, but we
must face the humiliation till we have removed the
misconceptions which have given to them a semblance
of reality.

The character of Cambridge studies seems to me to
make success in this respect comparatively easy here,
which elsewhere might appear difficult or hopeless.

The facts which arrange themselves round the three
final existences which consciousness reveals, self, the
world, and God, spring from different sources, are tested
by different proofs, and in their proper nature can *never*
interfere, because they move in distinct regions.

The judgment of conscience and the conception of
God are progressive and relative. Both claim to penetrate beyond the present order, and just so far as they
serve to realise to us the unseen and the eternal they
must transcend the criteria of sense, and introduce
elements not included in the constitution of our own
minds.

Materialism is an invasion of theology by physics:
pietism is an invasion of physics by theology.

Even if there is no actual trespass, it is as perilous to
study a lower subject without regard to the higher, as to
study a higher subject without regard to the lower.

Thus there is need in any engrossing intellectual
pursuit of a personal discipline, and (so to speak) of a
collective discipline. When once this is recognised,
Theology, the science of revelation, will be seen in the
grandeur of its true office ; and Metaphysics, the science
of introspection, and Science, popularly so called, the

science of observation, will be indefinitely elevated by the introduction of a moral element into abstract study.

The study of history shews the unity of life: the study of science shews the unity of thought: the study of action shews the unity of being: unities broken indeed by man's sin, but yet potentially restored by Christ.

To bring these out into a clearer and more commanding light is the highest work of education.

To inspire men with a sense of their sovereign grandeur is the spiritual office of the Universities.

The Universities have the Means ready before them

NOWHERE else can there be found the same full combination of contrasted pursuits controlled and fostered for one end.

Nowhere else can there be found the same grave harmony of things old and new which gives life to order and stability to progress.

Here the widest, calmest, grandest thoughts are most natural.

The speciality of teaching is relieved by the necessity of culture.

Education passes into life, for men, who are the hope of England, are brought under these moving influences at a time when they are most susceptible of permanent impressions.

Here only the chosen representatives of a generation meet as *men* enriching a society of equals with their different gifts.

Here only are they bound together by a common discipline and a common aim before they are scattered to the divided duties of their lives.

Here only are they able to realise on a wide scale by daily fellowship that deep sympathy in difference which is the strength of action.

In this aspect the general spirit of the Universities is of more importance than the special teaching which they afford.

The spirit is the life: the teaching is only one embodiment of the life.

Occupations close round us, and we necessarily exaggerate the magnitude of present cares because we see them near.

Our personal interests, by the force of their importunity, exclude all larger sympathies if these are not already matured before the conflict begins. In the press of the world we lose sight of life, if the life is not within us.

An ideal may seem unattainable, but when it is distinctly acknowledged as the object of aspiration, it will be found close at hand.

It seems to me that the total effect of the Universities, great as it is, is not at present commensurate with the sources which they command, because they do *not* set forth boldly their highest aim. There is a moral irony in those who give the tone to them which hides from many eyes the devotedness of the scholar's life.

Let the Universities only be seen to be what they are, let those who animate them confess openly their deepest thoughts, and the end is gained.

Each one who comes within their reach shall find in them a spiritual power, not "wasting the patrimony of faith," but enlarging, deepening, elevating the conception of religious life, and will go forth from them to his appointed place with the conviction that he stands between two ages, inheriting a boundless past, and fashioning, irrevocably fashioning, a boundless future.

There is very much in life which, externally at least, is dull and weary and mechanical: there is very much in life which brings us face to face with mysteries which our reason and our soul acknowledge to be final.

To feel no rude discords, no inexorable checks, no passionate and unfulfilled longings, to find, in a word, peace on earth, is to deny Christ: but to trust to a harmony as yet imperfect, to trust to failure as "a triumph's evidence," to trust that God will complete what we are sure that He has begun, is to know the power of Christ's Resurrection.

And when the universities have crowned the education of their sons with this knowledge, then will England be prepared to fulfil her mission for which, as it seems, the world is now waiting.

Symptoms of coming Struggle

WE cannot accept as final alternatives for man abject superstition or open unbelief, despotism or anarchy.

Our perils are obvious. Materially there is the concentration of wealth in fewer and fewer hands, while at the same time men are treated more and more as equal units in a sum total.

Intellectually there is the hasty and restless striving to fashion a system of the universe by the extension of one method to all things.

Spiritually there is the separation of thought from action, of philosophy from life, which ends in the substitution of a sentiment or a doctrine for religion.

In other words, we are threatened by the supremacy of a false standard which destroys the conception of order: by a false unity which destroys the conception of creation: by a false worship which destroys the conception of sin.

But, on the other hand, the thoughts which are quickened by the contemplation of these dangers, and by the endeavour to understand the causes out of which they spring, stir in us those aspirations through which wisdom comes; and, unless I am mistaken, we are already gaining livelier, fuller, deeper views of our Christian Faith than have been hitherto revealed. They may be vague, but at least they are full of light.

Never before have men been brought so near to the practical confession of the solidarity of life as they are now brought: never before have they been so firmly possessed by the sense of the ultimate cohesion of all that is unrolled in long succession through the slow experience of men: never before has it been possible for others to feel as we can now feel what is included in the communing of the individual soul with God.

These are truths which the discipline, the studies, the friendships of our University seem to be fitted to create and to develop.

The Intellectual Training of the Clergy

CHRISTIANITY is the absolute religion, and therefore the Christian minister must apprehend clearly the relation in which Christian theology, as a science, stands to all other sciences. Christianity is a historical religion, and therefore he must be conversant with the laws of investigation into the past. He needs, above all men, largeness of view and critical discipline. It follows, therefore, that his training must be, if I may use the term, encyclopædic in spirit and historical in method.

The theologian who studies theology only is really as liable to error, as unnaturally cramped, as imperfectly equipped for his work, as a philologer would be who confined himself to the knowledge of a single language.

It is his task to watch for the convergence of all the streams of truth, to gather every scattered ray of light, without hurry and without misgiving; without hurry, for time is to him only "the shadow which his *weakness* shapes"; without misgiving, for he knows, as no one else can know, that all truth, all light is one.

We shall all feel that this largeness of sympathy, this comprehensiveness of view, this patience of discrimination, must be gained before the student devotes himself to the special study of the master-science of his life. Theology, true theology, is inspired by such a spirit, but the pursuit of theology alone will not produce it any more than the pursuit of physics or of philosophy.

We shall feel also that this spirit is the natural product of the Universities. No other intellectual discipline besides that which they supply can present to men with equal efficiency the manifoldness of knowledge, and at the same time shew how all subserves in various ways to the same end.

The peculiar difficulties which beset faith now seem to spring from two sources—from supposed consequences of the study of physics, and from supposed consequences of the study of life. It is argued, on the one hand, to put the case in the broadest light, that we are placed under a system of inevitable sequences; and, on the other, that the forms of religious belief are functions, so to speak, of particular stages of progress, individual or national.

The problems which arrange themselves under these two heads are unquestionably grave and urgent. They are problems which Christian students alone, as I believe, can solve, so far as it is given to man as yet to solve them; and they are problems which all Christian students who desire to see far into the depths of the Gospel ought to face.

Neither in morals nor theology is ignorance the surest safeguard of lasting purity. Faith (our Christian faith) can, I am sure, use the conscious or unconscious services of every labourer for truth. It can claim and consecrate tribute from every region of the universe. It can move inviolate through every element and leave a blessing behind it. Faith is blanched and impoverished not in light but in darkness. It gains strength in the air and sunshine. Then it is crippled, dishonoured, imperilled, when it is isolated, when its supremacy is circumscribed, when its fresh springs of knowledge are stopped up. The true divine must be in sympathy with every science: the true son of faith is emphatically a son of light.

I cannot then but believe that it is an inestimable advantage for students of theology that they should accomplish the first stages of their work in the closest intercourse with those who are engaged in other fields of labour, and guided by other methods of inquiry. By so doing, and hardly in any other way, will they become intelligently conversant with the adverse forces which they have to meet: they will find scattered treasures which fall under their own domain. There may be some shipwrecks of faith in this mental commerce: the great deeps of thought cannot, in our imperfect state, be traversed without peril; but, on the whole, faith will grow stronger, and the interpretation of faith will grow wider and richer, as the manifold relations of Christianity with every fragment of life become more clearly seen.

And this wider vision cannot but be best gained in the Universities, where every form of intellectual activity ought to be freshest and most energetic.

The Mission of the Schoolmaster

HE gave gifts unto men, and the gifts which He gave were men, not primarily forms, or rites, or institutions, though these have their place, their necessary place, in a human society, but living men.

From age to age the relative importance of different forms of work changes as we imperfectly estimate their worth.

With the schoolmasters, I believe, more than with the clergy rests the shaping of that generation which will decide in a large degree what the England of the future will be, turbulent, divided, self-indulgent, materialised, or quickened with a power of spiritual sympathy, striving towards the realisation of a national ideal, touched already with that spirit of sacrifice which regards every gift of fortune and place and character as held for the common good.

Living contact with the young is a spring of youth.
As you enter into their thoughts you receive something of their freshness.
The true teacher can never grow old.
He always hears the children's voices and can understand them.
Thus to him the benediction of entrance into heaven is presented as a perpetual reality.

If, as some have most strangely said, elementary teaching becomes "narrowing," it is when all human interest has died out of it, when faith supports no enthusiasm, and hope sees no visions, and love rejoices in no sacrifices.

The Teacher's Duty to Educate, not to Furnish

Do not allow measurable, technical results to modify your own ideal, still less to shape it.

Resolutely maintain that you have to educate, not to furnish: to call out effort, self-control, observation, reflection: to prepare your scholars for the great school of after-life: to fit them to be not faultless fragments in a perfect machine, but thoughtful, struggling citizens in a present kingdom of God.

We need to learn as it has not yet been learnt that it is the prerogative of man to think, and not of any particular class of men: to learn that right doing involves in its completeness right reasoning: to learn that elevation of soul is for all.

The Nobility of Labour

We have at least learned in theory the foundation truth.

We have learnt the nobility of labour. Toil is not, as it was to Greek ears, synonymous with wretchedness or vice. But we have still to realise it in its moral beauty.

There can be, as far as I can see, no stable peace till it can be openly shewn on a large scale that the toiler with slender means may be rich in all that makes life worth living, filled with the joy of devotion to the good and the true and the beautiful and the holy.

The Teacher Himself a Spiritual Gift

In the deepest and truest sense, in respect of all that gives a living power to education, the teacher's work is concentrated in himself. He is the spiritual gift. What he is his work will be. More powerful than any subject or any words is that force of conviction by which the true teacher insensibly conveys his own estimate of the worth of things. As we listen to him we feel that we are in contact with that which is real; and his faith stirs ours.

Christian Teaching through the Classic Writers

IT was through the Greek historian or the Latin poet that I was taught most impressively what our Christian Faith means: taught that there is a divine counsel being wrought out about us in daily duties: taught that words and deeds are true if partial revelations of an abiding character: taught that the least difference of form or expression has a meaning which we can often interpret and may never disregard: taught that there is a truth in the world to which we owe the service of complete devotion: taught that there are effects, correspondences, of human action reaching beyond all thought: taught that we can find rest only in God, for whom we were made.

The Ministry of the Laity

EVEN under the old dispensation the greatest prophets were laymen—David, Isaiah, Daniel were laymen—and yet we have unlearnt, or failed to learn, in this later age, the law which imposes upon him who has found the truth the obligation of proclaiming it.

Let any one read the epistles of the New Testament as records of a real life, and he will find that the powers, the responsibilities, the victories of spiritual gifts, are not for a small section of the Church, but for all, to be used by each according to the circumstances of his position.

The Joy of Teaching and its Reward

I NEED not speak to you of the joy of teaching and its exceeding great reward; how our own thoughts grow clearer, fuller, wider, as we see them taken up, reflected, extended by our scholars; how difficulties frankly met become sources of fresh conviction; how sympathy opens the springs of unexpected enthusiasm; how a power of life enters into doctrines which are dead theories as long as we keep them to ourselves; how each point that is illuminated becomes a new luminary, for *everything that is made manifest is light.*

The Spirit of Teaching

I NEED not speak to you of the spirit of teaching; of that patience which, as was said of one of the noblest of modern Frenchmen, is "tender to dulness as to every form of poverty"; of that reality which refuses to advance by hearsay beyond the limits of personal conviction and experience; of that reverence which shields the purity of early faith from questionings born of human wilfulness; of that golden law which provides that we can only teach that which we know, and as we enter into the soul of our pupil.

The End of Teaching

I NEED not speak to you of the end of teaching; how we aim finally not at producing wide knowledge or great thoughts, but noble lives; how for us all nature and all history is a revelation of the being and will of

God offered, not for contemplation only, but for guidance in deed; how we remember that of the manifold stores which we accumulate by diligent study the character alone survives all earthly change, the character which is the last sum of the moral forces by which our labours have been ruled; how in this sense all teaching must be religious or irreligious, helping to fashion new links of sympathy between the seen and the unseen, or imprisoning our life in sense, making, as has been finely said, "our bodies the tombs of our souls."

The Trials of a New Age

"He that is near Me," the Lord is reported to have said, "is near fire." And we cannot hope to endure the splendour of a fuller, purer light without enduring the pain which necessarily comes from the removal of the veils by which it is obscured.

Gain through apparent loss; victory through momentary defeat; the energy of a new life through the pangs of travail; such has ever been the law of spiritual progress.

This law has been fulfilled in every crisis of reformation; and it is illustrated for our learning in every page of the New Testament.

In no apostolic writing is the truth unfolded with such pathetic force as in the Epistle to the Hebrews. And so it is, I think, that that mysterious "word of consolation" appeals to us with a voice of thrilling power in our time of trial, when the law of progress, the law of fruitfulness through death, seems to be hastening to fresh fulfilment.

Men who had lived in the light of the Old Testament, who had known the joy of a noble ritual, men who had habitually drawn near to God in intelligible ways, men who had but lately welcomed Him in Whom they believed that the glory of Israel should be consummated, were most unexpectedly required to face what seemed to them to be the forfeiture of all that they held dearest.

The letter of Scripture, the worship of the temple, the expectations of national triumph, had to be abandoned.

They could not but begin to reckon up their loss and gain. The fresh enthusiasm of their early faith had died away in the weary waiting of a lifetime.

They had in part degenerated because they had not grown.

The Trials of early Believers an Image of our Own

NOW when we read the apostolic words, and picture to ourselves the sorrows which they illuminated—when we feel that in the portraiture of the perils of early believers we have the record of true struggles, and know that the essential elements of human discipline must always be the same—we cannot, I think, fail to recognise in the trials of the Hebrews of the first age an image of the peculiar trials by which we are beset; and so by their experience we may gain the assurance that for us also there is the promise of larger wisdom where they found it in wider views of Christ's Person and Work, that *the removal of those things that are shaken* is brought about in order *that those things which are not shaken may remain* in serener and simpler beauty.

If we look at the circumstances of the Hebrews a

little more closely we shall notice that the severity of their trials came in a great degree from mistaken devoutness.

They had determined, in obedience to traditional opinion, what Scripture should mean, and they found it hard to enter into its wider teaching.

They had determined that institutions which were of Divine appointment must be permanent, and they found it hard to grasp the realities by which the forms of the older worship were replaced.

Now in these respects we cannot fail to recognise that the difficulties of the Hebrews correspond with our own. For I am speaking now of the difficulties of those who hold to their first faith, and are yet conscious of shakings, changes, losses, of the removing of much which they formerly identified with it.

Many among us, for example, tremble with a vague fear when they find that that "Divine Library," in the noble language of Jerome, which we call the Bible —"the Books"—"the Book"—cannot be summarily separated by a sharp unquestionable line from the other literature with which it is connected; that the text and the interpretation of the constituent parts have not been kept free from the corruptions and ambiguities which require the closest exercise of critical skill; that deductions have been habitually drawn from incidental modes of expression in Scripture which cannot be maintained in the light of that fuller knowledge of God's working which He has given us.

Others again find the historical problems raised by the study of the Bible carried into a wider region.

THE TRIALS OF A NEW AGE

They learn in the turmoil of action and they learn in the silence of their own souls that the Faith can no longer be isolated and fenced off from rude questionings as something separate from common life. They perceive that they must bear, as they can, to acknowledge once and again that formulas which, in earlier times, seemed to declare the Gospel adequately, no longer cover the facts of the world as they have been revealed to us in these later days.

And others have a more grievous trial still. As their view of the world is widened; as they come to understand better the capacities of humanity and the claims of Christ; as they are driven to compare the promises of the kingdom of God with the present fruits of its sway; as they feel that they cannot separate themselves from the race of which they are heirs; as they look upon the light, still after eighteen centuries struggling (as it appears) against eclipse, their hearts may well sink within them. We cannot wonder if such are tempted to ask with those of old times, *Where is the promise of His coming?* or to listen with little more than the sad protest of a lonely trust to the bold assertions of those who say that the Faith has exhausted its power in dealing with the facts of an earlier and simpler civilisation.

And what then shall we say? How shall we escape the double danger which besets us of hastily surrendering every position which is boldly challenged, or of rigidly refusing to consider arguments which tend to modify traditional opinion?

I do not doubt for one moment as to my answer. I bid those who are tempted to accept their trials with the frankest trust as the conditions through which they will be brought to know God better.

Each Region of anxious Trial fruitful in Blessing

I HAVE been forced, by the peculiar circumstances of my work, to regard from many sides the difficulties which beset our historic Faith. If I know by experience their significance and their gravity; if I readily allow that on many points I wish for fuller light; then I claim to be heard when I say without reserve that I have found each region of anxious trial fruitful in blessing: that I have found my devout reverence for every word of the Bible quickened and deepened when I have acknowledged that it demands the exercise of every faculty with which I have been endowed, and that it touches the life of man at every point, it welcomes, from its fuller understanding, the help which comes from every gain of human knowledge.

The Consolation of the Hebrew Christians ours also

IF our trials, the trials of a new age, correspond with those of the Hebrews, the consolation which availed for them avails for us also.

We shall find in due course, as they found, that all we are required to surrender—childlike prepossessions, venerable types of opinion, partial and impatient hopes—is given back to us in a new revelation of Christ; that He is being brought nearer to us, and shewn in fresh glory, through the "fallings from us, vanishing of sense and earthly things," which we had been inclined to identify with Himself.

Christus Consolator and Christus Consummator

THERE is a picture with which we are all familiar, in which Christ seated in glory is represented as dispensing His gifts to the representatives of suffering humanity.

From His hands the slave receives freedom and the sick health: the mourner finds rest in His sympathy, old men peace, children joy. "Christus Consolator" is indeed an image which touches every heart.

But it is not the whole Gospel; it is not, I venture to think, the particular aspect of the Gospel which is offered by the Spirit of God to us now for our acknowledgment.

Sin, suffering, sorrow, are not the ultimate facts of life. These are the work of an enemy; and the work of our God and Saviour lies deeper.

The Creation stands behind the Fall, the counsel of the Father's love behind the self-assertion of man's wilfulness. And I believe that if we are to do our work we must learn to think, not only of the redemption of man, but also of the accomplishment of the Divine purpose for all that God made. We must learn to think of that *summing up of all things in Christ*, in the phrase of St. Paul, which crowns the last aspirations of physicist and historian with a final benediction.

We must dare, in other words, to look beyond Christ the Consoler to Christ the Fulfiller. *Christus Consolator* —let us thank God for the revelation which leaves no trial of man unnoticed and unsoothed—leads us to *Christus Consummator*.

Progress still the Essence of Faith

LET us remember that progress is still, as in the first age, the essence of our faith. We have to gather little by little the fruits of a victory in which Christ has overcome the world. The Hebrews were in danger of apostasy because they failed to go forward. And that we may be shielded from the like peril, the words which were spoken to them are spoken also to us: *let us be borne on to perfection;* not simply "let us go on," or even "let us press on," as if the advance depended on the vigour of our own effort, but "let us be borne on"—"borne on" with that mighty influence which waits only for the acceptance of faith, that it may exert its sovereign sway, "borne on" by Him who is the Way and the End of all human endeavour.

And as we are thus "borne on," as we yield ourselves, yield every gift of mind and body, of place and circumstance, yield all that we cherish most tenderly, to the service of Him in Whom we are made more than conquerors, let us not fear that we shall lose the sense of the vastness of the Divine life in our glad consciousness of its immediate power.

We assuredly shall not fail in reverent gratitude to our fathers for the inheritance which they have bequeathed to us while we acknowledge that it is our duty to improve it.

We shall not disparage the past, while we accept the inspiring responsibility of using to the uttermost the opportunities of the present.

We shall cling with the simplest devotion to every article of our ancient Creed, while we believe, and act as believing, that *this is eternal life, that we may know,*—know, as the original word implies, with a knowledge which is extended from generation to generation, and from day to day,—the only true God and Jesus Christ.

Our Difficulties veiled Promises of coming Wisdom

BY the pursuit of this knowledge we come to recognise that the difficulties which press us most sorely are really the discipline through which God is teaching us: veiled promises of coming wisdom.

We learn through the living lessons of our own experience that the eternal Gospel covers the facts of life, its sorrows, its needs, its joys, its wealth.

Through every conflict the Truth is seen in the majesty of its growing vigour. Shakings, shakings not of the earth only but of the heaven, will come; but what then? We know this, that all that falls is taken away, *that those things which are not shaken may remain.*

The Sight of the Sorrows of Life

TIME has not softened the sharpness of the impression which is made upon thoughtful spectators by the sight of the sorrows of life. If the contrast between man made *a little lower than angels*—nay, literally *a little less than God*—and man as man has made him, was startling at the time when the Apostle wrote, it has not grown less impressive since.

Larger knowledge of man's capacities and of his growth, of his endowments and of his conquests, has only given intensity to the colours in which poets and moralists have portrayed the conflict in his nature and in his life.

Whether we look within or without, we cannot refuse to acknowledge both the element of nobility in man which bears witness to his Divine origin, and also the element of selfishness which betrays his falls.

Every philosophy of humanity which leaves out of account the one or the other is shattered by experience.

The loftiest enthusiasm leaves a place in its reconstruction of society where superstition may attach itself. Out of the darkest depths of crime not seldom flashes a light of self-sacrifice, like the prayer of the rich man for his brethren when he was in torments, which shews that all is not lost.

We cannot accept the theory of those who see around them nothing but the signs of unlimited progress towards perfection, or the theory of those who write a sentence of despair over the chequered scenes of life.

We look, as the Psalmist looked, at the sun and the stars, with a sense which he could not have of the awful mysteries of the depths of night, but we refuse to accept space as a measure of being.

We trace back till thought fails the long line of ages through which the earth was prepared to be our dwelling-place, but we refuse to accept time as a measure of the soul.

We recognise without reserve the influence upon us of our ancestry and our environment, but we refuse to distrust the immediate consciousness of our personal responsibility.

We do not hide from ourselves any of the evils which darken the face of the world, but we do not dissemble our kindred with the worst and lowest, whose life enters into our lives at a thousand points.

We acknowledge that *the whole creation groaneth and travaileth in pain together until now*, but we believe also that these travail-pains prepare the joy of a new birth.

We make no effort to cast off the riddles or the burdens of our earthly state, but we cling all the while to the highest thoughts which we have known as the signs of God's purpose for us and for our fellowmen.

The Sufferings of Christ as a Consummation of Humanity

THE currents of theological speculation have led us to consider the sufferings of Christ in relation to God as a propitiation for sin, rather than in relation to man as a discipline, a consummation of humanity.

The words in which Isaiah spoke of the Servant of the Lord as "taking our infirmities and bearing our sicknesses," were indeed fulfilled when the Son of man healed the sick who came to Him,—healed them not by dispensing from His opulence a blessing which cost Him nothing, but by making His own the ill which He removed.

The true Secret of Happiness

RESPONSIVE love transfigures that which it bears.

Pain loses its sting when it is mastered by a stronger passion. The true secret of happiness is not to escape toil and affliction, but to meet them with the faith that through them the destiny of man is fulfilled.

The Spirit of Divine Discontent

NO thoughtful person can seriously regard the circumstances of his life without feeling the need of forgiveness and the need of strengthening. He looks back upon the past and he sees not only failures, but unnecessary failures. He looks forward to the future, and he sees that while the difficulties of duty do not grow less with added years, the freshness of enthusiasm fades away, and the temptation to accept a lower standard of action grows more powerful. Perhaps in the words of Hood's most touching lyric, he thinks "he's farther off from heaven Than when he was a boy." At any rate, he does feel that in himself he has not reached and cannot reach that for which he was born, that which the spirit of divine discontent within him, a discontent made keener by temporal success, still marks as his one goal of peace. For when Augustine said, *Tu nos fecisti ad te, Domine, et inquietum est cor nostrum donec requiescat in te*, he proclaimed a fact to which every soul bears witness in the silence of its self-communings.

We know that we were made for God; we know that we have been separated from God; we know that we cannot acquiesce in the desolation of that divorce.

The Institution of the Priesthood

THE institution of the priesthood has been misused, degraded, overlaid with terrible superstitions, but in its essence it corresponds with the necessities of our nature. Therefore it has been interpreted and fulfilled in the Bible.

We can yet learn much from the figures of the Levitical system in which the priesthood *of this world* was fashioned by the Spirit of God in a form of marvellous significance and beauty. The law of the priestly service in the Old Testament is indeed a vivid parable of the needs, the aim, the benediction of human life.

The King-priest

THE kingly and priestly offices cannot be kept apart. He who makes atonement must direct action. He who demands the complete service of every power must hallow the powers of which He claims the ministry. The ruler who consecrates, the priest who rules, must be *merciful and faithful;* He must have absolute authority and perfect sympathy; authority that He may represent God to man, sympathy that He may represent man to God. And such is Christ made known to us, King and Priest, *Priest after the order of Melchisedek*, in whose mysterious person the old world on the edge of a new dispensation met and blessed the father of the faithful.

The apostolic words are true for us, true while there is one sin to vex the overburdened conscience, one struggle to strain the feeble will, *such a High Priest became us*.

If human priests compassed with infirmity could inspire confidence in the worshipper, then Christ, if we will lift our eyes to Him, a thousandfold more. Their compassion was necessarily limited by their experience, but His experience covers the whole field of life; their gentle bearing was tempered by the consciousness of failure, but His breathes the invigorating spirit of perfect holiness. They knew the power of temptation in part by the sad lessons of failure; He knew it to the uttermost by perfect victory. They could see dimly through earth-born mists something of the real hideousness of evil; He saw it in the undimmed light of the Divine purity. And He is tenderest, not who has sinned, as is sometimes vainly thought, but who has known best the power of sin by overcoming it. His love is most watchful who has seen what wrong is in the eyes of God.

Can we not then boldly proclaim that here also the Gospel covers the facts of life? that in the prospect of the conflicts and defeats which sadden us, and which we dare not disguise or extenuate, *such a High Priest became us*, strong with the strength of God, compassionate with the affection of a friend?

We must cling to both these truths, and wrestle with them and win their blessing from them.

"Earth's Children cling to Earth"

"EARTH'S children cling to earth," and there are many among us who feel keenly the very trials which the Hebrews felt; who long for some visible system which shall "bring all heaven before their eyes," for some path to the divine presence along which they can walk by sight, for recurrent words of personal absolution from some human minister, for that which shall localise their centre of worship; who labour, often unconsciously, to make the earthly the measure of the spiritual; who shrink from the ennobling responsibility of striving with untiring effort to hold communion with the unseen and eternal; who turn back with regretful looks to the discipline and the helps of a childly age, when they are required to accept the graver duties of maturity; required to listen, as it were, like Elijah on the lonely mountain, when the thunder of the earthquake is stilled and the violence of the fire is spent, for the still small voice.

These are not, I know, imaginary temptations; but if we are tried and disquieted by their assaults, the writer of the Epistle enables us to face them. He brings Christ near to us, and he brings us near to Christ. He discloses the privileges to which we are all admitted by the ascended Saviour. He gives an abiding application to the Lord's words, *He that hath seen Me hath seen the Father*. And He does this without hiding one dark trait in the prospect of life.

The Spectacle of divided and rival Churches

THE spectacle of divided and rival Churches is as sad and far vaster than the spectacle of unbelieving Israel. It is hard for us to bear the prospect of Christendom rent into hostile fragments as it was hard for the Hebrews to bear the anathema of their countrymen. It is hard to look for peace, and to find a sword; to look for the concentration of every force of those who bear Christ's name in a common assault upon evil, and to find energies of thought and feeling and action weakened and wasted in misunderstandings, jealousies, and schisms; to look for the beauty of a visible unity of the faithful which shall strike even those who are without with reverent awe, and to find our divisions a commonplace with mocking adversaries. It is hard; and if what we see were all, the trial would be intolerable.

But what we see is not all: what we see is not even the dim image of that which is. The life which we feel, the life which we share, is more than the earthly materials by which it is at present sustained, more than the earthly vestures through which it is at present manifested.

That is not most real which can be touched and measured, but that which struggles, as it were, to find imperfect expression through the veil of sense: that which to the All-seeing Eye gilds with the light of self-devotion acts that to us appear self-willed and miscalculated; that which to the All-hearing Ear joins in a full harmony words that to us sound fretful and impatient; that which fills our poor dull hearts with a love and sympathy towards all the creatures of God, deeper than just hatred of sin, deeper than right condemnation of error, deeper than the circumstances of birth and place and temperament which kindle the friendships and sharpen the animosities of human intercourse.

If the outward were the measure of the Church of Christ, we might well despair. But side by side with us, when we fondly think, like Elijah, that we stand alone, are countless multitudes whom we know not, angels whom we have no power to discern, children of God whom we have not learnt to recognise.

How we may become one

WE shall become one, not by narrowing and defining the Faith which is committed to us, but by rising, through the help of the Spirit, to a worthier sense of its immeasurable grandeur.

How the first Christians conquered the World

THE character of a generation is moulded by personal character. And if we have considered some of the temptations of the first Christians; if we know a little of the terrible environment of evil by which they were encircled; we must not, as we too often do, forget how they conquered the world.

It was not by any despairing withdrawal from city and market; not by any proud isolation in selfish security; not by any impatient violence; but by the winning influence of gracious faith, they mastered the family, the school, the empire. They were a living Gospel, a message of God's good-will to those with whom they toiled and suffered.

Pure among the self-indulgent, loving among the factious, tender among the ruthless, meek among the vainglorious, firm in faith amidst the shaking of nations, joyous in hope amidst the sorrows of a corrupt society, they revealed to men their true destiny, and shewed that it could be attained.

They appealed boldly to the awakened conscience as the advocate of their claims. They taught as believing that He who had stirred their heart with a great desire would assuredly satisfy it.

They offered not in word but in deed the ideal of spiritual devotion, and "the soul naturally Christian" turned to it, as the flower turns to the light, drew from it, as the flower draws from the light, the richness of perfect beauty.

Yes; that was the secret of their success; and it is the secret of our success. The words are true now as they were when addressed by Zechariah to the poor remnant of Jews struggling to rebuild their outward temple: *Not by might, nor by power, but by My Spirit, saith the Lord of Hosts.* Not first by material change, not by intellectual culture, but by spiritual sympathy will our work be done.

PART III

Aspects of Life

A POET'S VIEW OF LIFE

Browning

IN my undergraduate days, if I remember rightly, I came across the description of a poet which speaks of him as one "who sees the infinite in things." The thought has been to me from that time forward a great help in studying the noblest poetry.

The true poet does, I believe, of necessity, see the infinite in his subject; and he so presents his vision to his readers that they too, if their eyes are open, are enabled in some degree to share in its lessons.

The same gift belongs in a certain degree to the artist. But the range of the poet is unlimited; while the artist's choice of subject is conditioned by the requirement that its treatment shall come within the domain of the beautiful.

The ground of this difference obviously lies in the different means which the poet and the artist use to express what they see with the eyes of the soul. The mode in which words and the melody of words (not now to speak of music) affect us is different in kind from the action of form and colour.

All life, all nature, is therefore the legitimate field of

the poet, as prophet. There is an infinite, an eternal meaning in all, and it is his office to make this intelligible to his students.

No modern poet has more boldly claimed the fulness of his heritage of life than Browning. He has dared to look on the darkest and meanest forms of action and passion, from which we commonly and rightly turn our eyes, and he has brought back for us from this universal survey a conviction of hope.

He has laid bare what there is in man of sordid, selfish, impure, corrupt, brutish, and he proclaims, in spite of every disappointment and every wound, that he still finds a spiritual power in him, answering to a spiritual power without him, which restores assurance as to the destiny of creation.

As has been well pointed out, Browning occupies a position complementary to Wordsworth.

He looks for the revelation of the Divine as coming through the spiritual struggles of man and not through Nature.

Both poets, however, agree in this, that they assert the sovereignty of feeling over knowledge, of that within us which they hold to have affinity with the heavenly and eternal, over that which must be earthly and temporal.

The key-note of Browning's teaching, in a word, is not knowledge, but love.

This learning of love, this acquisition of the power of self-sacrifice, involves a long and painful discipline:

> *Life is probation, and this earth no goal,*
> *But starting-point of man. . . .*
>
> *To try man's foot, if it will creep or climb,*
> *'Mid obstacles in seeming, points that prove*
> *Advantage for who vaults from low to high,*
> *And makes the stumbling-block a stepping-stone.*

A POET'S VIEW OF LIFE—BROWNING

> *Why comes temptation but for man to meet*
> *And master, and make crouch beneath his foot,*
> *And so be pedestalled in triumph.*

The poet teaches that life must be treated as a whole; that learning comes through suffering; that every failure felt to be failure points to final achievement; that the visible present is but one scene in an illimitable growth.

Our present life is to be taken in its entirety. The discipline of man is to be fulfilled, the progress of man is to be secured, under the conditions of our complex earthly being.

These lets and limitations are not to be disparaged or overborne, but accepted and used in due order.

No attempt must be made either to retain that which has been, or to anticipate that which will be.

Each element in human nature is to be allowed its proper office.

Each season brings its own work and its own means.

This conception is wrought out in many-sided completeness in *Rabbi Ben Ezra*, which is, in epitome, a philosophy of life.

Here are the lessons of advancing years:

> *Let us not always say*
> *"Spite of this flesh to-day,*
> *I strove, made head, gained ground upon the whole!"*
> *As the bird wings and sings,*
> *Let us cry, "All good things*
> *Are ours, nor soul helps flesh more now, than flesh helps soul."*

. . . . .

> *Grow old along with me!*
> *The best is yet to be,*
> *The last of life, for which the first was made:*
> *Our times are in His hand*
> *Who saith "A whole I planned,*
> *Youth shews but half; trust God; see all, nor be afraid."*

The capacity for moral progress, thus recognised in the law of outward growth and decay, is indeed laid down by Browning to be the essential characteristic of man:

> *Getting increase of knowledge, since he learns*
> *Because he lives, which is to be a man,*
> *Set to instruct himself by his past self.*

Hence the mutability of things may become a help to his growth:

> *Rejoice that man is hurled*
> *From change to change unceasingly,*
> *His soul's wings never furled.*

The very infirmities of later years, incapacity to receive new impressions, dulness of sight by which far and near are blended together, have their peculiar office in revealing the lessons of life:

> *So at the last shall come old age,*
> *Decrepit as befits that stage;*
> *How else would'st thou retire apart*
> *With the hoarded memories of thy heart,*
> *And gather all to the very least*
> *Of the fragments of life's earlier feast,*
> *Let fall thro' eagerness to find*
> *The crowning dainties yet behind?*

The true human life will therefore present a just balance of powers in the course of its varied progress.

In the strangely fascinating *Epistle of Karshish* Browning has drawn the portraiture of one to whom the eternal is sensibly present, whose spirit has gained prematurely absolute predominance:

> *Heaven opened to a soul while yet on earth,*
> *Earth forced on a soul's use while seeing Heaven:*

and the result is not a man but a sign; a being

> *Professedly the faultier that he knows*
> *God's secret, while he holds the thread of life.*

Lazarus, therefore, while he moves in the world, has lost all sense of proportion in things about him, all measure of and faculty of dealing with that which sways his fellows.

In this crucial example Browning shews how the exclusive dominance of the spirit destroys the fulness of human life, its uses and powers, while it leaves a passive life crowned with an unearthly beauty.

On the other hand, he shews in his study of Cleon that the richest results of earth in art and speculation and pleasure and power are unable to remove from life the desolation of final gloom.

Thus over against the picture of Lazarus is placed that of the poet who by happy circumstances has been enabled to gather to himself all that is highest in the civilisation of Greece.

The contrast is of the deepest significance. The Jewish peasant endures earth, being in possession of heaven : the Greek poet in possession of earth feels that heaven some future state,

> *Unlimited in capability*
> *For joy, as this is in desire for joy*,

is a necessity for man ; but no,

> *Zeus has not yet revealed it ; and alas,*
> *He must have done so, were it possible!*

Flesh and spirit each claim recognition in connection with their proper spheres, in order that the present life may bear its true result.

We must, that we may live human lives, loyally yield ourselves to, and yet master the circumstances in which we are placed.

This is an arduous task, but it is fruitful :

> *When pain ends gain ends too.*

Doubt, rightly understood, is just that vivid, personal, questioning of phenomena which breaks "the torpor of assurance," and gives a living value to decision.

In this sense, and not as if doubts were an absolution from the duty of endeavour, we can say,

> *I prize the doubt,*
> *Low kinds exist without,*
> *Finished and finite clods, untroubled by a spark.*

In such a view of life, as it is thus outlined, no room is left for indifference or neutrality.

There is no surrender to an idle optimism.

A part must be taken and maintained. The spirit in which Luther said *pecca fortiter* finds a powerful expression in *The Statue and the Bust*:

> *Let a man contend to the uttermost*
> *For his life's set prize, be it what it will!*
>
> . . . . .
>
> *And the sin I impute to each frustrate ghost*
> *Is, the unlit lamp and the ungirt loin.*

In the midst of strenuous endeavour or of patient suffering, the lesson of life, the lesson of love, is brought within man's reach. It is finally taught, perhaps, by a sudden appeal of distress (*Caponsacchi*); or by human companionship (*By the Fireside*); or by a message felt to be divine (*Easter Day*).

There are also other sharper ways of enforcing the lesson. One illustration I cannot forbear quoting, for it brings out the basis of Browning's hopefulness, and combines two passages which, in different ways, for grandeur of imagery and for spiritual insight, are unsurpassed in Browning—I will venture to say in literature.

I need not recall the character of Guido, which Browning has analysed with exceptional power and evidently with the deepest interest. This, at last, is the judgment which the Pope pronounces on him:

> *For the main criminal I have no hope*
> *Except in such a suddenness of fate.*
> *I stood at Naples once, a night so dark*
> *I could have scarce conjectured there was earth*
> *Anywhere, sky, or sea, or world at all ;*
> *But the night's black was burst through by a blaze,*
> *Thunder struck blow on blow, earth groaned and bore*
> *Through her whole length of mountain visible:*
> *There lay the city thick and plain with spires,*
> *And, like a ghost dis-shrouded, white the sea.*
> *So may the truth be flashed out by one blow,*
> *And Guido see, one instant, and be saved.*

Degraded and debased, Guido is seen to be not past hope by the true spiritual eye. And what is the issue? Up to the last, with fresh kindled passion, the great criminal re-asserts his hate. He gathers strength to repeat his crime in will. I grow, he says, one gorge

> *To loathingly reject Pompilia's pale*
> *Poison my hasty hunger took for food.*

So the end comes. The ministers of death claim him. In his agony he summons every helper whom he has known or heard of—

> *Abate, Cardinal, Christ, Maria, God—*

and then the light breaks through the blackest gloom :

> *Pompilia, will you let them murder me?*

In this supreme moment he has known what love is, and, knowing it, has begun to feel it.
The cry, like the intercession of the rich man in Hades for his five brethren, is a promise of a far-off deliverance.

In this case the poet shews how we may take heart again in looking at the tragedies of guilt.

But there are wider and more general sorrows in life. There is the failure, the falling from our ideal, of which we are all conscious; there is the incompleteness of opportunity, which leaves noblest powers unused. Browning states the facts without reserve or palliation:

> *All labour, yet no less*
> *Bear up beneath their unsuccess.*
> *Look at the end of work, contrast*
> *The petty Done with the Undone vast,*
> *This Present of theirs with the hopeful Past!*

In dealing with the difficulties which are thus raised, Browning offers what appears to me to be his most striking message. Acknowledged failure is, he teaches, a promise of future attainment; unfruitful preparation is the sign of the continuity of life. And these two principles rest on another: imperfection is the condition of growth:

> *What's whole can increase no more,*
> *Is dwarfed and dies, since here's its sphere.*

And hence comes (as may be noticed parenthetically) the contrast between works of art and living men:

> *They are perfect—how else? they shall never change:*
> *We are faulty—why not? we have time in store.*
> *The artificer's hand is not arrested*
> *With us—we are rough-hewn, nowise polished:*
> *They stand for our copy, and once invested*
> *With all they can teach, we shall see them abolished.*
>
> *'Tis a life-long toil till our lump be leaven;*
> *The better! what's come to perfection perishes.*

Failure, as Browning treats it, may come in two ways. It may come from what he does not scruple to call "the corruption of man's heart," or it may come from the want of necessary external help.

The first form of failure is in various degrees universal.

But as long as effort is directed to the highest, that aim, though it is out of reach, is the standard of hope.

The existence of a capacity, cherished and quickened, is a pledge that it will find scope.

There will yet be, as we believe, a field for the exercise of every power which has been trained and not called into service. What has been consecrated cannot be wasted:

> *Earn the means first—God surely will contrive*
> *Use for our earning.*

The preparation and discipline of intellect is subordinate to the preparation and discipline of feeling.

The end of life is learning love—the learning God—and that in a large degree through human fellowship. *Omne vivum ex vivo*—"life is the one source of life"—is an axiom true in the spiritual as in the physical order.

An intellectual result may be the occasion, but it cannot be the source of a moral quickening.

And what does the poet say of the end? For that which is evil there is judgment of utter destruction; for that which is good, purifying. So it is that chastisement is often seen to come through the noblest part of a character otherwise mean, because in that there is yet hope:

> *You were punished in the very part*
> *That looked most pure of speck,—the honest love*
> *Betrayed you,—did love seem most worthy pains,*
> *Challenge such purging, as ordained survive*
> *When all the rest of you was done with?*

And on the whole

> *There shall never be one lost good! what was shall live as before;*
> *The evil is null, is nought, is silence implying sound;*
> *What was good shall be good with, for evil, so much good more;*
> *On the earth the broken arcs; in heaven a perfect round.*

The high that proved too high, the heroic for earth too hard,
The passion that left the ground to lose itself in the sky,
Are music sent up to God by the lover and the bard;
Enough that He heard it once; we shall hear it by-and-by.

These thoughts interpret the fulness of our lives, our trials and falls and aspirations, and help us to understand better some parts of our Faith in which alone, as far as I can see, they find their solid foundation.

STEPS IN THE CHRISTIAN LIFE

ADDING on your part all diligence, in your faith provide virtue; and in your virtue knowledge; and in your knowledge self-control; and in your self-control patience; and in your patience godliness; and in your godliness love of the brethren; and in your love of the brethren love (2 Peter i.)

Bringing all Diligence

WE are apt to live at random. We are swayed by the circumstances which we ought to control. We find it a relief when we are spared (as we think) the necessity for reflection or decision: a book lightly taken up, a friend's visit, a fixed engagement, fill up the day with fragments; and day follows day as a mere addition. There is no living idea to unite and harmonise the whole.

Of course we cannot make, or to any great extent modify, the conditions under which we have to act; but we can consciously render them tributary to one high purpose. We can regard them habitually in the light of our supreme end.

In your Faith supply Virtue

HEATHEN philosophers had drawn a noble ideal of what man ought to be. The Gospel—the Truth—

furnished the power by which the ideal could be wrought out by all.

The first stage in the spiritual life is the fulfilment of the natural type of virtue.

Religion is stamped first with the mark of manliness in its highest sense. Whatever is false, or mean, or cowardly, or ungenerous is utterly at variance with it.

On the other hand there is nothing true, or lofty, or heroic which does not find its proper place—and more than that, its unfailing support—in the life of faith.

It rests with us to shew each in our little way that all that moves the instinctive admiration of men flows of necessity from our Creed.

Our Faith has among its natural fruits those qualities which mankind are constituted to approve.

It extends also to the fulness of life.

The virtue of the cloister, or of the school, or of the closet is not all. There is the virtue also of the market and of the council chamber. And this too is a growth of faith.

In times of great confusion it has often happened that there has been a sharp division between the religious life and the secular life, to the grievous injury of both. Many symptoms both at home and abroad point to the danger of such a separation coming again.

It is, then, of the deepest moment that we should keep our sympathies wide and keen; that we should guard against indifference towards any object of human interest.

Every fragment of life belongs to us. Every social movement, every political change affects in some way the advent of that Kingdom of God for which we pray.

We neglect our duty if we deliberately stand aloof

from any pursuit, from any conflict, in which we are fitted to engage.

We are poor judges of great and small.

The little service which we can render may be all that is required to complete the circle of some greater work. That which is poorest in appearance may be most necessary.

At least our duty is plain: not to pretend to be what we are not: not to leave our place at will in search of another: not to measure ourselves by others: but to offer to God just what we have and what we are.

In Virtue Knowledge

THE effort to realise what we have learnt will drive us forward.

"Knowledge for knowledge" is parallel with "grace for grace" in the divine economy. And it is not, I think, without significance that the Greek term for absolute scientific knowledge finds no place in the New Testament.

There is, I fancy, always about us a spiritual indolence which springs from an intellectual indolence. We have seen and felt something of the Truth; and we are tempted to rest in the first imperfect experience.

It is not so, however, that we can really hold that which we have gained. Life is only another name for progress.

St. Peter tells us that the prophets themselves "*sought and searched diligently*" as to the further meaning of the message which they were inspired to deliver.

Even for them the striving after knowledge was not made superfluous by a divine illumination; or rather, the greatness of their gifts made the striving more unremitting and intense.

It is true that knowledge in itself is not an end still less the end of life.

But none the less it is impossible not to feel how every access of knowledge gives distinctness and reality to our Faith: how we are enabled to see fresh harmonies in the Bible, as we apprehend with a more simple trust the interpretation of the outward facts of life.

The Christian works that he may learn, and learns that he may work.

Avoid controversy. There must be some whose work it is to meet adversaries in debate. But, as Archbishop Leighton said, "it is a loss to them that they are forced to be busied in that way," and this work is not for the young. It is their privilege to be able to seize the Truth in all its freshness.

It is immeasurably better to spare no pains to understand the truth by which a false system lives, than to gain a victory over it at the price of disregarding this fragmentary good.

Nothing can be more perilous than to use weapons which we have not proved. If we win with them, we shall be tempted to treat the Faith as a question of words when it is a question of life; and every success so obtained will leave behind it a sense of failure and doubt.

There is a terrible, a crushing retribution for him who ventures to maintain a just cause by arguments which he does not feel in the depths of his soul to be sufficient; and few—very few—can put into formal language without long experience the real grounds of their belief.

It may often be our duty to keep silence: it can never be our duty to defend our faith in a way which does not bring conviction to ourselves.

As we know anything better in any real sense of the word, we know Christ better. *Ex uno Verbo omnia, et unum loquuntur omnia:* *"All things proceed from one Word, and all things have one utterance."*

Whatever may be the immediate subject of our study, we can see Him through it.

A moment's pause will be enough, and the light of His presence will flash over our work. In this light we can live and die: without this light all knowledge is unsubstantial and unsatisfying.

In Knowledge Self-control

TEMPERANCE. The original term describes that sovereign self-mastery, that perfect self-control, in which the mysterious will of man holds in harmonious subjection all the passions and faculties of his nature.

Selfwill is to mind what self-indulgence is to sense, the usurpation by a part of that which belongs to the whole.

In knowledge temperance. The Apostle counsels temperance, the just and proportionate use of every faculty and gift, and not the abolition or abandonment of any.

It is easier in many cases to pluck out the right eye or to cut off the right hand than to discipline and employ them.

Sometimes also it may be a clear duty to cast wholly away what we are no longer able to consecrate. But this is to accept by a sad necessity the less noble course, and to render a maimed offering to God, though it is the best in our power, seeing what we have become.

St. Peter therefore calls us to the fulfilment of a loftier ideal. He bids us, while there is yet time and opportunity, strive to bring every fragment of our nature, every power by which we are carried towards the good and the beautiful and the true, under the sovereign sway of the Christian conscience, and to render their manifold fruits as the rational service of our whole being.

"The prize is noble and the hope is great," so Plato spoke. The words gain a practical force by the teaching of St. Paul: *Every man that striveth for the mastery is temperate in all things.* Now they do it to *obtain a corruptible crown, we an incorruptible.*

In Self-control Patience

THERE is something to be borne with resolute endurance, as well as something to be conquered by energetic effort.

Patience—that calm strength which sustains courageously the burden which cannot rightly be thrown off, which waits in sure confidence, as knowing that the darkness cannot last for ever—has its own victories. *In your patience*, the Lord said to His disciples in the prospect of unparalleled trials, *ye shall win your souls.*

This lesson of patience is one, I think, which we greatly need to lay to heart at the present time.

Many obvious causes combine to make men restless under the pressure of uncertainty, to tempt them on the one side to take refuge in some system which may free them from the responsibility of judgment, and on the other to renounce inquiries which seem to admit of no decisive issue.

We have all, I fancy, known in our own experience the perils of the impatience which calls out dogmatism, and of the impatience which calls out scepticism.

The one claims to be devout humility, and the other to be absolute love of truth.

But Christian patience is more rightly humble than the one, and more sincerely truth-loving than the other, being, as it is, the necessary result of a just survey of our position and of our hopes.

For if our immediate circumstances suggest thoughts of impatience, a wider view of life will banish them.

Do what we will we cannot take away the sad stern mysteries of life, the mysteries of birth and death, the one central mystery of our finite personal being. These must remain, however we may regard them or refuse to regard them; and they must remain unsolved.

They are not less real because we close our eyes to them. They are not less insoluble because we refuse to discuss them.

Christianity does not bring them into the world; and to reject the message of Faith is not to do away with the subjects to which it is directed.

It is impossible to reduce human life to elements which will furnish certain conclusions.

Reason, then, no less than faith, forces upon us the duty of patience in the face of the problems of existence.

But though we cannot, from the nature of the case, ever remove the mysteries of life, yet as time goes on, and the purposes of God grow clearer with the lapse of ages, we are enabled to see them under new lights, to group them together, to feel, as it were, the end to which they are pointing.

In this aspect, therefore, we really impoverish ourselves if we thrust back unreflectingly, by an effort of will, each difficulty which presents itself to us.

To claim completeness for our opinions is to abandon the encouragement of progress; and on the other hand difficulties frankly met reveal new paths of truth.

They stimulate us to strive for fuller knowledge, and they prepare us for gaining it.

The patience which regards with clear untroubled vision *all* the parts of our being, so far as they are visible, which sets the weakness of man side by side with what is made known in the long ages of the loving power of God, which learns neither to haste nor to rest in a pursuit for the good which lingers, disciplines and quickens our faculty of spiritual discernment.

The temper which patience is calculated to form is best fitted for the apprehension of the widest truths which are in our reach.

It is not, we can see, the Divine method to answer at once every sincere questioner, or to guide every one to the good on which his soul is fixed.

It is not always good for us to be spared the stern discipline of failure, the desolate silence of doubts unsatisfied, the weariness of delays and the dull pressure of loneliness. It is through these that patience has her perfect work, and finds that the sense of unrest is a promise of progress.

Let us not yield to the seduction of some dogmatic definition which often on the side of the intellect usurps the place of a personal, vital, progressive appropriation of the corresponding truth.

In patience Godliness

THE term *godliness* is far more than "*godliness*" in our common acceptation of the word. It is that spirit of devout reverence which springs out of the recognition of God's immediate Presence, or, to present part of the truth from the opposite side, that spirit of devout reverence which springs out of a sense of the true divinity of things as created by God and sustained by God.

A "godly reverence," a profound yet childlike conviction of the Divine Presence in us and around us, unchanged and untouched in its ineffable holiness and beauty by the sin and evil and sorrow which mar our perception of it, supports us in our conflict with our own temptations, and enables us to look without despair upon what seems to our eyes wide and inevitable waste and loss.

We have all known occasions when we have been possessed, as it were, with the fulness of mere physical pleasure.

The flooding sunlight, the immeasurable sky, the sea, or the mountains, have entered into our souls : happy then shall we be if we have consecrated the joy with the faint assurance that all this is but a faint reflection of His glory *in whom we live and move and have our being.*

In sorrow and loss and failure we turn instinctively to God for the consolation which we have not found and cannot find elsewhere.

If we have not learnt before to recognise the signs of His Presence, it may be hard to see Him in our extremity. But if we have looked for Him at other times : if by various experience we have been enabled to pierce beneath the veil : if we have referred our joys to Him : He will not hide Himself from us in our need.

The godly reverence which has hallowed our brighter hours will bring light to us in our darkness : *at evening time it shall be light.*

In Godliness love of the Brethren

AFFECTATION, censoriousness, hardness, unreality, are naturally repulsive to the young; and on the other hand there is, I think, no time when a kindly and courageous word spoken in Christ's name and for Christ is wider or more enduring in its effects.

Too commonly a natural reserve becomes chilled into a hard irony under which we are content to dissemble our real feelings and aspirations.

How often a single word of genuine sympathy will embolden another to cast off the burden which he has borne silently, and set forth his difficulties and doubts, and face them and overcome them.

How often a word of counsel spoken out of our own experience will inspire the wavering will of a companion with strength and purpose, and guide him rightly where the ways of life part.

How often a word of expostulation tempered with that gentleness which the sense of our own failure gives, will call out the true self in a man, and help him to conquer the temptation which was on the point of overpowering him as he stood alone.

Now all these—this sympathy, this counsel, this expostulation—are simple acts of that *love of the brethren* which we owe one to another, because we are united in *one Lord, one faith, one baptism.*

Perfect fellowship in Christ teaches the believer to reckon not only the failings of others as his own, but their successes also.

In love of the Brethren, love

"LOVE" in the most comprehensive sense is individualised for the Christian. There is no injunction of a general love of men—a vague "philanthropy." He who is not our "brother" is still our "neighbour."

The widest love, in other words, is personal, not an undefined sentiment, but the practical recognition of a real claim.

The love of Christ in its twofold sense is the support of the Christian's love, and growing conformity to Christ is the fruit of love. "To be made like to God" was the noblest aspiration of heathen moralists; and the spirit of Christ converts the aspiration into a fact.

Nothing, perhaps, is more injurious to the influence of Christianity on those without than our own unreadiness to apply to ourselves in the common calls of business, as the motive and measure of our exertion, the frank confession, *the love of Christ constraineth us.*

It is idle and far worse than idle for us to speculate why the world was not made other than it is.

The Christian Faith at least reveals to us a love as great as our need, and calls out in us love to answer love.

Without dissembling the evil which has overspread the world, love will gain and hold the assurance that what is begun shall he consummated, and *God shall be all in all.*

In this sense also it is true that *perfect love casteth out fear.*

He that loveth not hath not known God. It must be so. All ignorance and all error comes from that selfishness which is the opposite to love. But in love self is transfigured, and faith has its perfect work. Faith is the foundation, and love the highest crown. All that comes between is a preparation for that which reaches up to heaven and abides there.

The Incarnation and the Creation

OUR fathers by the teaching of the Holy Spirit saw the Truth, but they did not see all the Truth. And it is, I think, impossible to look at modern writings without perceiving that the teaching on Christ's Person which is current in the most reverent schools falls short in many ways of the living fulness of the Bible.

For in Holy Scripture He is shewn to stand essentially in some ineffable yet real connection with all finite being. In Him, and through Him, and unto Him were all things made. He is the "first-born," "the beginning" of all creation.

The Incarnation is commonly made to depend upon the Fall. And the whole tenor of revelation, as I conceive, leads us to regard the Incarnation as inherently involved in the Creation.

God's image was given to man that he might gain God's likeness.

The marvel is that the purpose of creation was wrought out in spite of that wilful self-assertion of the creature which might have seemed to have fatally thwarted it.

We gaze for an instant on the Majesty within the veil that we may go forth again into the world, *to our work and to our labour*, and still bear about with us the strong assurance that the powers of the heavenly order are placed within our reach; that above the clouds and darkness which beset our path He is throned Who has borne our nature to the right hand of God; that *in many parts and in many fashions*, through sufferings and chastisements, the Divine purpose is being fulfilled; that behind the veils of sense, which perplex and distract us, burns the serene glory of the Divine Presence; that beyond the spectacle of failures and conflicts which flow from selfishness, glows the prospect of a holy unity passing knowledge,—a holy unity which shall hereafter crown and fulfil creation as one revelation of Infinite Love when the Father's will is accomplished, and He has *summed up all things in Christ, the things in the heavens and the things upon earth*.

The Incarnation and the Fall

EVERY one recognises in himself the two conflicting truths which are expressed in the narrative of the Fall: the power of evil and the prerogative of personal responsibility.

There is, we feel, a "baseness in our blood," and we feel also that we have embodied the corruption "by our fault, by our own fault, by our own great fault."

The tendency, indeed, is our inheritance, but we have made the issues our own by deed, we are actually, and we know ourselves to be, guilty, enthralled, alienated from God.

We look around us, and we see the double sentence of our own consciences written on a larger scale in the crimes and judgments of classes and nations, in the deeds of selfish violence which betray a common taint, and in the clear, unquestioning appeal of suffering souls to the majesty of a violated law.

Man did not lose the image of God by the Fall. His essential nature still remained capable of union with God, but it was burdened and hampered. The Word, therefore, could still become flesh, but if He was pleased to realise this fellowship of the Divine and human, He took to Himself, naturally, humanity with its immeasurable obligations, life with its untold temptations and sorrows. But some one will say, "How can another's suffering avail for my offence?" Here the apprehension of social unity is most fertile in suggestion. Fifty years ago the term "solidarity," and the idea which it conveys, were alike strange and unknown. We had not apprehended in any living way that we are, as St. Paul says, literally *members one of another*, as men and nations. We are beginning to understand that in the unity of the body it is possible for one member to take away the infirmity and disease of another by taking them to himself.

We are coming to understand why the human instinct has always rejoiced in the stories of uncalculating self-devotion which brighten the annals of every people: why our hearts respond to the words of a Chinese king, contemporary with Jacob, who said to his people: "When guilt is found anywhere in you who occupy the myriad regions, let it rest on me the One man;" and faithful to his prayer said again, when a human victim was demanded to avert a drought: "If a man must be the victim, I will be he:" why we do not think lives wasted which are offered in heroic prodigality to witness to a great principle: why the blood of the martyrs is indeed seed, not idly spilt upon the ground, but made the vital source of a teeming harvest: we are coming to understand, in a word, what is the true meaning of that phrase "vicarious suffering" which has brought at other times sad perplexity to anxious minds; how it excludes everything that is arbitrary, fictitious, unnatural, external in human relationships: how it expresses the highest energy of love, which takes a friend's sorrows into the loving heart, and taking them by God's grace transfigures them, satisfying every claim of righteousness, justifying every instinct of hope, quickening the spirit of self-surrender, offering within the sphere of common life a faint image of forgiveness, of redemption, of reconciliation.

We cannot, if we would, gain our happiness alone: we cannot be saved alone.

There is a wonderful Indian legend which tells how a Buddhist saint had reached by successive lines of sacrifice the stage next to Nirvâna. At that point he could by one effort of will obtain for himself eternal and untroubled calm. But when the decision had to be made he set aside the tempting prize, and chose rather to live again in the world while conflict could bear fruit. "Not," he said, "till the last soul on every earth and in every hell has found peace can I enter on my rest."

Do we not feel the Christain truth which is enshrined in the splendid story?

The Incarnation and Nature

IN revelation, no less than in science, man is the representative of Creation who gathers up into himself and combines in the most perfect form the various manifestations of life and being which are seen dispersed tentatively, as it were, through other orders.

Mr. Herbert Spencer writes: "Scientific progress is a gradual transfiguration of Nature. The conception to which the explorer of Nature tends is much less of a Universe of dead matter than that of a Universe everywhere alive." Such a calm summary of the latest results of unbiassed research helps us to understand the words of St. Paul in which he tells us that *the earnest expectation of the Creation waiteth for the revealing of the sons of God. . . . For we know that the whole Creation groaneth and travaileth in pain together until now:* words which distinctly lay down the dependence of Creation upon man, both in his fall and in his restoration.

The sympathy of Nature with man is written on the first page of the Bible and on the last. In the spiritual history of Genesis the earth is said to have been cursed for man's sake. In the spiritual vision of the Apocalypse new heavens and a new earth are prepared for redeemed humanity.

It would be easy to shew that, if according to the beautiful Greek fancy, the clay of which man was moulded was moistened not with water but with tears, every strain of natural music dies away into a dirge: easy to paint the ashy tint of death which follows the glow of burning purple on the mountain-side when the sun has set: easy to round all in gloom, if we pause in our first experience. But we may not pause here.

St. Paul recognises the deep voice of grief in the Creation, but he does not rest in it. *The whole Creation*, he says, *groaneth and travaileth together until now.* The sorrow is unto joy at last. Out of that which appears to us to be a confused struggle shall come a new and more perfect life. The pains which we witness are the very conditions of the birth of the new order.

Let the thought of the Incarnation come in, the thought that it was the Father's good pleasure from the first to rear through the ages a living shrine for His Word which became conscious in man, and every token of inner and manifold life in *all things in heaven and upon the earth* assumes a fresh significance.

The progress of the past is the sign and not the measure of that which shall be when the glory of the sons of God shall be reflected by the scene of their finished labour; or rather when we with pure and opened eyes shall see the world as God made it.

> *O world, as God has made it! All is beauty:*
> *And knowing this is love, and love is duty.*
> *What further may be sought for, or declared?*

Not one secret won from Nature by unconscious interpreters of the Divine will, not one fact shewn to have been realised in history by the students of human progress, not one cry of penitence, or one aspiration of faith, which rises from the solitary soul, fails to find a place in the majestic range of the Gospel of the Word made flesh,—fails, if we look aright, to shew it in more sovereign grace.

We are tempted to say "The will of God will be fulfilled. What can we do?" True, most true. The execution of the will of God does not depend upon our endeavour. But O the difference for each one of us if we behold it, if we enter into it, if, in our poor measure, we make it our own, if we offer ourselves without reserve for its service. And so the truth of the Incarnation reaches to the innermost recesses of the single life.

The Incarnation and Life

FOR the noblest truths are not given us for an intellectual luxury, still less for a moral opiate or a spiritual charm.

They are for the inspiration of our whole being, for the hallowing and for the bracing of every power, outward and inward, with which we are endowed, for use in the busy fields of common duty.

If there were found in Christ one trait which belonged to some transitory phase of human growth, to a sect, a class, a nation, an age, if there were wanting in Him one characteristic which belongs to the essence of humanity; one virtue which is the peculiar glory of man or woman; we might then *look for another* to fulfil the higher type which we should be able to imagine. But as it is, there is nothing which we can remove from His portraiture, nothing which we can add to it, without marring the ideal in which each soul can find the satisfaction of every desire that it would lay open in the light of heaven.

We gain no relief from labour by lowering our standard. We do not rid ourselves of enigmas by abridging our hopes.

We cast away the Faith; and what then? The sufferings of earth remain, but they are emptied of their redemptive potency.

Disciplined Life—A Call

WE live commonly at random, without plan, without discipline. We trust to an uncultivated notion of duty for an improvised solution of unforeseen difficulties.

It is as though while "pilgrims and strangers" we cared to learn nothing of the region which we must traverse: as though while "soldiers of Christ" we awaited blindly the attack of an unknown enemy: as though while "fellow-workers with God" we were content to use no training for the fulfilment of our part of His designs.

The East has done her ascetic work: the Romanic nations of Europe have done their ascetic work: it remains for the Saxon race to do their ascetic work, nobler, vaster, richer than any which has gone before.

There is, indeed, much in the earlier forms of asceticism which appears unnatural and repulsive now, simply because they were adapted to achieve a special work, *not* for our age, or race, or country.

But you must look in each case at the principle and not at the system.

The system is transitory while the principle is eternal.

The Stoic counselled suicide as the remedy for overwhelming evil: the Christian found the remedy in the creation of a new life of the soul out of the completest subjection of the body.

Anthony and Benedict

WE may despise from our position the rude and fierce simplicity of Anthony's devotion, but the two great representatives of the East and West witness to his immediate power. Athanasius, his biographer, counts it among his chief glories that he had been allowed to minister to the saint. Augustine was inspired by the study of his life when he heard the words that decided him to become a Christian.

Anthony shewed the foundation of individual freedom in self-conquest: Benedict shewed the foundation of social freedom in self-surrender. It may seem a paradox, but all experience teaches us that perfect obedience coincides with perfect liberty, and that he is strongest who seeks *not to do his own will, but the will of Him that sent him.* To forget or dissemble the work which was achieved for us by the brethren of Benedict, is not only to mutilate history, but to impoverish the springs of our spiritual strength. We owe to them nearly all that remains of the literature of Rome. We owe to them our English Christianity. We owe to them our greatest Churches and Cathedrals. We owe to them no small share of our national liberties. Their corruption came, not because they clung to their principle, but because they abandoned it; and no later failure can obliterate the debt which is due to their early heroism and love.

Our Need of Ascetic Devotion

THE unparalleled achievements of the Jesuits, always imperfect and often disastrous, shew no less clearly than the purer victories of which we claim to be heirs what can be done by faith, by devotion, by discipline.

History teaches us that social evils must be met by social organisation. A life of absolute and calculated sacrifice is a spring of immeasurable power. In the past it has worked marvels, and there is nothing to prove that its virtue is exhausted.

God has blessed the spirit of ascetic devotion, and no less clearly has He shewn that it must not be confined to one form. One type after another has lost its vitality when its work has been accomplished.

It is clear, indeed, that that which is specially suited to one order of things must so far necessarily be unsuited to another. And thus nothing from old times will meet our exigencies.

We want a rule which shall answer to the complexity of our own age. We want a discipline which shall combine the sovereignty of soul of Anthony, the social devotion of Benedict, the humble love of Francis, the matchless energy of the Jesuits, with faith that fears no trial, with hope that fears no darkness, with truth that fears no light.

"There is," says Lamennais, "nothing fruitful but sacrifice." But whether Christ offers you this prerogative of sacrifice, or leaves to you the calmer offices of common duty, at least be sure, from the examples of the saints, that life is not easy.

Disciplined Life—A Suggestion

LUXURY is no longer one of the natural consequences of privilege, or culture, or birth, but is a common object offered to open competition.

It is an expression of wealth; and fortune, as we are often reminded with a most sad complacency, is now within the reach of every man.

Each rank affects the mode of life of that which is immediately above it; and the connection between the two is still more closely knit by individuals who pass from the one to the other.

The spirit of luxury with which we have to deal is socially universal and levelling, morally depressing and disorganising.

The Family the true Unit of Society

A RULE constructed with the individual for the unit can never satisfy the mature wants of humanity. The true unit of society is the family, and not the man.

If we wish to be faithful to the teaching of self-sacrifice which our fathers have bequeathed to us, we must carry it forward to some completer shape.

If we wish to do our own work we must use our examples, not as copies, but as stimulants to exertion, and as pledges of hope.

Nothing is more significant in later history than the persistent recurrence of attempts to deal with the growing evils of life by social organisation.

The family offers the only complete pattern of life: all other groupings of men or women must in themselves be imperfect, and partial in their influence, though, in dependence on that, they can fulfil offices of inestimable importance.

It presents in the most powerful and natural form the relations of essential authority and subordination, and lays the basis of a graduated society.

Celibate forms of life cannot be offered for general acceptance. On the contrary, they sanction most injuriously the definite recognition of manifold standards of Christian duty.

Thus while they are calculated to act with concentrated power on any special point, they are essentially unfitted to elevate the whole form of social life by the exhibition of a pattern in which its ordinary temptations are seen to be met and overcome.

And this defect of celibate rules is the more serious now, when the disorders of society spring for the most part from the disregard of the laws which the family can best interpret; when extravagance and display descend from class to class with a fatal and accelerated speed; when it seems impossible, except by isolation, to modify or even to avoid the sway of fashion which yet finds few open defenders.

What might be done by an Organisation of Families

IN all these respects it is easy to see how an organisation of families might place openly before all a noble type of domestic life; not so costly as to be beyond the aspirations of the poor; not so sordid as to be destructive of simple refinement; strong by the expression of sympathy; expansive by the force of example.

One of our most urgent needs is to realise the existence of permanent differences between men as the foundation of the divine government of the world.

However much a celibate rule may intensify special powers, it sacrifices sympathies, feelings, faculties, which may be disciplined, and which must play an important part in the general life of men.

The cloistral character, as such, is beset with inevitable weaknesses and imperfections.

In the family there can be no danger of such inherent incompleteness: in that there must be constant movement, conflict, growth.

No one who has not tried, however feebly and imperfectly, the efficacy of systematised religious exercises in the midst of busy occupation, can judge how they tend to concentrate, intensify, increase power.

It is obvious, to suggest no other consideration, what it must be to pause from painful endeavours, and for a few moments to lie open and receptive, as it were, before the source of all strength and knowledge and love.

There are few among us who do not sadly regret that they cannot enjoy the lessons of genial courtesy, of tender forbearance, of large sympathy, which society can best teach, because they are unable or unwilling to pay the material price exacted from them.

The present waste of the educational power of women is one of the saddest and most fruitful of evils.

Nothing, I believe, is more unjust than to call the spirit of modern English thought irreligious. On the contrary, even in its scepticism it clings to religion. There never was a time when men have had a keener sense of what religion ought to be and do. There never was a time when the demands upon religion were greater.

It is assumed, and assumed rightly, that if it be real, if it be human, it will control and discipline the outward conduct of men; that it will welcome and harmonise every fact which represents, at least to us, some one detail of the Divine action; that it will unite and employ in social service the manifold powers of every individual. And when it is seen that the Christian society—for the individual Christian life must for the most part be hidden —does not, as such, stand in the van of moral and spiritual progress, doubts arise whether the Christian faith is adequate to meet the requirements of a later age. Such a deduction is not unnatural. The fault lies with us if it remains unrefuted.

Disciplined Life—An Opportunity

WE shall all confess that the general estimate and use and distribution of material wealth present the saddest problems for our thought, not fearing to maintain that the abundance of the rich is as perilous to the purity and grace of life as the indigence of the poor.

We shall all confess that as believers we proclaim that the highest life is not for the few, for a class, but for all for whom Christ died; and therefore that every circumstance which hinders this issue is an evil against which we must contend to the uttermost.

There are on every side tokens of noble self-denial and labour, but efforts which are isolated fail of their full effect. The levelling, depressing, disorganising power of modern luxury neutralises their influence.

We require, therefore, something which shall strike

DISCIPLINED LIFE—AN OPPORTUNITY

the imagination; which shall shew the breadth and grandeur of the Faith; which shall continue and consolidate the impulses to sacrifice that are lost in unobserved diffusion; which shall make it clear that as Christians we do indeed believe, and live as believing, that the toiler with scanty means has within his reach all that makes life worth living.

Laws are inoperative where they do not answer to dominant opinion. Even at the best they can only restrain and not inspire.

The energy which stirs a nation must come from the spirit and not from the letter. It must be the result not of constraint, but of a spontaneous offering.

Those whom no personal necessity forces "to live laborious days" can alone display in unquestioned supremacy the energy of self-forgetful ministering love.

The purifying and ennobling of family relations includes in essence all that is required for the stable adjustment of the larger relations of national life.

No celibate organisation can reach the evils from which we suffer, or furnish a pattern for general acceptance.

All experience tends to shew that an abiding, a progressive morality must be inspired by theology.

I know that there is about us the deep swelling of a noble discontent ready to sweep away much that mars the surface of society. I know that there are aspirations after generous service in those for whom the choice of duty is yet open, which need only to be confessed and concentrated that they may become a trumpet-call of quickening enthusiasm.

I know that there is beneath the frivolous shows of fashion and the misleading irony of untried natures a true and touching sense of the infinite issues of conduct, of the awful swiftness of opportunity, of the invigorating "blessing of great cares" among those to whom God has given great endowments of wealth and station and mind, that they may render to Him more costly offerings.

Life Consecrated by the Ascension

CHRISTMAS is the festival of the family, for then Christ, by being born, hallowed all the ties of home.

Easter is the festival of the Church, for then Christ, by the victory over death, established a spiritual power among men invincible for ever.

Ascension-tide is the festival of the race, for then Christ, by raising all that belongs to the perfection of humanity to heaven, gave us a glorious sign of our true destiny as men.

If we enter into the spirit of Ascension-day, we shall be enabled to realise practically that Christian life is essentially one. Over all the hands of Christ are raised to bless.

We are always tempted to break up life into little fractions; to separate routine and effort; to contrast secular and spiritual; to assign this part to the duties of the world, and that to the service of God. But such a division is faithless and vain. As the body is one, so also is the life.

Physical health is the harmonious action of every member according to its proper law, and religion is the true health of our whole being.

If we once see that it is in the silent, unnumbered, unnoticed trivialities (as they seem) of daily business that character is formed which in due time a crisis will reveal: then already something of a divine harmony is re-established among the elements which sin has disordered.

Whatever is inchoate, imperfect, discordant, becomes a sign of that fuller being into which all our efforts and all our achievements are destined to pass.

That only which is wholly of the earth can find its satisfaction on earth; all which belongs essentially to some vaster whole must as yet bear about with it the marks of incompleteness, and to our eyes the appearance of failure.

The weaknesses, the littlenesses, the incoherences of daily life, so long as they are felt and struggled with, are evidences of a victory yet to come. They bear witness to us that we cannot rest till we rise to the level of Him in whom we live. They never cease to teach us that the end to which we are called is not now or here.

The same spirit which leads us to isolate parts of our life as alone religious, leads us also to construct one type of religious work, so that all action which does not fall within this narrow boundary is left out of account.

Those whom Christ sent, as the Father sent Him, fulfilled their commission not after one pattern but after many.

Even in that first outburst of renovated life each believer worked according to his natural gifts. One ministered, another preached, another wrote: one satisfied an immediate want, another laid up treasures for a later time. Every form of service was hallowed, because all were rendered to God. And this is the image of Christian activity which we are at present called to imitate according to the measure of our power.

If we were all alike in our highest attributes, if religion were in all the same exercise of the same gifts, then the defection of one or another would make little difference to the general result; but if, as we see it must be, the faithlessness of one subtracts from the whole that which no other can supply, all is changed; we feel at once the overwhelming majesty of life even in its ultimate details.

Many Gifts—One Spirit

THERE is something very sublime and at the same time very awful in the thought of the marvellous complexity of our modern life, even in its outward aspects; and if we penetrate below the surface and come to feel that the same law holds in the spiritual as in the material relations of men, we shall readily acknowledge that we are in the presence of a truth which it concerns us most nearly to apprehend as far as we can do so.

If religion be the most complete harmony of life with the seen and the unseen, the modes in which it will be embodied will vary with the varying modes of life.

All the causes which tend to stereotype or separate or narrow our lives, tend equally to stereotype and separate and narrow our religion.

And if, on the other hand, we see that by the counsel of the Divine Love the highest forms of earthly good spring from the co-operation of the most diverse elements, so we believe is it also in religion.

There are diversities of gifts, but the same Spirit. There is an essential difference in all lives, and there is in them also, by the gift of God, an essential unity.

The law of progressive variety is forced upon us by all the conditions under which we act and think.

It is called into play equally by the natural endowments with which we are born, and by the circumstances under which we use our powers.

MANY GIFTS—ONE SPIRIT

It is the spring of all that is most impressive in national character: it is the spring of all that is most energetic in personal influence.

A great people stamps the history of the world with the impress of its special traits.

A great man sways his fellows by the gifts through which he differs from them.

There is nothing from which a true patriot would shrink more than from the endeavour to obliterate the marks which represent in his countrymen all the issues of the past. They may be transformed, ennobled, transfigured, but in them lies the pledge that the nation has still something to do for the race.

Remove the difference, slender it may be, by which citizen is distinguished from citizen, and something is lost to the fulness of the body which nothing can replace.

External equality is uniform degradation.

But while this principle is acknowledged unhesitatingly in social and political life, we do not commonly apply it to religious life. Religion is regarded as something abstract, uniform, colourless. Here it is supposed that the rich variety of function which marks the development of man finds no place. He is *unclothed*, to use St. Paul's image, and not *clothed upon*, that so he may fulfil his highest work.

We suddenly abandon the law which has guided the magnificent growth of life when it approaches its last fulfilment.

We trust to no generous spontaneity when we come as sons to our heavenly Father. We painfully mould and repress ourselves after one fashion; and enemies say, not without the semblance of excuse, that our religion looks traditional, formal, dead, powerless to claim all human interests for its domain, all human faculties for its instruments.

And still if we reflect that what we are called upon to offer to God is nothing less than ourselves, our souls and bodies, it must at once be seen that in that *perfect, holy, living sacrifice* is included every element of character, of endowment, of circumstance, by which each one of us is made to differ from others.

Other offices may appear to us to be more fruitful than our own: we may wish for an ampler field on which to shew the devotion which we sincerely feel: our time, we may argue, is so engrossed by necessary routine that all nobler aspirations are dulled.

But if followed to their spring such thoughts come simply from faithlessness and impatience.

The results of silent service, of complete self-surrender, of patient trust, cannot be measured by our present experience. They survive us on earth, and they follow us before the very throne of God.

We work each in our own way with untiring and truthful effort, and because we do so, a higher unity is possible. There can be no unity in an aggregate of atoms.

Our diversity of gifts is reconciled in one supreme destination.

Our religion finds its true expression in the consecration of our special gifts.

All our natural endowments, all our personal histories, all our contrasted circumstances, are so many opportunities for peculiar work.

We are all different, and therefore we *may* be one. We are all united in Christ, and therefore, unless we be unfaithful, we *must* be one.

The Gospel of Christ's Death and Resurrection

IN the Gospel, as the Apostle calls it, of Christ's Death and Christ's Resurrection we stand; by that we are saved. It accompanies us from the beginning of our lives to the end. It is the voice which welcomes the unconscious infant to his Saviour's love: it is the voice which commits the unconscious dead to his Maker's keeping.

The message of the Resurrection which the apostles were charged to proclaim has lost none of its significance, but we, I think, perplexed by the necessary growth of later thoughts, are often in danger of missing the grandeur of its simple outline.

At least the unnatural barriers of separation which we all fix in various degrees between parts of our duties and our pleasures: the conventional banishment of our highest desires from ordinary intercourse: the unreal triviality which first veils and then smothers passionate longings for sympathy: the sense of weakness which drives us in upon ourselves: the sense of weariness which forces us again to frivolity; shew that we have not yet fully learnt the lessons which it can teach, or the strength which it can give; for the faith in the Resurrection can harmonise life: can inspire life: can transform life.

There is about us on every side, in the midst of much that is simply ostentatious and false and selfish, a restless striving for the truth, a stern impatience of hypocrisy, an eager desire to do something to raise the masses of men to their proper dignity. And in the meantime popular religion seems to stand aside from these great stirrings of national life. Adversaries even venture to urge that Christianity is, at least in certain aspects, hostile to truth, to sincerity, to freedom. The sphere of its action and its hopes is said to be transferred by tacit consent to a remote region, inaccessible even to the imagination.

So true it is that at first we neglect our gifts, and then we deny them.

Our first prayer teaches us to ask not that we may be transferred into the kingdom of God, but that the kingdom of God may come among us.

We are placed, as it were, in the presence of a veiled glory. The practised eye can habitually pierce beneath the covering, and even we of duller vision come to feel, first perhaps in seasons of darkness, the reality of its effulgence.

In a word, heaven is not for us so much a "yonder" towards which we have to move, as a "here" which we have to realise.

If we try to form a distinct conception of what we call vaguely our soul, we shall find that we include in the idea all the details of circumstance and action and feeling and thought which go to make up that which we feel to be ourselves.

We know each how, as life goes on, its stream grows stained and turbid. Dark memories from distant years come unbidden and mingle with its current. We cannot stay the source once opened.

And for the infinite future, is there then no release, no restoration, no purifying power? Must we for ever carry with us not only the impress of the past, but that ever-springing fount of sorrow, if not of sin, which lies in the bitter recollection of good neglected or of evil done?

The answer comes to us from the Cross and from the sepulchre. *Beloved now are we the sons of God, and it doth not yet appear what we shall be: but we know that, when He shall appear, we shall be like Him; for we shall see Him as He is.* The open vision of God in Christ will then transform us into His image.

By that the most amazing miracle of Divine love and Divine power will be consummated, the complete forgiveness of sin crowned by the transfiguration of the sinner.

To make of life one harmonious whole, to realise the invisible, to anticipate the transfiguring majesty of the Divine Presence, is all that is worth living for.

Death, after earthly duty, loyally, humbly, patiently fulfilled, is not the end but the beginning of life.

Social Aspects of Christianity—the Foundation

I DO not think that our real controversies in the immediate future are likely to be speculative: they threaten to be terribly practical. Behind the disputes of words, the abstract reasonings about the Being of God or the constitution of man, which occupy a large place even in popular literature, lie the fundamental questionings of social duty. What is the basis and measure of our mutual obligations? What is the source of our weakness and of our strength? What is or ought to be our aim, our ideal, as men living human lives? What, in other words, is the foundation on which a kingdom of God can be built, and how can we do our part in hastening its establishment?

The answers to such questions as these are, I believe, to be found—to be found only as they always have been found since the first age—in the Christian life answering to the Christian Faith.

But, I repeat, they are to be found. They are not permanent and uniform. They are not ready for our use without effort. They must be sought for, shaped, realised. They must answer to our time, our education, our place in the order of the world.

If it be said that the problems which the coming generation will have to face, problems of wealth and poverty, of luxury and want, of capital and labour, of population, of class, of national responsibility, of peace and war, are to be solved irrespectively of the Faith, I can only reply that if I am a Christian I must bring every interest and every difficulty of man within the range of my religion.

When we look to Christ's Birth and Death and Resurrection, are we not constrained to confess sadly that we have in Him a revelation which has not yet found that social expression which sooner or later it must find?

As Christians we are not left as other men to quicken our impulses by noble abstractions or splendid guesses.

As Christians we are not constrained as other men to acquiesce in the presence of unconquerable suffering. As Christians we are not condemned as other men to gaze with stern resignation upon the spectacle of lost good.

On us the duty is laid of shewing openly to the world that our one Foundation is able to support the fabric which answers to the present needs of society, that it marks out lines of enduring effort, that it gives unity to the varied strivings of all who are looking towards the dawn.

Our relationship one to another does not depend on any remote descent: it is not perilled by any possible discovery as to the origin or the antiquity of man: it is not measured by the course of days and years: it is not closed by death. The brotherhood of men seen in Christ is a question not of genealogy but of being. It rests upon the present and abiding fatherhood of God, Who in His Son has taken our common nature to Himself.

The mystery of forgiveness is unveiled to us, as far as our sight can look at it, in the fact of a Redemption answering to the fact of a Fall, in death endured and death overcome.

For the rest it is enough for us to know that an enemy hath done this which covers the earth with gloom, and that One stronger than he hath spoiled him. It is enough for us to know that evil is foreign and intrusive, and therefore conquerable.

The Family

WE feel at each moment that we are responsible, responsible for the past which we recall and for the future to which we look forward. And at the same time we recognise that we are dependent on our descent and on our environment, limited both in action and in thought by laws which we cannot evade.

Further reflection opens the vision of an underlying harmony between these conflicting experiences. We come to see that the completest conception which we can form of moral freedom is the willing fulfilment of the absolute law of our existence. He is free, he alone is free, who discerns the end and the method of his being, and follows with glad obedience the course which he finds marked out for him.

Each fragment of the great order in which we are placed brightens and grows more glorious as we study it; and if we offer ourselves to the influence of that divine teaching which is for the moment within our reach, we shall stand in a right attitude towards the undiscovered sum of heavenly mysteries by which we are surrounded on all sides.

We are not made to live alone.

Even our communion with God must be through the fulness of life. There may be times when hermit-isolation becomes a duty, as it may be a duty to cut off the right hand, or to pluck out the right eye, but it exhibits a mutilation and not an ideal of life.

All anarchy and half the social errors by which we are troubled spring from placing the individual, the self, at the centre of all things.

No view can be more flagrantly false. It is impossible to resolve the world into a multitude of isolated men.

It is impossible to picture in imagination even one isolated man. A man who had grown up alone would not be a man. When we come into being we are sons. When we first begin to act we have been necessarily in some degree disciplined and educated. To the last what we have inherited immeasurably outweighs what we have acquired.

Man, in a word, is made by and made for fellowship. The Family and not the individual is the unit of mankind. This fact is the foundation of human life to which we must look for the broad lines of its harmonious structure.

In the Family, as has been nobly said, *living for others* becomes the strict corollary of the patent fact that we *live by others*.

In the Family we learn to set aside the conception of right, and to place in its stead the conception of duty, which alone can give stable peace to peoples or to men.

SOCIAL ASPECTS OF CHRISTIANITY

So it is that the popular estimate of the Family is an infallible criterion of the state of society.

Heroes cannot save a country where the idea of the Family is degraded ; and strong battalions are of no avail against homes guarded by faith and reverence and love.

Classical history is a commentary on this truth. The national life of Greece lasted barely for three generations, in spite of the undying glory of its literature and the unrivalled triumphs of its art, because there the Family fell from its proper place. A constitution and laws reared on a lofty estimate of the Family gave Rome the sovereignty of the world. And more than this : Roman legislation, which was based on the Family institutions of the old Republic, survived the dissolution of the Empire, and after more than two thousand years is still powerful in the civil courts of Europe.

Man or woman alone represents only half of the powers and capacities and feelings of humanity. And no real approach can be made to the consummation of our common nature by any attempt on the part of woman to cultivate these elements in it which are characteristic of man, or on the part of man to make his own that which is truly womanly.

Such attempts only impoverish the race. Nothing less than the union of man and woman in their developed diversity gives us the image of a perfect human being, and raises our thoughts to a higher existence than that of our divided personalities.

The husband grows more manly, the wife grows more womanly, as they realise each in the other the possession of that which they severally need, and yet cannot provide from within themselves.

If trust be incomplete, Marriage, we know, cannot have its perfect work. If trust be broken, Marriage perishes. But, by interchange of thought and hope and prayer, in Marriage trust ripens into faith. And that faith, carried out into the world, is the secret of the blessedness of life.

Marriage, in a word, is the divine pattern and ground of human communion, the original sacrament of completed manhood.

Fatherhood is the pattern or the original sacrament of authority: sonship, of reverence and obedience.

The lesson of Fatherhood passes at once within the Family to the connection of masters and servants, which cannot with impunity be degraded into a mere bargain, and which may be ennobled by real sympathy.

It passes on without to the connection of employer and workman, which ceases, I cannot but say, to be human if it is made to mean only so much labour for so much money.

It passes to the connection of owner and occupier, which cannot be stable if an inherited right is supposed to dispense with present duties.

It passes to the connection of government and citizen, which is simply a compact of limited slavery unless we recognise above us that which we may modify but which we cannot make, a manifestation of eternal authority which we are born to treat with loyal reverence.

The ties of blood may be dissembled, disregarded, disgraced, but they cannot be destroyed. "Brothers are brothers evermore."

The sense of equality which home blesses is most perfect, not when we make the claim to receive the payment of a debt owed, but when we feel the power to pay a debt acknowledged.

The idea of Brotherhood reveals to us the great depths of our being in which we are all equal. It enables us to claim and to realise a fellowship with those who are separated from us. It gives hope under the consciousness of the fragmentariness of our individual work. It keeps fresh the generous impulses which bind kinsmen together though scattered through distant lands. It tends to counteract that spirit of isolating competition which is eating away the old repose and nobility of English life.

Thanks be to God the teaching of the family is still left to us in England rich in gracious lessons of authority and reverence and service. The ties of the Family are still held sacred by popular sentiment. So may we study them while there is yet time, study them in the light of God's presence, and we shall need no other school of social duty. May we by the Spirit's help labour to fulfil them, and we shall need no other preparation for the greater offices of life, no other pledge that for these also the *Father from Whom every Family in heaven and earth is named* will give us the strength which we need.

The Nation

ALL attempts to explain the continuance of states by the necessities of individual protection and convenience leave out of account the social instincts which are not less real, if at first they are less prevailing, than personal instincts.

The generating, the sustaining force of states is not material but spiritual.

The soul at its noblest is the witness to its destiny.

We are born and live, and we feel that we are born and live, not for ourselves only, not for our families only, but for all about us.

The poet and the legislator, the statesman and the evangelist, achieve their work by interpreting and not by creating thoughts in many hearts. The humblest human experience goes to form the oracle of the prophet.

These four, if we will but listen to their voice— language, law, government, religion—remind us at every moment of a larger being in which we share and to which we may minister.

We cannot, if we would, start afresh from our simple manhood. Our national characteristics surround us with an atmosphere equally subtle and pervading. What we are and what we can be has been determined for us by our English ancestors. They have stored up for our ready use, by toil and thrift, by insight and love, material and spiritual treasures which no one generation could amass.

They have, in a word, transmitted to us their life; and this life is the heritage not of a party, or of a class, but of all; and all have entered upon it.

Two occasions, now in the distant past, rise before me still with unchangeable freshness, when every Englishman, I believe, rejoiced to know even through anxiety and sorrow that the nation was still one, one in the maintenance of law, one in the devotion of loyalty.

Five and twenty years ago, when peace or war hung upon the answer to a claim made as the deliberate assertion of a legal right, the issue was awaited throughout the empire with calm resolution; and when the claim was yielded, not one expression of pride or selfishness marred the thanksgiving for a bloodless victory.

Again, at a later time, when it seemed that the succession of our royal line would be broken, the heart of the whole people was moved as the heart of one man, not for a son or a husband or a father only, but for a prince, who was felt to represent to his people something far more than personal qualities, and to bind us all, as no other could do, to a glorious past.

That memorable season of suspense and deliverance and grateful joy was, I cannot doubt, a crisis in the history of our monarchy; and when I think of it my thoughts go back not to the august ceremonial of a nation's thanksgiving at St. Paul's, but to a plain white cross in the churchyard at Sandringham, on which are inscribed the words which tell the story of death and life—"*One is taken and another left,*"—the servant taken and remembered: the lord left and not unmindful of the awful presence in which he has been.

Surely this most touching and open confession of equality reveals to us the secret of that

> *Sober freedom, out of which there springs*
> *Our loyal passion for our temperate kings.*

For such revelations of national life as these we may well thank God.

There could be no true nation, even as there could be no true family, without wide differences in power, in fortune, in duty, among those who compose it. And the aim of the Christian patriot will not be to obliterate these differences, but to harmonise them in their ripe development by shewing that they can minister to the vigour of one life. He will strive not to confound class with class, but to bind all classes together in their characteristic distinctness by the consciousness of mutual service.

He will labour to establish everywhere the central truth of morals, the central truth of faith, that man is stronger and more blessed through sacrifice than through self-assertion. He will seek to realise—last triumph of noble souls—that the brightest crown of action is the feeling of good done for which there is no reward.

> *Paid by the world,—what dost thou owe*
> *Me? God might question: now instead,*
> *'Tis God shall repay! I am safer so.*

The nation again, no less than the family, is organised and controlled by an inherent authority. Through whatever instruments the authority may be administered, it is in itself not of man but of God. Authority is not created but recognised even in a successful revolution.

Authority may be graced or obscured by the character of him who wields it, but essentially it can receive no glory and suffer no loss from man. St. Peter and St. Paul, as we remember, honoured it in the tyrant Nero: Christ Himself acknowledged it in the selfish Pilate.

There have been times when the sacredness of the divine ordinance has been transferred to the person of the sovereign; and now, on the other hand, we are tempted to derive the sanction of the authority itself from the character of the person who wields it.

But it is possible to avoid the falsehood of both extremes. And the Christian patriot will keep the divine and human elements in the ruler separate in thought, while he prays ardently that they may be brought into the truest unison. He will know, and he will help others to know, that the stability of society is assured when we believe that its structure is not wholly of earth. He will rejoice to teach that reverence is the parent of self-respect and dignity.

The Christian patriot will not tire in urging others to confess in public, what home makes clear, that love and not interest is alone able to explain and to guide our conduct: that self-devotion and not self-assertion is the spring of enduring and beneficent influence: that each in his proper sphere—workman, capitalist, teacher—is equally a servant of the state, feeding in his measure that common life by which he lives: that work is not measured but made possible by the wages rendered to the doer: that the feeling of class is healthy, like the narrower affections of home, till it claims to be predominant: that we cannot dispense, except at the cost of national impoverishment, with the peculiar and independent services of numbers and of wealth and of thought, which respectively embody and interpret the present, the past, and the future: that we cannot isolate ourselves as citizens any more than as men, and that if we willingly offer to our country what we have, we shall in turn share in the rich fulness of the life of all.

The Race

TRAINED by the happy discipline of our homes to feel the need of fellowship, the grace of authority, the joy of service, we soon recognise the divine lineaments of the state. We perceive naturally how the life of this larger body is sustained and purified and ennobled by the forces which are first revealed in Marriage, in Fatherhood, in Brotherhood. We gladly acknowledge that the forms of political order are something more than convenient provisions for the satisfaction of material needs.

But we cannot rest here. As the teaching of the Family leads us to the idea of the Nation, so the teaching of the Nation leads us while the ages go forward to the idea of the Race. While the ages go forward: for the old Roman had but one word for stranger and enemy. The Greeks sharply separated from themselves all other peoples as essentially inferior. The Hebrews alone of ancient peoples, in this respect true children of Abraham, though in others the most exclusive of all, provided from the first for the admission of strangers to a full share in their most sacred privileges.

But none the less the experience of life gradually leads men towards a larger communion. The sense of national friendships is slowly established between peoples not unequally matched; and still more slowly the strong are inspired with regard for the rights of the weak. In this way, little by little, the nations are brought to realise that there is in the order of the world a sacred fellowship between them as members of one Race.

We are tempted by the spirit of domination, by the spirit of imitation, and by the spirit of affected indifference; and these three spirits must be effectually exorcised before we can serve our Race, or indeed have any true sense of its vital unity.

Our first impulse is to claim universal supremacy for our own customs and opinions and forms of government: to regard each variation from our own standards of thought and action as the result of ignorance or degeneracy: to urge the adoption of our social institutions as the remedy for evils in other lands: to press patriotism into arrogant self-assertion.

But then a reaction follows. As our intercourse with neighbouring peoples is increased we are struck by their grace or their versatility or their vigour. At once all that is strange in them grows attractive. We endeavour to copy what is not natural to us, that we may gain what we have learnt to admire.

We disguise and disparage our own tastes. We assume habits which have not grown out of our circumstances.

We treat the characteristic results of our past training as insular prejudices.

It soon, however, becomes clear that we cannot make others like ourselves or make ourselves like others, and so in our disappointment we aspire to be "citizens of the world," regarding with a lofty indifference the various types of human life by which we are surrounded, using and discarding according to our convenience the fashion of the hour; accepting without conviction and abandoning without regret the customs of our neighbourhood, finding nothing more precious or stable in the form of society than in the many tints of earth-born clouds which veil the immeasurable sky.

But here again we are disappointed. This temper brings no satisfaction or rest: we find ourselves dwarfed and chilled by the narrowing of our sympathies. We are poorer, and we feel ourselves to be poorer, as men in proportion as we have succeeded in our endeavours after domination, imitation, indifference.

Happy are we if we confess that these self-willed interpretations of the facts of the world are vain; for then God opens *the eyes of our hearts* to see a little more of His wider counsel: to see how the principles which bring harmony to the life of the Nation, bring harmony also to the life of the Race.

Such thoughts cannot but affect us as Englishmen most deeply. England stands, as no other country stands, in a threefold relation to great families of men. She stands face to face with the most powerful empires as their peer, bound to guard her heritage and to commend to others by courage, by generosity, by self-control, the blessings which she has received. She stands face to face with the weakest tribes as their sovereign, bound to protect, to foster, to develop human forces which have not yet reached their full growth.

She stands yet again face to face with daughter-peoples, jealous of their independence and loyal in their affection, through whom, as their parent, she is called to mould a new world to sober freedom, not by rigid control, but by spiritual quickening.

Never has any nation received a charge of authority

so far-reaching and so complex. There is not a social problem of the future of which the elements are not included within its range.

A single nation, moved by one thought, could alter the fortunes of the world. And, as has been said by one not of us, "the power of love as the basis of a state has not yet been tried."

The true patriot seeks the highest good of his own country, not at the cost of other countries, but through their corresponding advance.

The Church

THE Church holds before us the end for which we were made, even to become like God. It quickens again the noblest thoughts of our hearts by the calm of holydays, by the fellowship of solemn services, by the silent eloquence of stately temples in which the dead still living proclaim the victories of faith: it hallows through the institution of the sacraments every object of sense with something of a sacramental value as a sign of unimaginable glory. It peoples the solitude of our hearts with innumerable hosts of heavenly beings. It makes the communion of saints the pledge of a life of which sight is no measure and no test. It gives us, when we look upon the vastness of the sea and the sky and the mountains, instead of a vague feeling of mysterious grandeur, a vision of the Presence of God.

No one will question that the Church of England occupies a historical position which is without parallel. It has borne with the nation the pressure of foreign conquest and domestic revolution, and drawn breadth and vigour from both.

It has received the treasures of alien thought and experience, and vindicated its independence. It has never broken with the past, and yet it has put off the accretions of age.

I confess that the Church of England has failed, if it be failure to fall short of the ideal. The Church of England has failed as Christianity itself has failed. It has failed through the imperfection of the men who have represented it. But it has not failed so as to abdicate its charge.

We have forgotten that the Church is a Body in which an appropriate office belongs to every member; and so we have suffered grievously from a loss of power and from a loss of mutual understanding.

We have suffered grievously from loss of power. Those who are set to be teachers among us, who need ample leisure for calm reading and high thinking, in order that they may follow the swift currents of opinion, have been overwhelmed with labours not their own, with anxieties of finance, and with details of parish organisation.

And those again who have a practical knowledge of affairs, a wide influence in business, a rich endowment of "saving common sense," have found no proper sphere for the exercise of their gifts.

The Kingdom of God

IN every part of the New Testament, in every region of early Christian labour, the teaching is the same. The object of Redemption is set before us not simply as the deliverance of individual souls, but as the establishment of a Divine Society: the saving not only of men but of the world, the hallowing of life, and not characteristically the preparation for leaving it.

Morning and Evening we all pray in Christ's own words that "Our Father's Kingdom may come, on earth as in heaven": that it may "come," not that we may be carried away to it far off, out of this stormy tumult of common cares as to some tranquil haven of rest: that it may come to us "on earth as in heaven."

The Lord points forward, if I may gather up what I would say in one sentence, to a transfiguration of human society which corresponds to the Resurrection of the individual.

Mediæval Efforts: the Franciscans

FRANCIS of Assisi spoke in life, so that his work can never cease to move. He built up, purified, ennobled what he found, overcoming evil by the good. Through Francis of Assisi the mediæval efforts after the Kingdom of God found their most characteristic embodiment. Bright, joyous, enterprising, thoughtlessly lavish by nature, untrained in scholastic learning, instinct with poetic enthusiasm, Francis came to men simply as a man. He knew but one pattern, the Lord Himself. He knew but one lesson, the story of the Cross. He offered to the simple outward faith of the middle ages a visible image of love, of love to God and love to man. He brought Christ out of the student's cell into the wild and sordid conflicts of life. He was, if I may so speak, a living *Imitatio Christi*. He sought and touched the leper in body or in soul. He took to him Poverty, or rather Humanity bleeding from a thousand wounds "whom none had chosen for his own since Christ Himself," to cherish to his life's end with unfailing tenderness.

The power of the example soon made itself felt. Francis drew to him a few followers, who found in the new life the Gospel for which they looked, the Gospel for the poor.

Francis, in answer to the prayer of eager inquirers,

drew up a rule for men and women living in the world. Those who subscribed it were bound to renounce all ill-gotten gains; to abstain from aggressive war and litigation: to observe the utmost simplicity in dress, intercourse, and amusements: to give themselves according to their opportunity to works of devotion: to meet for common worship and almsgiving. By the institution of this Third Order of the "brothers and sisters of penitence," as they were called, the work of Francis was consummated. It seemed for a short space as if the Kingdom of God were indeed about to be established on earth. Then followed a swift decline.

Francis aimed at an ideal which neglected essential facts of life. He sought to destroy individuality. He disregarded also the divine office of nations for the race.

Yet once again the tender devotion of Francis to the Lord's manhood became the occasion of grievous error. Everything that is compassionate in the character of the Lord was separated from His sovereign righteousness, and then these attributes of tender love were transferred to His human Mother, who seemed to be more within the reach of rude and simple minds. In this way a system of Mariolatry was shaped with what consequence they know who are familiar with the popular religion of modern Italy. Even Francis himself was set by some in the place of the Lord. The evil spread far and wide; and many who hear me must have looked with shuddering, as I have looked, on a picture at Brussels, painted by Rubens for the Franciscan Church at Ghent, in which Francis and the Mother of the Lord are shielding the world from the thunderbolts which the Divine Son is directing against it.

The order of Francis failed in its issue, and it is well to take account of the causes of its failure; but it is far more welcome to mark the causes of its first splendid success.

Modern Efforts: the Quakers

THE Jesuits and the Quakers both aimed at establishing a Kingdom of God upon earth. They did this in different ways, with different aims, and with different results; and they both failed.

The Quakers appear to me to express with the greatest force and exclusiveness the new thought of the Reformation, the thought of individuality. They give us in a striking form one side of the Gospel, if one side only.

Fox judged that the words of God could not supersede the Word of God.

No religious order can point to services rendered to humanity more unsullied by selfishness or nobler in far-seeing wisdom.

William Penn was, I believe, the only colonist in America who left his settlement wholly unprotected by fence or arms, and his settlement was the only one which was unassailed by the Indian tribes.

Francis sacrificed the individual: Fox left wholly out of account the powers of the larger life of the Church and the race. For him the past was "a long and dismal night of apostasy and darkness." He had no eye for the *many parts and many fashions* in which God is pleased to work. He had no sense of the action of the Holy Spirit through the great Body of Christ.

He had no thought of the weak and immature, for whom earthly signs are the appropriate support of faith; no thought for the students of nature for whom they are the hallowing of all life.

He disinherited the Christian society and he maimed the Christian man.

But he made clear beyond question the power of the simplest spiritual appeal to the consciences of men. He made clear beyond question the efficacy of a childlike trust in the reality of a divine fellowship to cleanse the rudest and coarsest life.

The principle of life fashions the organism, and sustains it. No organism, however delicately constructed, can summon to itself the principle of life.

Present Problems

WE are suffering on all sides, and we know that we are suffering, from a tyrannical individualism. This reveals itself in social life by the pursuit of personal pleasure: in commercial life by the admission of the principle of unlimited competition: in our theories of life by the acceptance of material standards of prosperity and progress.

The "great industries" have cheapened luxuries and stimulated the passion for them. They have destroyed the human fellowship of craftsman and chief. They have degraded trade, in a large degree, into speculation. They have deprived labour of its thoughtful freedom and turned men into "hands." They have given capital a power of dominion and growth perilous above all to its possessor.

So it has come to pass that in our fierce conflicts we are in peril of guiding our conduct by a theory of rights and not by a confession of duties: of losing life in a search for the means of living.

The first words attributed to man born outside the Paradise of God are words which disclose the secret of all social evil. *Am I*, said the earliest murderer, *my brother's keeper?*

And the answer came from the unfruitful earth, silent witness of the deed of violence; came from the soul, filling with remorse the fugitive, who could not flee from himself.

Yes: and the same answer must come as often as the thoughtless, the self-indulgent, the idle, propose the question now.

We are our brothers' keepers even as they are ours; and unless we accept the charge, the scene of our toil and the inexorable sovereign of our hearts will condemn us to unsatisfied desires.

Behind every social question there lies not only a moral, but also a religious question. And the final solution of every question belongs to the highest sphere.

"You cannot," in the words of the noblest leader of modern democracy, "change the fate of man by embellishing his material dwelling."

We must touch the soul, if we are to change the mode of living.

Many who allow that Christianity can deal with individuals deny that it has any message for classes or states.

Its virtues, they say, are the petty virtues of private life: its promises, the gratification of the small objects of personal aim: towards the struggles of society, of the nation, of the race, it can at the best produce nothing better than a temper of benevolent neutrality.

We know that the charge is false, essentially false, but we must admit without reserve that we have given occasion to it.

If we cannot improvise peremptory judgments, we can always affirm an eternal principle: we can quell in our hearts that spirit of self-assertion which fills us with restless jealousy till our present demands are fully paid, and that spirit of larger, deadlier self-assertion, miscalled patriotism, which tempts us to think that the power of a nation is the power of dictation and not of service, and that every failure must be washed out in blood. We can do this, and shall we venture to say we have done it?

We need yet once more to gain and to exhibit a great ideal. We are troubled on the one side by a spirit of irony, which shrinks from the avowal of its loftiest aims; and on the other side by the spirit of confidence, which assumes that all will be well if we go with the stream.

We play with noble thoughts. Now we want insight, and now we want courage. In both cases we want faith in men, and, that which alone can give it, faith in God.

No word is used more familiarly than "progress," but it is very hard to see the goal towards which we are supposed to be moving.

The greatest triumphs of modern science are, as we have seen, fruitful in evils no less than in blessings. They have increased our power, our opportunities, our resources: but in themselves they cannot open the heavens and shew *the glory of God and Jesus standing at the right hand of God:* they cannot give us that vision of immeasurable majesty which fills the whole soul with the consciousness of its destiny, and that vision of sovereign love which brings the assurance that attainment is within our reach.

For we do not think too much of life, too much of humanity, too much of men, but infinitely too little, because we allow that which can be seen by the eye of sense to furnish the data of our estimate.

But let us bring the Gospel of Christ, Maker and Heir of all things into connection not with ourselves only, but with the world, and then there will rise before us a spectacle which must move the dullest with enthusiasm and touch the most disconsolate with hope: a spectacle of a life unfolded through the ages in which, in spite of every partial loss and every-temporary check, a divine counsel of *righteousness* is fulfilled: of a humanity through whose discipline and victory, won by sacrifice offered in the ministry of every member, the end of the whole creation is reached in the *peace* of an indissoluble harmony: of men who, each in their appointed place, receive the inheritance of the fathers, and transmit it, enriched by their own toils, to a new generation, and enter living and dying into the *joy* of the Lord.

What ideal can be offered to the spirit which is greater or more true?

The sense of responsibility, the energy of spiritual force, the power of a divine ideal: how can we gain them? To this question, which is for us the question of all questions, the past returns no uncertain answer.

Each new revelation of Christ among men has hitherto found expression in some social movement, in some form of disciplined life, which has embodied and interpreted it.

And Christ is revealing Himself through the very needs which trouble us. We can see now, as men could not see in earlier times, how there has been a law in the growth of the race: how man was taken from himself by the ancient organisations of the state: how he was taken from the world by the dominant religious communities of the middle ages: how he has been taken from society by the isolating narrowness of many forms of popular Protestantism; and seeing this we can see also, when we let the Incarnation give its perfect message, that he is given back to himself, to the world, to society, in the Risen Christ.

This then is the revelation which we have to embody:

to embody in the eyes of all by some fellowship which shall strike the imagination; which shall teach by manifold experience the power of social relationships and social obligations in commerce, in politics, in religion; which shall claim for the family and the nation their proper parts in preparing the Kingdom of God on earth, in bringing to redeemed humanity the fulness of its life in Christ.

The fellowship must be natural. It must not depend for its formation or its permanence on any appeals to morbid or fantastic sentiments. It must accept the facts of life, as seen in the relations of the family, for the ground of its constitution. It must be an attempt not to realise the counsels of perfection for a select few, but to give a healthy type of living for all.

The fellowship must be English. The nation is to the race what the family is to the nation.

And England, alone among the nations, has received the power which is essential for the task which we contemplate, the power of assimilating new ideas without breaking with the past.

The fellowship must be comprehensive. It must deal not with opinion or feeling or action only, but with the whole sum of life. It must proclaim that God is not to be found more easily in "the wilderness and the solitary place" than in the study or in the market or in the workshop or by the fireside.

It must banish the strange delusion by which we suppose that things temporal and spiritual can be separated in human action, or that we can render rightly to Caesar that which is not in the very rendering rendered also to God.

The fellowship must be social. Every member of it must hold himself pledged to regard his endowments of character, of power, of place, of wealth, as a trust to be administered with resolute and conscious purpose for the good of men.

The fellowship must be open. The uniform of the soldier is at once a symbol and a safeguard.

It reminds others of his obligations, and supports him in the endeavour to fulfil them.

It makes some grave faults practically impossible. So too a measured and unostentatious simplicity, a simplicity in dress, in life, in establishment, wisely adopted by choice and not of necessity, will be an impressive outward witness to the Christian ideal, and it will help towards the attainment of it.

The fellowship must be rational. It must welcome light from every quarter, as found by those who know that every luminous ray, reflected or refracted a hundred times, comes finally from one source.

The fellowship, above all, must be spiritual. It must rest avowedly on the belief that the voice of God is not silent among us, and the vision of God not withdrawn from His people.

It must labour in the assurance that the difference of our age from the first age is not the difference of the dull, dim twilight from the noon, but that of common earth, flooded with sunshine, from the solitary mountain-top kindled to a lamp of dawn.

It must find occasion for continual praise and thanksgiving in victories of faith, from that of the first martyr St. Stephen to that of the last boy in Uganda who knew at least how to die for his Saviour.

We can estimate fairly the resources of the race. No dark continents, no untried peoples, fill the dim background of our picture of the world with incalculable possibilities. The whole field lies before us. We look upon all the provinces of the kingdom of God. We can communicate to others the noblest which we have, and save them from the long pains of our discipline. All things are ready.

Let nothing rob you of the conviction that the voice of God can be heard, and is heard '*To-day:*' that the vision of God can be gained, and is gained '*To-day.*'

We know in Part

WHEN St. Paul says "We know in part" he does not disparage knowledge; on the contrary, he reveals it in its true nobility. He opens to us one view of the meaning of the Lord's words—that sustaining motto of the scholar—in which He declared (John xvii. 17) truth to be the medium of man's consecration.

This necessary incompleteness of our knowledge, which is at first sight disappointing and discouraging, is, when duly weighed, fitted to bring stability to the results of labour, satisfies the conditions of progress, offers hope in the face of the problems of the present age, is briefly a consolation, a promise, a prophecy for us as we strive to fulfil our work in the shadow of time:

> *For thence—a paradox*
> *Which comforts while it mocks—*
> *Shall life succeed in that it seems to fail.*

The angel who was seen in Augustine's vision emptying the ocean with a shell gives no untrue image of the disproportion between the possibilities of humanity and the attainments of individual labour.

No one who has considered the slow development of the powers which man now enjoys in what appears to us to be his maturity, would be willing to admit that his faculties exhaust in kind or in degree the possible action of being.

No one supposes that the most encyclopædic mind could grasp all that is capable of being known at the moment, not to speak of those remoter consequences of all that we do, which often reveal first the true meaning of thought and action.

Our knowledge is inevitably partial in regard of the object and of the subject and of the conditions of its acquisition. In each respect an infinite mystery enwraps a little spot of light.

It requires a serious effort to enter with a living sympathy into the character of another man, or of another class, or of another nation, or of another course of thought: to feel, not with a sense of gracious superiority, but of devout thankfulness, that here and here that is supplied which we could not have provided: to acknowledge how peculiar gifts or a peculiar environment, how long discipline or an intense struggle, have conferred upon others the power of seeing that which we cannot see.

There is on all sides an overpowering passion for clearness, for decision, for results which can be measured on demand. Art and history are trammelled by realism. A restless anxiety for fulness and superficial accuracy of detail diverts the forces which should be given to an interpretation of the life. We begin to think that when we can picture to ourselves the outside of things we have mastered them.

So it is also in many respects with opinion. We are told that we must make our choice definitely between this extreme and that; that there can be no mean; that a logical necessity demands one precise conclusion or the other.

In this way we lose insensibly the present consciousness of the great deeps of life; we lose the genial influence of the vital play of thought and experience; we lose the chastening power of those unutterable strivings of the soul to which language gives witness but not shape. Portraiture becomes photography, and faith is represented by a phrase. The reflections from the mirror, the shadows on the wall of the cave, are taken for the realities which these fleeting signs should move us to seek.

We must indeed, for purposes of use, define our conceptions. We accept the necessity cheerfully, but we will not willingly forget that in doing so we mutilate them; that we convert into abstractions what are elements of life.

There is no outline in Nature, however convenient or even necessary we may find it to draw one.

However paradoxical the statement may appear, physical study more than any other brings the invisible vividly before us. The world of the man of science is not the scene of conflict and disorder which we look upon with our untrained eyes, but an order of absolute law which he finds by the interpretation of a larger experience. He pierces beneath the scene to that which it indicates. So far he has read the thought of God. His partial knowledge is a sign for the moralist and for the theologian. His triumph encourages us to study the phenomena of spiritual disorder in the sure hope that here also something of the perfection of the Divine counsel will be disclosed to us in due time, as we gaze and ponder and wait.

The Present and the Past

IT needs but little observation to notice how swiftly an exclusive fashion of opinion passes away; how a partial philosophy reigns for a space as universal and then is neglected and then despised. But our Christian faith is the heir of all. It can welcome a new lesson, and it can shelter one which has grown unpopular. It is hospitable to forces whose claims to supremacy it combats. It draws strength from truths with which its enemies have assailed it. Even when it is impressed most deeply by the spirit of the age it never lays aside its catholicity.

We are tempted to linger with a vain regret round that which is ready to vanish away or to hasten prematurely the advent of that which is not yet mature.

The present is for us not only the result, but also the epitome of the past. It gathers up into one scene the forces which have been called into play in successive ages.

It is no disrespect to our fathers if we allow that their words were not final: it is no flattery to our sons if we bid them make good new conquests.

We can use old phrases, but we cannot in that way recall old thoughts. Each generation has its own work; and the condition of performance is that the successive labourers should feel that their work has not been done hitherto, and that it will be carried out to its completion after them.

———

WE have looked away from earth in order that we may see heaven more purely; we must still look back to earth that we may make the truth of heaven more effectual.

It is a commonplace that the planets are globes: we have yet to discover, as it has been well said, that our globe is a star.

———

OUR faith is light: not the lamp only in the sepulchre, but the sun shining on the broad fields of life.

We can feel that the darkest riddles of life lose their final gloom when we refuse to acknowledge that their solution must be found in the facts which we have been so far able to grasp.

Do what we will, we cannot empty life of its mystery. Each one of us is in himself a mystery than which there can be nothing greater.

We forget the harvest reaped from others' labours while we murmur that the seed which we have cast upon the ground remains long hidden.

To wait, even with dim eye and dull ear, for the coming of the Kingdom of heaven is for us a sign that the Spirit is active within us.

We have learnt again and again from that feeding of the five thousand to see in a blessing given not only the promise, but the provision for a blessing yet to be—the sign of a love not exhausted by exercise.

When all past wants had been amply fulfilled beyond all expectation, there remained a store for the future great out of all proportion to that which had been offered from human resources.

When the disciples might have been tempted to rest as if all had been done, the voice came, *Gather up the fragments that remain, that nothing be lost*—fragments, let us remember, which do not represent what was left from man's imperfect or capricious use, but the fresh superabundance of the divine bounty.

And it is added, *Therefore*—because they accepted the labour, because they trusted the word—*they gathered them together, and filled twelve baskets with the fragments of the five barley-loaves, which remained over and above unto them that had eaten.*

We cannot mistake the spiritual meaning of the history. It is the abiding benediction of means, gifts, endowments, faithfully used without "nice calculation of less and more."

It shews us how that which we have, if brought to God with a single heart, is made fruitful beyond our utmost thought,—fruitful not only to meet wants which are felt to be urgent, but fruitful also to anticipate wants which we have not yet foreseen.

It is most characteristic of the Bible that in its loftiest promises there is no suppression, no dissembling of pain and sorrow.

In the Lord's life triumph and suffering go side by side. The last sign in which He manifested His glory was the recognised prelude to the agony of the Cross. His words of power were preceded by His bitter weeping.

Christ announces to us the unbroken continuity of all life which is truly life. There is no likelihood that we shall ever underrate the changes which we can see, the separations which sadden us, the losses which mar our capacity for action; but, on the other hand, we lose much by not dwelling day by day on that which as yet we can grasp of the permanence of our being; we lose much by constructing a future out of some fragments of the present, and transferring it to some remote scene which serves to obscure the solemn beauty of earth. We lose much by not striving to behold, little by little, it may be in fleeting visions, the eternal which is about us and in us, and which remains unaltered by all vicissitudes.

CHRIST promises to the believer without reserve a freedom from death. We have no warrant for an arbitrary dilution of the promise. We may confess that we cannot comprehend all that it embraces, but we dare not say that it means only what we can comprehend. "Whosoever believeth in Me," He says plainly, "shall never die;" not some part of him shall live hereafter, but he—the living, loving person—all of him that truly is—"shall never die."

THE strength of a church, the strength of a nation, the strength of a family, lies for the most part in the unseen yet living members which the past has inscribed for ever in its roll.

WE need not go from our proper place in order to discipline ourselves for God's service; we need not strive after gifts which He has not entrusted to us, or forms of action which are foreign to our position, in order to do our part as members of His Church.

It is enough that we grow and wax strong under the action of those forces by which He moves us within and without, if we desire to fulfil, according to the measure of our powers, the charge which He has prepared for us.

GREAT occasions do not make heroes or cowards; they simply unveil them to the eyes of men.

Silently and imperceptibly, as we wake and sleep, we grow and wax strong; we grow and wax weak; and at last some crisis shews us what we have become.

From small beginnings flow the currents of our lives, from constant and unnoticed impulses we take our bias;

the stream is ever gathering strength, the bend is ever being confirmed or corrected.

There is not one act, not one purpose, which does not leave its trace, though we may be unable to distinguish and measure its value.

There is not one drop which does not add something to the flowing river, not one blast which does not in some way shape the rising tree.

QUESTIONS are ripening for discussion by which all we hold most precious is imperilled. Evil forces are gathering with which battle must be done. It will be for us or for our children to shew that our faith can solve fresh problems and win new victories.

But while we feel all this keenly, it is not our part to anticipate with anxious curiosity what the future will bring; we can best prepare for that by doing in quietness and confidence what we find prepared for us.

SPIRITUAL service lies in the consecration of simplest duties.

KNOWLEDGE is only a vantage-ground and not a victory. If we neglect to turn to use the superiority which it gives us, our defeat will only be the more disgraceful because we were so richly furnished for the battle.

CAN any one sincerely believe that God the Father made the world, and not regard all creation, even in what we call its lowest forms, with reverence?

THE Christian differs from the patriot and the philanthropist not so much in the immediate ends which he seeks as in the impulse by which he is moved to seek them.

NOT one difficulty, one pain, one contradiction of life is removed by the spirit of denial. Only the treasury of heaven is closed at its bidding.

THE higher, nobler, fuller, comes to men only as the fruit of the lower and the less.

"Light after light well used they shall attain."

OF all the perils of advancing age none is greater than that of losing the faculty of wonder. That which is commonest is indeed the most real cause of wonder.

AS a whole human life is not like a straight line, it is not like a circle; but it is a widening and ascending spiral. There is progress without return; there is resemblance without repetition.

HE who loves the Church of Christ fears not the investigation but the neglect of its records.

NEVER forget that in the inner life feeling is the herald of knowledge. Never despond when you find that to suffer is often the synonym for to work.

THOUGH a man may become more incisive in action in proportion as he grows narrower, the cost of success is a maimed humanity.

THEOLOGY and physical science are, and it is vain to deny or extenuate the fact, separated for the time by a profound jealousy and misunderstanding.

We have been reminded very frequently of the errors of theologians as to the office and method and results of physics; to me the errors of physicists as to the office and methods and results of theology are more surprising; and, if I may venture to express my whole mind, the practical neglect of history—the only record of the complete life of man—by both, appears to be still more wonderful and still more disastrous.

THE science of life, which deals with the whole experience of men, must be restored to its proper place between the science of experiment, which deals with matter, and the science of revelation, which deals with God.

Then, and not till then, shall we see how the Gospel is illuminated by our progress, and itself is illuminated by our darkness.

IT is of the utmost importance that in all intellectual labour we should remember that every expression of truth is the resultant of many forces which are perpetually changing, so that an identical formula cannot long preserve its original significance.

ASPIRATIONS without faith are powerful only for destruction. They can kindle a revolution, but they cannot mould a new order.

The recognition of duty is the surest protection of rights.

A SAINT falls in some obscure conflict, and forthwith he is manifested with a multiplied energy, and stirs the heart of men with an irresistible force which he had not before. A warrior or a statesman shews that he can dare or suffer or forbear great things for his country and his name; his life through his name becomes a power to inspire, to support, to control later generations.

At one time the change from the seen to the unseen comes swiftly, in the full vigour of action, that so we may learn that there must yet be scope in some new and unknown field, in some new and unknown shape, for the energy which is instinct with promise.

At another time the change comes through "calm decay": first one faculty and then another is withdrawn, while love abides, that so we may learn that the person whom we love is more than those qualities through which he has been outwardly revealed to us.

He would be less than man who could exist in the world and not be ennobled while he blesses the countless multitude of silent benefactors who at every moment are stirring him to follow great examples; less than a man who did not feel that his self-denial would be joyous if he could foresee that in some later age another would thank him for having removed one stumbling-block from the path of right. Our soldiers at Badajos laid their bodies on the sword-blades that their comrades might find a path to the breach; that is an image of what our fathers have done for us.

Even now we have not fully learnt what the Greek Scriptures and Greek speculation, classical and Christian, have to teach; but at least we can feel that, with all its faithlessness, with all its hypocrisy, with all its violence, the classical Renaissance has left a blessing behind it; and so we can await with thankful expectation the renaissance inspired by physical thought with which society is travailing now.

The way of God is the way of sacrifice. But let us not mistake the meaning of the word. It has been well said that "in the hours of clear reason we should say that we had never made a sacrifice"; and again it may be said no less well that all which we delight to recall is sacrifice. For sacrifice properly describes not loss to man but devotion to God : not suffering but dedication : not the foregoing of that which we might have enjoyed, but the conversion of that which was offered to us for a time into an eternal possession; the investment of things unstable and fleeting with a power of unchangeable joy.

The poorest mother who clasps her new-born infant to her breast has found, if but for a moment, the secret of life. To live for others, to suffer for others, is the inevitable condition of our being. To accept the condition gladly is to find it crowned with its own joy.

The failure of every selfish pleasure to satisfy the soul, the weariness which follows self-indulgence, the sense of weakness and distrust which comes from powers unused and duties unpursued, confirm the sentence which is executed, sooner or later, by the conditions of society. We were made to serve one another. We are happiest when we fulfil the law of our being, "It is more blessed to give than to receive." The Lord does not say it is more natural or more pleasant.

To love is better, nobler, more elevating, and more sure, than to be loved. To love is to have found that which lifts us above ourselves; which makes us capable of sacrifice; which unseals the forces of another world. He who is loved has gained the highest tribute of earth; he who loves has entered into the spirit of heaven. The love which comes to us must always be alloyed with the sad sense of our own unworthiness. The love which goes out from us is kept bright by the ideal to which it is directed.

He who has turned aside from the march of the great army to bring help to one who has fallen, he who has yielded a foremost place that he might restore another, has felt something of the joy of his Lord—the joy of absolute self-surrender,—and knows that there is a priceless victory in what seems to be failure in the eyes of men.

The return for labour is the power of fresh activity.

In the symbol of the Friendly Society the open hand is the minister of the open heart. There the wreath round the world foreshadows the conquest of all earthly claims. There, over the speaking signs, which represent the facts of this life and the hopes of the future, is laid the golden cross, the emblem of true service unto death. There, around all, faith and hope and love are busy with gracious duties; there, above all, the eye of light is opened, which tells of a presence that never fails and of a care that never slumbers. It is enough, then, that these symbols be translated into deeds. By love serve one another, and you will know—know with deeper thankfulness as the service is more perfect—that "it is more blessed to give than to receive."

LET any one looking to his own home, put on one side the trivial, commonplace occasions on which he has sacrificed others to himself, and on the other those in which he has sacrificed himself to others, and he will see that life is indeed the discipline of love, and that love is the soul of life.

WE have not only a domestic ancestry and a domestic heritage. We have also a national ancestry and a national heritage. A great part of our life is made up of that which we have, every one, received in common as Englishmen. And this splendid patrimony is not for display, not for pride, but for most laborious and solemn employment. Patriotism, like affection, may unhappily degenerate into selfishness; but it may, by God's grace, be the devout expression of a duty to humanity.

THE greater body has its grievous sicknesses, its fevers and its frenzies, even as the less. But the ocean lies deep and still below the storms which trouble its surface.

THERE is much, very much, in the circumstances of life which requires readjustment; but as we believe in the one life in Christ, we shall not attempt to deal directly with symptoms, and achieve superficial reforms.

We shall seek to overcome the disease by quickening the healthy energy of the vital forces. To this end we can all contribute. In this labour we are all called to be fellow-workers with God.

What the issue may be we are not careful to prejudge. But we are sure that the spiritual life of a people will find an outward form corresponding to its power and beauty.

For of the soul the body form doth take,
For soul is form and doth the body make.

THERE is, I think, nothing sadder in the world than the waste of Christian influence. From one cause or another we shrink from the responsibility of avowing our deepest convictions. Partly it is from fear of ostentation and singularity, partly from self-distrust and sincere humility, partly from more unworthy motives. But from whatever cause it may be, by so doing we wrong our friends. We leave unspoken the word which might have cheered or guided or turned them. By our coldness we suffer them to remain in doubt whether God has visited us. If the heart be full, men argue, its feelings will find utterance. If the Christian creed be accepted as the Truth, it cannot but colour the whole life of the believer. Not to speak, then, of our highest hopes, not to talk, one with another, of what, as we trust, God has done, and will do, for us, is to cast discredit on our name. When that is at stake we may well forget ourselves.

NO one, I fancy, has ever ventured to cast aside his religious reserve without meeting with sympathy for which he had not looked, and gaining courage from the sense of spiritual fellowship. How can it be otherwise? It is not of any special prerogative we make boast, but of a blessing which is offered as the common heritage of men.

The Christian Society

ALL the images under which the religious life is figured bear witness to this its twofold character. The power and beauty of the Christian society are always shewn to us in manifold subordination. At one time we are taught to regard it as a temple reared through long ages, each stone of which fills its special place and contributes its share to the grace and stability of the fabric. At another time as a vine, where, by the complicated and delicate machinery of Providence, earth and air and water are fashioned into leaf and flower and fruit. At another time as a body, where a royal will directs and disciplines and uses the functions of every member. At another time as a vast army, where each soldier, trained and strengthened, acts no longer for himself, but even to absolute self-sacrifice submits to the sovereign control of his leader. It is impossible to mistake the meaning of such images, which teach us our mutual dependence in every aspect.

We are dependent on the past, which determines our relative positions. We are dependent on the present, which supplies the materials for our action and the law by which we can appropriate and employ them. We are dependent even on the future, which may require that we perish, as some forlorn hope, to ensure the triumph of those who shall come after us.

Noblesse Oblige

THE aspect of the blessing of Church work which is brightest with promise is that which presents it as the firstfruits of a dedicated life. It is the end which determines the character of the work. What we do is generous or base in consideration of the object at which we are aiming as we do it. I remember to have read a most touching story in which a man is represented as preserving through every vicissitude of declining fortune the sense that he was serving his country. He fell outwardly lower and lower, but he never ceased to be noble. The story is a parable. What his country is to the citizen, the universal Church is to the Christian: the visible representation of all that is loftiest in duty, and of all that is most august in power. To work for that Society in whose life ages are but as days, to whose fulness nations are contributory elements: for that Society which is indeed the Body of Christ, is a privilege which gives inexpressible dignity to the humblest ministry. If we are often led to think too highly of ourselves, we always, I believe, think too poorly of that to which God has called us. *Noblesse oblige*—the inspiring necessity of position—has at all times stirred men to splendid efforts. And the nobility of the Christian—if our eyes are open to see—rises supreme even now. He traces his descent through a line of Martyrs and Saints; he holds the charter of an eternal kingdom.

To what Purpose was this Waste?

WHY is it that we build splendid churches and decorate them beyond the necessities of use? "To what purpose is this waste?" Would it not be better to multiply buildings of the simplest character, which would offer adequate shelter to crowds of worshippers? Has Art, in other words, a place in spiritual service? It is common to seek a reply to these questions from the Old Testament, from the divinely-ordered magnificence of the Temple, from "the ark of the covenant overlaid with gold," and "the cherubim of glory overshadowing the mercy-seat," on which even the writer of the Epistle to the Hebrews dwells with lingering affection. But no valid argument can be drawn from that source. The Jewish system was external, and consequently the natural embodiment of all its teaching was external. Christianity is spiritual; we might, therefore, be tempted to conclude by analogy, that its teaching will always be presented in a spiritual form. This being so, we must look deeper for our answer. We must look to the very constitution of man, which our Faith hallows in its fulness—body, soul, and spirit—and then at once we can see that we are made to love the beautiful no less than the true and good. There are harmonies of form and colour and sound which not only give us keen delight, but minister to pure and noble thoughts. No doubt the beautiful differs widely from the true and good in this—that it is liable to corruption. It deals with those objects of sense through which we are most openly and readily led astray. But it may be said that for this very reason it stands in greater need of consecration; and at least it is clear that we shall not have rendered ourselves wholly a sacrifice to God till we have in some way found for every power with which He has endowed us a satisfaction consistent with His will. All life, all instinct, proves that we cannot but seek to gratify the different organs of sense. We cannot close them against the beauty and the wonder and the power; the shapes of things, their colours, lights and shades, changes, surprises; and God made them all. And the impulse to dwell on them belongs to us as men, and not as fallen men. The few ornaments carefully arranged on the cottage shelf, the few plants brightening the window, the feeling which finds expression in the simple melody, bear witness to the working of pure and tender elements in our nature which claim to be recognised, satisfied, interpreted. Even before Christian worship emerged into open daylight, the early believers decorated their tombs with such skill as they could command. The vine spreading over the vault, as the emblem of the graceful fruitfulness of the divine life, the figures of the Good Shepherd or of the Lamb, shewed that they wished to enlist art in the service of their faith, and they gave gladly even of their slender means for the adornment of its sanctuaries. There is, I have admitted, a danger in this use of art. I do not forget that some would seek in this distraction of outward beauty a substitute for spiritual devotion. I do not forget that the most lavish display of ecclesiastical splendour in England heralded forth the struggles of the Reformation. I do not forget that all that is of the world passeth away. But this is the great trial of our earthly discipline, that we must save, that we must hallow, that which is ready to perish; that we must strive even now to bring to creation something of the glory of the sons of God. In this effort art is our minister. Art, rightly studied and employed, brings the ideal before us in material shapes, reveals something of the underlying, eternal lessons of things transitory, saves us from turning away from that which lies about our feet to an unimaginable future. As, then, we acknowledge the peril of art and the office of art, we look for guidance in the offering of gifts for the gracing of worship.

The Study of Art

THE study of art generally enlarges, invigorates, and refines very important powers, both of feeling and thinking.

The cultivation of some art is not only necessary for enjoyment, but that we may fulfil our own part in life.

If this is the function of art is it not a part of the spiritual teacher's duty to put art in its true light before those with whom he has to deal?

It is a principle we are constantly losing sight of. One result is that we are trying to divide our life into two spheres which have no connection with one another. So it is that there enters into our religion something of unreality.

We clergy are apt to forget that the message entrusted to us was a message to man as man; that we are bidden to bring perfection to man as created, and not only redemption to man as fallen.

Music is essentially the social art. The painter and sculptor can work alone, but the highest effects of music can only be brought out by thorough combination.

Music gains in movement and variety what it loses in permanence and directness; it is a living thing; painting and sculpture, without disrespect, may be described as dead things. Music is a human art—a creation of man, not an imitation.

True Art, like Nature, appeals to all. The pleasure which it brings is common property. The waving cornfield, the purple blush of the budding elm trees, the changing glory of the sunset over our wide plains, speak alike to every one who looks on them.

And so it is with a great picture, or a great piece of music, or a great building.

These also are a public endowment. They address various minds and various moods, it is true, in different ways, but for all they have an intelligible voice.

Peterborough Cathedral

TO speak only of that which is most directly before us, I will venture to say that there is not one here to whom our Cathedral has not spoken, not one who has not felt that it has been well for him to listen to the message which it bears from a distant age. It may have been the majestic front, with its promise of catholic welcome, or the smaller porch, which shews a danger boldly made into an occasion for a fresh beauty, or the long nave with its lesson of self-forgetful faithfulness, or some smaller part, telling of thought, of reverence, of sacrifice, by which we have been touched; but do we not know that the influence has been real?

The Value of Life

How few of us pause to consider what life is, not in its circumstances but in its energy, in its capacities, in its issues.

We all know, even if the knowledge has little practical effect, that no measure of time or sense gives a standard of its value.

Life is more than the sum of personal enjoyments and pains through which it finds expression; more than the length of days in which it is visible to human eyes; more than the fulness of means which reveal to us its power. All these pass away, but in the process of their vanishing a spiritual result has been fulfilled. The soul of the man has been brought into fellowship—a fellowship welcomed or disregarded—with men and with the world and with God. It has consciously or unconsciously learnt much and done much. It has shaped a character for itself; it has helped to shape a character for others. It is at the end, most solemn thought, "as it has been used."

Providence on the Side of the strongest Convictions

The saying that Providence is on the side of the strongest battalions was found false by the experience of the man who said it, false by his greatest triumphs, and false by his fatal overthrow, if multitude is the measure of success.

Providence—if we dare so to speak—is on the side, not of the strongest battalions, but of the strongest convictions.

The devotion of faith can change a defeat into a victory, and overbalance at the instant the weight of numbers.

The Swiss, at St. Jacob, conquered a force twenty times as great as their own, not for a day, but for centuries, by simply dying. When Cromwell burst into the words of the 68th Psalm, as the sun just rose over the rout of Dunbar, he had decided the fate of the Empire with an army half as large as that opposed to him. So it will ever be.

Bossuet's funeral Oration on Louis XIV

I REMEMBER that one of the greatest orators of France began his sermon on the death of her most brilliant sovereign with the solemn words, "My brethren, God only is great." I often have wished that he had also ended there. In the magnificent periods which followed, he drew in unconscious irony a picture of warlike glory, of ostentatious luxury, of successful persecution, by which, in spite of his own confession, he sought to establish the title of "great" for the departed king.

The orator was sincere in his pleading, and his contemporaries affirmed his judgment. But for one hundred and fifty years the nation of the "great monarch" has reaped the fruits of his "greatness" in a disastrous cycle of revolution and anarchy and despotism. The pride of class trampled under foot, unparalleled victories more than compensated by unparalleled defeats, wealth dissipated, confidence destroyed, have left the opening sentence of the panegyric almost startling in its isolated truth. Over all its lofty boastings, over all its august prophecies, the words stand written, luminous and ineffaceable—"God only is great."

Napoleon III

NEVER before, not even in the defeat of the first Napoleon, have men been allowed to look upon so swift and total an overthrow of personal dominion as that which has finally been consummated in a lonely death. Of all that kept Europe in awe for twenty years, nothing remains except burning memories of shame and disaster. The armies which were fabled to be invincible have endured surrender and captivity. The city, which boasted herself the indefeasible queen of pleasure, has twice borne the extremities of war. The chief in whose silent thoughts the destiny of nations was supposed to lie, has acknowledged defeat and with patient dignity passed before a tribunal loftier than man's. We may give sentence as severely as we dare upon the self-seeking which compassed a throne, and upon the self-indulgence which occupied it; but we must admit that, in man's measure, the penalty did not fall short of the sin. Where there was no sacrifice there was no permanence. The rain descended, and the floods came, and the wind blew, and beat upon that pleasure-house of Majesty; and it fell: and great was the fall thereof. For sovereignty came exile; for luxury the long tortures of exquisite pain; for statecraft utter and hopeless discomfiture. And if we try to represent to ourselves what must have been the sufferings of that last campaign to him who led it, the most just condemnation will be lost in pity.

Two special Blessings of English Society

NOT to dwell on blessings, which we all rightly regard as natural constituents in an Englishman's birthright, parts, that is, in God's gifts to him, such as freedom of speech and act, tenacity of purpose, self-restraint, I will mention two others, which are, perhaps, less obvious, and which, nevertheless, seem to me to characterise the part which we have to play in the conflict of opinions, rather than of peoples, which is threatening to break over Europe.

The first is the vital unity of English society. The second is the combination of reverence with self-respect in popular opinion. I do not forget that there are forces at work among us which tend to separate class from class, and to set one against another in fratricidal rivalry.

I do not forget that some would represent loyal homage to rank and blood as derogatory to the generous spirit which it purifies. But I am sure that the great heart of England is sound still.

I am sure that the unity of which I speak is real, if often concealed, and that reverence is as yet powerful among us, if often dissembled.

There is a living circulation between our many ranks which makes mutual understanding easy. On the other hand there is an age-long tradition gathered round each one which preserves its distinctions intact.

We do not yet think that we have made, or that we can unmake the dignity of the Throne.

We are not yet persuaded that level uniformity is the type of grace, or an adequate expression of the constitution of human nature.

England as a Teacher

IF Europe is to learn that manifold service is the true condition of unity, that order is the one foundation of progress, I cannot doubt that England must be the teacher.

We must make clear among ourselves, so that all men may see the animating spectacle, that there can be a society free without confusion, reverent without servility, strong without selfwill, devout without superstition.

The part is not of our seeking: it is not matter of self-gratulation or arrogance, but for self-questioning and self-abasement.

What are we that such issues should be left in our hands? No one can recognise more gladly than I do, the priceless benefits which the great nations of the Continent have conferred upon mankind at large, and upon ourselves; but now (as it seems to me) they, in turn, are looking to us. They want what we have been trained to offer, if we have not wasted the heritage of our fathers, in the example of an energetic, a multiform, a harmonious national life.

It may be that dangers seem to be more urgent and more alarming, because they are brought nearer to us by the conditions of modern intercourse, but I confess that I tremble for the future when I hear of a wide and growing organisation abroad, which pledges its members, on the penalty of expulsion, to reject the sacraments of Christianity for themselves and for their children: when I hear of societies of youths and schoolboys banded together to assail the Faith of their fellows: when I see one great people still trammelled by the traditions of feudalism, which claim no respect in the popular conscience, and another united only in the deep passion for far-off revenge, and another torn asunder by a succession of civil wars, till the conception of the nation has become an idle name, and another sadly despairing of the reconciliation of civil duties and catholic belief, and another driven by a restless ambition to seek in conquest the semblance of strength which domestic intrigues consume at home.

The Miseries of War

OF these the fierce, mad struggle, the swift and honourable death are the very least. Gather together every ingredient of suffering, all the agony of suspense, and all the despair of foreboding; fancy that whoever is dearest to you—brother, husband, son—is called away to trials which are not uncertain but only undefined; conjure up the indescribable deeds which men will dare to do, who know that their lives are in the balance; look forward to the heritage of desolation which a great battle leaves alike to conquerors and to conquered; and acknowledge, prostrate before the throne of God, that of all the mysteries which encompass us, that is the greatest, that at the bidding of one or two men, of whose good faith there can be no warranty, thousands should be consigned to swift destruction, and tens of thousands to hopeless bereavement.

There have been, and there yet may be, times when principles were and will be maintained not too dearly even at this cost. Freedom, faith, religion, the integrity of an empire, the fulfilment of a trust, claim as a ready sacrifice all that we are and all that we have. But often there is no principle at stake. The combatants meet in a mere trial of strength. It is at the best a duel, and not a conflict of nations. Some plea of wounded honour, some rankling of old grievances, some strained susceptibility as to damaged influence, is all that is urged to justify the irrevocable defiance.

We should not forget that even war may be a duty—a duty on both sides. Sharp swift blows may prove to be a less evil than the suppressed and slumbering passions of which they are the open avowal.

It may be that through bloodshed lies the surest way to peace; it may be that after the paroxysm of concentrated suffering is over, the peoples will be left torn, enfeebled, half-dead, but yet freed from the evil spirits of pride and domination by which they were before possessed. But in the meantime, What is our duty as spectators of the struggle? Some things there are which we must guard ourselves from doing.

As far as I can judge, there are three principal temptations to wrong-doing or wrong-thinking in this matter which we must overcome. There is in the first place a temptation to claim for ourselves the interpretation of the methods of Providence. We are inclined to be over-hasty in deciding that in this or that lies an evident retribution for something in the past. But the ways of God are not as our ways. He works upon a wider field than we can embrace with our vision. Virtue is not always prosperous before our eyes; the champion of justice is not always triumphant. There may be martyred nations as well as martyred men. They too may fall, and falling, bequeath their cause, consecrated by a baptism of blood, to those who shall come after them.

The temptations to read the Divine judgments may be strong, but if you love right, and as you love right, do not peril your convictions on transitory and precarious tests. Every sin, we may be sure, sooner or later, brings its harvest of sorrow, but the harvest ripens slowly. The third or fourth generations may have to bear the inevitable punishment of the iniquity of their fathers, who have themselves enjoyed a terrible impunity.

THERE is, in the next place, an appalling selfishness roused in us at the prospect of two great nations engaged in a death struggle together.

We calculate instinctively what we have to gain or lose by the success of either side; we allow considerations of interest to cloud our views of truth; we accept combinations in the spirit of gamblers, which promise to leave us the largest profit. This one, we think, may become a formidable rival; that one may become a powerful ally. We grow almost content with the sacrifice of lives and fortunes, if it appears that some advantage may accrue to us while we idly watch. Every one's experience will bear witness that what I say is true. In the American War this feeling found an unabashed though partial utterance. Strike down the ignoble impulse, if you perceive it is rising within you. Security, repose, prosperity, may be enjoyed in thankfulness if we hold them, under God, by the exertion of those powers which He has given us; but to look complacently for the increase of such blessings, through the toils of those with whom we have not laboured, and through the tears of those with whom we have not wept, is something meaner than cowardice.

A THIRD temptation yet remains, still more coarse, and yet still more subtle, which every one of us will have to meet. In the straining after some new excitement, we convert the most overwhelming tragedies of life into food for our passing curiosity; we are impatient for tidings which will enrol one more among the blood-stained names of history; we watch the movements of armies as if they were representing a drama for our amusement; we almost feel ourselves aggrieved if a day fail to add a startling incident to the progress of the action; we willingly forget that that glorious battlefield, as men speak, is one loathsome sepulchre; we forget that that triumphant march is accompanied at every step by bitter, lingering wails of sorrow, which outlast the trumpet-call; we forget that the story which makes our pulse beat quicker and our eye flash brighter has darkened for ever homes which till that was told were as happy as our own. Strive against this temptation also. Do not try by an inhuman alchemy to turn the pangs of others into your pleasure. They too, who perish unknown in strange lands, are our brethren—for them too Christ died.

THE individual is not an isolated unit, but a complicated result of an enormous past, inspired at the same time with a personal will, which makes him a source of influence for an immeasurable future.

I HAVE good hope that when all wealth is felt to be a trust the blessing which lies in poverty will be recognised.

What we need for the purification of society is, as was said long since, plain living and high thinking.

CHRISTIANITY is not an etherealised Judaism, but its spiritual antitype.

LIFE is filled with awe. Its solemnity grows upon us. We may wish to remain children always, but we cannot.

IF it be true that a prophet is not received in his own country, it is equally true that he is not received in his own age.

NOT all at once, not in blinding glory, not in overpowering might, but in many parts and in many fashions, God trains His children to a riper understanding of His counsels.

A CLEAR and harmonious view of the elements of truth is not necessarily a complete view.

OUR power of apprehension is no measure of the fulness of the Divine message.

CAREFUL reflection will at once shew that our bodies are nothing more than the outward expression of unseen forces, according to the laws of our present existence.

THE real sign of the supremacy of the Christian society is not that it spreads everywhere, but that it embraces the whole truth. This is the sure pledge of the Church's dominion.

OUR efforts must be directed not to materialising heaven, but to discerning the divine, the eternal, in earth.

THE efficacy of a pattern obviously must depend upon its fitness for imitation.

THE loftiest aspirations and the most difficult labours

have in the home-hearth that which may kindle them with a homelier glow and direct them with a steadier light.

BEYOND the crowded thoroughfares which bewilder us, beyond these crushing palaces of commerce which overwhelm us, this sordid glare which dazzles and saddens us, rises before the believer the holy city pure and still.

TO live is hard; and there is not one of us, I fancy, who has not again and again been tempted to despair of life when he has dared to look upon its dark mysteries; but again, there is not one of us who has not found a great sorrow, a great disappointment, a great trial, an avenue to unexpected joy.

THE rejection of the mysteries of Christianity will not eliminate the element of mystery from life.

HOWEVER repulsive the ostentation of religion may be, the suppression of faith is more perilous. Who can believe that the heart is full when the lips are silent?

THE hallowing, the preservation, the transfiguration of every faculty of sense and thought and intuition with which we are endowed, is God's will.

IT is not our part to idolise or to disparage our fathers. It is our part to seek to understand that we may honour them.

WE should strive without reserve and without ostentation to lay open the spring of our hope and strength.

WE cannot always keep at the level of our loftiest thoughts.

WHAT men call success and failure are no more than changing lights in the prospect of the accomplishment of God's will.

TYPES OF APOSTOLIC SERVICE

Saintship

THE commemoration of Saints is one of the provisions which has been wisely made by our Church to bring home to us our connection with the invisible life: to help us to confess that they who once lived to God live still: to know that we are heirs not of a dead past, but of a fresh past with new lessons; to learn that consecrated gifts become an eternal blessing; to understand that Christ is pleased to reveal Himself little by little *in many parts and in many fashions*, in the persons of His servants.

The mark of a saint is not perfection but consecration. A saint is not a man without faults, but a man who has given himself without reserve to God.

Westminster Abbey has been called "a temple of silence and reconciliation." It is far more truly an altar of human endowments.

The Chapel of Henry VII. has its own peculiar message. It is, as it were, the tomb, the monument, of mediævalism. Designed to be the shrine of a canonised king it became the resting-place of three dynasties separated outwardly by sharp differences from his Communion. In both relations it speaks to us something of the nature of the eternal and the unseen. It speaks to us in the long line of statues which encircle it—unique in England—in which for the last time the middle age expressed its faith in the great communion of saints. It speaks to us in the costly structures and plain stones of later times which cover the dust of those to whom for a brief space earthly empire was committed.

We can hardly look upon that long line supported by the cornices of angels without feeling the conviction which it expresses of the manifoldness of consecrated service.

Philosophers, kings, priests, warriors, doctors, apostles, holy maids and matrons, lead up to the central figure of the enthroned Lord, blessing the world which He rules.

We can hardly look upon the strange contrast of splendour and bareness in the royal graves without feeling that the soul is not measured by "glory of birth and state."

Authority

THERE is a fundamental difference between heathen and Christian morality. On the one side there is the supreme authority of force: on the other side the supreme authority of service.

In the light of the Gospel and, may I not say, in the deep consciousness of the heart which it illuminates, reverence is the acknowledgment of a transforming grace, labour is the glad return for healthy vigour, dependence is the joy of fellowship, service is the secret of prevailing authority.

The Lord's words make clear beyond doubt that the blessing of power is "the blessing of great cares," that the sign of authority is the readiness to serve.

It is an old maxim that we can rule Nature only by obeying her.

Insight which is the inspiration of science comes from service.

It lies in our nature that we should respond to the voice which interprets us to ourselves.

We cannot but rejoice to obey him who proposes to us that ideal as our own which often we have not the courage to confess, though we inwardly strive towards it.

Christ Himself confirms the law in its widest application. He shews that His sovereignty is established on His individual knowledge of His servants.

His many sheep are not to Him a mere flock. His eye discerns in each that which modifies the common features.

We must serve in order that we may understand. We must not overpower by our own force the character which we wish to appreciate and guide in its mature vigour.

He is no true leader who drills his subjects into mechanical instruments of his designs. The true leader gains the devotion of the soul and spirit. Sympathy, which is the strength of government, comes by service.

Christian service is not the inconsiderate scattering of our gifts, but the deliberate bestowal of them in such a way that we *may take them again.*

If the terrible saying of the Roman historian is true that "it is characteristic of human nature that we should hate those whom we have injured," it is no less true that we love those whom we have helped.

In this way then by serving God in man and man in God we bring ourselves into harmony with all about us.

Freedom which is the soul of individual life comes through service.

Suffering: St. Paul

WHAT we can do for another is the test of power: what we can suffer for another is the test of love.

We can see, to use St. Paul's own words, how *the things which happened unto him*—the things which overthrew his cherished designs and condemned him to bear and to wait—*fell out rather unto the progress of the Gospel*. We can see how his service was, in those parts in which it proved most fruitful, the service of suffering.

The service of suffering: St. Paul learnt the lesson. It is a paradox of faith which we find it hard to learn. We would do some great thing, and God, by an unlooked-for change of health or fortune or position, forces us to sit still. So His will is accomplished; and in due time we find that our true end also is gained. Our robes are *washed and made white—in blood*.

The service of suffering: by this God equalises our circumstances. All are on a level of advantage in respect to this ministry. All can accept the place of patient learners in the school of affliction; and more things are wrought by quiet, uncomplaining endurance than the world knows of.

For a time the eloquence of adversity meekly borne may be unheard, but when it is heard it prevails.

The service of suffering: it is the comprehensive fulfilment of the Lord's promise, *Whosoever shall lose his life for My sake shall find it*. It gives to us in simple ways, in the accomplishment of our common work, in looking calmly, it may be, upon insoluble problems, in surrendering our will to the claims of social duty, the opportunity of gaining the true life.

The service of suffering: it is the revelation of peace. The man of restless ambition undergoes a thousand martyrdoms. But the trials which are accepted as God's gift, to be borne for His name's sake, are transformed by the acceptance.

Doubting: St. Thomas

IN the other Gospels St. Thomas is a name and nothing more: in St. John he is a living man, hampered by human infirmities and ennobled by human devotion, a living man nearer perhaps to ourselves, in our day of trial, than any other of the disciples.

St. Thomas doubted, and through his experience we can learn the legitimate issues of doubt.

Thomas saith unto Him, Lord, we know not whither Thou goest; and how know we the way?

The difficulty which is thus raised is a real and a natural one. It is true in common life that the knowledge of the end enables us to judge of the road. But it is not so in spiritual things. There the end belongs to another order. It lies beyond our power of distinct apprehension. It is enough therefore for us to know the road, as it is opened for us step by step.

And here fresh light is given. Christ shews that for us the end and the road are one. "*I am*," He says—"I am" and not "I reveal" or "I point to," as herald or prophet—"*the Way, and the Truth, and the Life.*"

Doubt as to the end is no reason for refusing to move along the opened way.

Doubt as to the validity of historic evidence is no obstacle to the victory of faith.

Waiting: St. John

IN St. John there is a calm strength, a power of spiritual vision which looks on all the riddles and sorrows of life, and looks through them, though it cannot arrange in familiar forms the glory which it sees beyond. The characteristic of St. John is "waiting"; and it is useful for us to meditate on this grace of "waiting," as it is seen in *the disciple whom Jesus loved*.

Can we not feel that it is well for us to pause and think of the blessedness of "waiting," hurried, as we are, to and fro, by the inevitable tumult of modern life?

For it is still through long watching that at last the opportunity is found for mastering the truth towards which our thoughts have been turned. It is still not unfrequently through sorrow that we gain little by little the power of insight by which the meaning of familiar facts is disclosed.

It is still by silent ponderings, in the solitude of the inner chamber, or in the solitude of the crowd, that we learn the lesson of communing with God. And our anxiety for results which we can measure, our restlessness under conditions which we hold to be unfavourable to our progress, our passion for excitement, tend to deprive us of these highest fruits of life.

We cannot remove the conditions under which our work is to be done, but we can transform them. They are the elements out of which we must build the temples wherein we serve.

In one sense God gives nothing, while in another sense He gives all things. He requires us, that is, to make His gifts our own by using the power which He inspires. Not all at once, and not as we should have expected, and not without many delays, does that which indeed is ours become ours.

So it is that waiting itself becomes a work; and of all the promises of Scripture none I think speaks with fuller encouragement to such as seem to find no fruit of labour, or no scope for it, if only they wait for the Lord who will not leave the desolate, than this, *In your patience ye shall win your souls.*

PART IV

Lessons of Literature and Art

LESSONS OF LITERATURE & ART

The Dramatist as Prophet: Aeschylus

THE Athenian, the typical Greek, learned the practice of life from the debates of the public assembly; he learned the theory of life from the poems of the theatre.

The Greek tragedies were poems, not illusions: they were interpretations and not pictures of life. The facts, so to speak, were given; the business of the writer was to explain their meaning and their lessons. The outline of the plot was a familiar text; the filling up was the sermon of the preacher. And so it is that the remains of the Greek tragedians furnish a remarkable picture of the history of popular religion during the period over which they reach.

Æschylus is the prophet of Greek tragedy, as Sophocles is the artist, and Euripides the realist. The succession of character is one which reappears in every literature, but in this first example it is most marked and most spontaneous. Events are first viewed on their divine side, then on the side of order or beauty, and lastly on the side of nature. The same story which furnishes Æschylus with an occasion for reconciling the claims of revenge and forgiveness, the powers of earth and the powers of heaven, furnishes Sophocles with a powerful dramatic study of female character, and Euripides with a graceful picture of life.

The poems of Homer betray, as we believe, the work of different hands: the religious teaching of Æschylus exhibits equally a diversity of sources.

It was his task to harmonise, as best he might, the claims of fate and will, of law and life, of God and man, in this present world; to connect suffering with sin, and strip guilt of the boast of impunity; to indicate the majesty of Providence, and the absolute wisdom of the Divine voice revealed in appointed ways.

As a religious poet, Dante alone stands by him; both were children of their age, both were schooled in sorrow, but both were above all that was merely personal and local, and remain, to those who will read them, prophets for all time.

However wide the field which Æschylus covers, he sees all equally in the light of a divine presence. Primitive myths, ancient traditions, historic events, are alike regarded by him from a spiritual point of sight. His view of life and society is in every case theocratic; and it is only by keeping this truth steadily in view that we can gain the central idea of his separate plays.

The "Prometheus" is necessarily the foundation of his system, for it treats of the original problem of life and revelation, the relation of the free will of a finite being to the supreme will, of limited reason to divine wisdom, of their first dissension, of their open antagonism, of their final reconciliation.

Unhappily the central piece of the trilogy alone survives.

We know little more of "Prometheus the Firebearer" than the name: of "Prometheus Released," than the most meagre outline of the plot. So it is that the "Prometheus Bound" is in danger of being misunderstood. Throughout we are spectators of what seems to be an undecided conflict. There is no calm. From first to last the storms of earth hide the clear light of heaven. While Zeus is represented chiefly by the words of his adversaries, Prometheus is represented by his own. We forget that his sufferings were the consequence of an act of faithless distrust in Zeus, and of disobedience to his counsels. We forget again that his daring boasts were afterwards exchanged for lamentations, and that his threats against Zeus were mere idle vauntings. For the time he appears as a martyr; but he was first a rebel, and afterwards a pardoned subject.

This true view of his character is illustrated by the appearance of Io, the second figure in the play. In Prometheus we have reason challenging Zeus: in Io Zeus making himself known to men. The contact in both cases brings for the present overwhelming suffering, but in all other respects the fate of the sufferers is contrasted. Prometheus, strong in will and power, has seized a divine boon; he is reckless of consequences; he forgets his own sufferings: the consciousness of his immortality assures him of final deliverance: such is reason. Io has been the involuntary recipient of divine fellowship; she is lost in the greatness of her own suffering; she has no self-dependence, no foresight: such is feeling. And yet it was from Io that the hero sprung by whose vicarious sufferings Prometheus was in due time delivered. The weak woman was in the end stronger than the Titan.

According to an early and constant tradition Æschylus was accused of publishing the Eleusinian mysteries; and, strange as it may seem, the charge is in itself likely to be true. For him divine mysteries were "open secrets."

He lived face to face with them, and they became axioms of life. For while he is a believer he is a poet and a prophet too. He looks beneath the manifold to the one: he translates, unconsciously it may be, the symbol into the lesson.

His work, as he seems to have understood it, was to reconcile and combine the conflicting factors of fate and will of which life is made up,—the offspring of earth and the offspring of heaven,—and not to ignore their antagonism, or suppress either element in the great battle.

The passions and temptations with which he deals are of overwhelming magnitude; the situations which he plans are of terrible grandeur; the persons whom he exhibits are gigantic: but yet there are present everywhere the two conflicting elements of fate and will out of which all action rises. The scale of representation is magnified, but the moral, when reduced to its simplest principles, is that of common experience. The life is human life, though the actors are heroes.

It is commonly said that the key to the moral understanding of the tragedies of Æschylus is the recognition of an inflexible fate by which families are doomed to destruction, without regard to the guilt or innocence of the victims. If this were true their highest value would be lost. But in fact the statement is as false to Æschylus as it is to life.

All life includes the element of fate and circumstance as well as the element of will and choice.

The traditions and beliefs in which we are reared, the memories which we inherit, the tendencies and impulses which go to form our character, the reputation in which we are held for the deeds of others who belong to us, all lie out of our power. If we allow our thoughts to rest on these only, we can conclude that we are mere puppets, whose conduct is determined by the action of forces wholly external.

But if we look within, there is the consciousness of responsibility, the sense of victory and defeat, the energy of opposition, which by its elasticity and continuance bears witness at least to the possibility of success,—in a word, the intuition of personality, which supplies a power not less strong than circumstance, by which we know that our life is a struggle and not an evolution of consequences, that if its purpose fails *we* are overcome.

And thus it is that Æschylus paints life. He sets fate by the side of will and lets them work. Before our own eyes fate, or as we say circumstance, constantly prevails over infirmity if will, more rarely heroic will, recognises its work and achieves it.

A first sin is swelled by neglect to reckless infatuation; an inheritance of sorrow crushes the selfish sufferer who rejects the discipline of woe; a noble soul trustfully obeys the voice of divine warning, and wisdom is justified in the issue.

This is the teaching of Æschylus, and the teaching of natural experience. For us, indeed, the area of life is widened; the faint lights of an earthly government of God grow into the brightness of a kingdom of heaven; the strength of man is perfected by fellowship with a divine Redeemer; but none the less we can see in the Greek poet the outlines of the never-ending conflict of man with evil, and marvel at the invincible constancy with which he holds his faith in the sure supremacy of good, even when he looked upon the region beyond the grave as shrouded in dismal gloom, and felt the littleness of each single life.

Plato clothed in a Greek dress the common instincts of humanity; Æschylus works out a characteristically

Greek view of life. Thus it is that his doctrine is most clearly Homeric. As a Greek he feels, like Homer, the nobility of our present powers, the grandeur of strength and wealth, the manifold delights of our complex being.

It is often said, and even taken for granted, that the severer aspects of the Christian creed are due to some peculiarity of the "Semitic" mind; that they are foreign to the more genial constitution of the "Japhetic" type; that here at least the instinct which revelation satisfies is partial and not universal. Against such assumptions the tragedies of Æschylus remain a solemn protest. The voice of law addresses us even from Athens. There is a stern and dark side to the Greek view of life. The "Prometheus," the "Seven against Thebes," and the "Orestea," contain a "natural testimony of the soul" to the reality of sin and the inevitable penalty which it carries in itself, and to the need which man has of a divine deliverer. And the testimony comes with the greater force because it is given by the poet who had witnessed the most glorious triumphs of Greek power.

The Dramatist as Thinker: Euripides

EURIPIDES was of honourable descent, and had enjoyed the discipline of most varied culture. He is the true representative of democratic Athens. Gymnast, artist, and student, he had made trial of all the city had to teach; and in holding a sacred office in the service of Apollo he had an inheritance from older religious feelings. It may almost be said that Euripides lived and died with the Athens which had moved the world. His lifetime included the highest development of Athenian art and literature, the rise and the fall of Athenian supremacy. He was born on the day of Salamis (480 B.C.) He produced his "Medea" in the first year of

THE DRAMATIST AS THINKER—EURIPIDES

the Peloponnesian War (431 B.C.) His "Trojan Women" was exhibited in the year of the expedition to Sicily, and the recall of Alcibiades (415 B.C.) He died in 406 B.C., the year before Ægospotamos. He belonged wholly to the new order which is represented by the age of Pericles. Though he was only a generation younger than Æschylus, his works, when compared with those of his predecessor, represent the results of a revolution both in art and in thought.

But however different Æschylus and Euripides are in their views of existence, and in their treatment of life upon the stage, they are alike interesting to the student of the history of religious thought. Both speak with deep personal feeling. Both offer a partial interpretation of mysteries which fill them with an overwhelming awe. For both life with its infinite sorrows is greater than art.

In this respect they both differ from Sophocles, by whom they are naturally separated. Sophocles is not the poet as prophet, but the poet as artist. For him all that is most solemn, or terrible, or beautiful in human experience becomes an element in his work. He shews the perfection of calm, conscious mastery over the subjects with which he deals, but he does not speak to us himself. He has no message, no questionings, no convictions, beyond such utterances as harmoniously complete the consummate symmetry of his poems. It is otherwise with Æschylus and Euripides. Both are deeply moved, and shew that they are deeply moved, by religious feeling, as a spiritual and not an æsthetic force. But the feeling in the two cases is widely different.

Euripides is essentially a poet, and not a speculator. He deals with the mysteries of being from the side of feeling rather than of thought. A passionate fulness of human interest is the characteristic mark of his writings, and the secret of his power. He touched the common heart because he recognised the different phases of its ordinary sorrows and temptations and strivings. The brusque lines of Philemon are a unique testimony to his personal attractiveness :—

> *If, as some say, men still in very truth*
> *Had life and feeling after they are dead,*
> *I had hanged myself to see Euripides.*

The significance of Euripides as a religious teacher springs directly from his position and his character.

He looks from the midst of Athenian society, a society brilliant, restless, sanguine, superstitious, at the popular mythology, at life, at the future, with the keenest insight into all that belongs to man.

In order to understand the treatment of the popular mythology by Euripides, we must bear in mind the place which was occupied by the Homeric poems in contemporary Greek education. It is not too much to say that these were (if the phrase may be allowed) a kind of Greek Bible. Every Athenian was familiar with their contents; they furnished the general view of the relations of God and men, of the seen and the unseen, which formed a fixed background to the common prospect of life.

Euripides regarded the human and the divine as factors in life, alike real and permanent. He aimed at dealing with the whole sum of our present experience. He was therefore constrained to bring the popular creed in some way into harmony with absolute right and truth; to give a moral interpretation to current legends; to shew that life, even as we see it, offers ground for calm trust on which men may at least venture to rest.

He practically anticipates Browning's judgment that "little else is worth study than the incidents in the development of a soul."

Euripides takes account of the manifold fulness of human existence, but the whole effect of life, as he sees it, is, in its external aspect at least, clouded with great sorrow. There is no music to charm its grief. At the best it is chequered, like the face of the earth, with storm and sunshine—

> *Not wholly happy, nor yet wholly sad,*
> *Blest for a while, and then again unblest.*

Man has a hard struggle to maintain, but he is able to maintain it. There is no ever-present, overwhelming weight of physical or moral necessity which crushes him. He is allowed from time to time to see that greater labours are the condition and the discipline of greater natures. And in spite of the obvious sorrows of life, he can discern that a divine purpose is being wrought out which will find accomplishment. "There is at present great confusion in the things of God and men." But the source of the disorder lies not with God but with man.

One chief cause of the sufferings and failures of men lies in the partial and inadequate view of the claims of being which is taken by those who are noble and good within a narrow range. This truth is brought out with impressive power in the characters of Pentheus and Hippolytus. Both are, up to a certain point, blameless and courageous, but they are unsympathetic to that which lies beyond their experience and inclination. They contemptuously cast aside warnings against selfwill. They refuse to pay respect to the convictions of others, or to admit that their view of life can fall short of fulness.

With tragic irony Pentheus is led to his ruin by a guilty curiosity, and Hippolytus, in the pathetic scene of his death, lays bare his overwhelming self-confidence. He can forgive his father, but he is defiant to the powers of heaven, and in the terrible line—

> *Would that the curse of men might reach the gods,*
> (Hippol. 1415.)

he reveals at once the strength and the weakness of his character.

In this connection Euripides appears to indicate one use of suffering. The discipline of life as he regards it is fitted to give to men a truer and larger sense of human powers and duties than they were inclined to form at first.

This lesson comes out prominently in the *Alcestis*.

In one aspect the drama is the record of a soul's purification.

Admetus obtains life at the price which he was ready to pay for it, and he finds that it ceases to be the blessing which he sought. He sees in his father the full image of himself, and fiercely condemns the selfishness which he has shewn. Little by little he fully realises that what he has gained by consciously sacrificing another to himself is of no avail for happiness, and he is prepared to receive, cleansed in heart, that which has been won for him by the spontaneous effort of Hercules.

The contrast of the two sacrifices and the two prizes is of the deepest meaning. Man cannot simply use another at his will for his own good; but he can enjoy the fruits of another's devotion. The life which Alcestis gave for her husband at his entreaty proved to be only a discipline of sorrow; the life which was wrested from death by human labour could be imparted to one made ready to welcome it.

A hero like Heracles is raised to heaven, but what has the unseen world for common men? To this question Euripides has no clear answer. He looks for the vindication of righteousness on earth. His references to another order are few and vague.

In this respect he holds the common attitude of the Athenian in the presence of death. There is, as Professor Gardner has pointed out, no trace of future scenes of happiness, or misery, or judgment, on early Greek funeral sculptures. The utmost that is represented is the farewell of the traveller who is bound for some unknown realm. And in the inscriptions which accompany them the future practically finds no place. The world to come is not denied so much as left out of sight. It is not a distinct object either of hope or of fear.

Euripides indeed has recognised, twice at least, in memorable words the mystery of life and death, the powerlessness of man to attain to a true conception of being:

Who knows if Life is Death,
And Death is counted Life by those below?

Who knows if Life, as we speak, is but Death,
And Death is Life?

But in the latter place he seems to shrink from the positive hope which he has called up into mere negation, and he continues:

Nay, lay the question by;
But this at least we do know: they that live
Are sick and suffer; they who are no more
Nor suffer further, nor have ills to bear.

We can study in Euripides a distinct stage in the preparation of the world for Christianity. He paints life as he found it when Greek Art and Greek thought had put forth their full power. He scatters the dream which some have indulged in of the unclouded brightness of the Athenian prospect of life; and his popularity shews that he represented truly the feeling of those with whom he lived, and of those who came after him. His recognition of the mystery of being from the point of sight of the poet and not of the philosopher, his affirmation of the establishment of the sovereignty of righteousness under the conditions of earth, his feeling after a final unity in the harmonious consummation of things in the supreme existence, his vindication of the claims of the fulness of man's nature, are so many testimonies of the soul to the character of that revelation which can perfectly meet its needs.

Let any one carefully ponder them, and consider whether they do not all find fulfilment in the one fact which is the message of the Gospel.

It cannot be a mere accidental coincidence that when St. Paul stood on the Areopagus and unfolded the meaning of his announcement of "Jesus and the Resurrection," he did in reality proclaim, as now established in the actual experience of men, the truths which Euripides felt after—the office of feeling, the oneness and end of humanity, the completeness of man's future being, the reign of righteousness, existence in God.

Ventures of Faith—Myths of Plato

PLATO, more than any other ancient philosopher, acknowledged alike the necessary limits of reason and the imperious instincts of faith, and when he could not absolutely reconcile both, at least gave to both a full and free expression. And so Platonism alone, and Platonism in virtue of this character, was able to stand for a time face to face with Christianity.

The myths of Plato are not, in essence, simply graceful embellishments of an argument, but venturous essays after truth, embodiments of definite instincts, sensible representations of universal human thoughts, confessions of weakness, it may be, but no less bold claims to an inherent communion with a divine and supra-sensuous world. They are truly philosophic, because they answer

to the innate wants of man : they are truly poetic, because
they are in thought creative.

A myth in its true technical sense is the instinctive
popular representation of an idea. "A myth," it has
been said, "springs up in the soul as a germ in the soil :
meaning and form are one: the history *is* the truth."
Thus a myth, properly so called, has points of contact
with a symbol, an allegory, and a legend, and is distinguished from each. Like the symbol, it is the embodiment and representation of a thought. But the
symbol is isolated, definite, and absolute. The symbol,
and the truth which it figures, are contemplated apart.
The one suggests the other. The myth, on the other
hand, is continuous, historical, and relative. The truth
is seen in the myth, and not separated from it. The
representation is the actual apprehension of the reality.
The myth and the allegory, again, have both a secondary
sense. Both half hide and half reveal the truth which
they clothe. But in the allegory the thought is grasped
first and by itself, and is then arrayed in a particular
dress. In the myth, thought and form come into being
together : the thought is the vital principle which shapes
the form : the form is the sensible image which displays
the thought. The allegory is the conscious work of an
individual fashioning the image of a truth which he has
seized. The myth is the unconscious growth of a common mind, which witnesses to the fundamental laws by
which its development is ruled. The meaning of an
allegory is prior to the construction of the story : the
meaning of a myth is first capable of being separated from
the expression in an age long after that in which it had its
origin. The myth and the legend have more in common.
Both spring up naturally. Both are the unconscious embodiments of popular feeling. Both are, as it seems,
necessary accompaniments of primitive forms of society.

The legend stands in the same relation to history and life as the myth to speculation and thought. The legend deals with a fact as outward, concrete, objective. The myth deals with an idea or the observation of a fact as inward, abstract, subjective. The tendency of the legend is to go ever farther from the simple circumstances from which it took its rise. The tendency of the myth is to express more and more clearly the idea which it foreshews. Yet in many cases it seems almost impossible to draw a distinct line between the myth and the legend. The stories of St. Christopher, of St. Bonaventura and his speaking Crucifix, of Whittington and his Cat, and generally those which may be called *interpretative* myths, will be called myths or legends according as the thought or the fact in them is supposed to predominate.

The Platonic myths, while they are varied in character, and present points of similarity with the legend and the allegory, yet truly claim for the most part to be regarded as essentially genuine myths. If they are individual and not popular, they are still the individual expression of a universal instinct. Plato speaks not as Plato, but as man.

A universal instinct has led men to imagine a golden age of peace and wealth and happiness, before the stern age of struggle and freedom in which they now live. Plato draws out the picture at length. We might be tempted to think that he has a vision of Eden before him when he describes the intercourse of man and animals, the maturity of each new-formed being, the rural ease of a life which is a gradual disrobing of the spirit from its earthly dress. But even so he shews that the perfect order of a divine government, and boundless plenty, may leave man's highest nature undisciplined.

The popular notions of Platonism are almost exclusively derived from the myths. And it is easy to see why it is so. The value of a method may be estimated differently at different times. The delight of mere discussion without result at last ceases to charm. But there are subjects of positive belief on which the soul is never wearied in dwelling; and it is with these the myths deal.

In bold and vigorous outlines they offer a philosophy of nature, a philosophy of history, and a philosophy of life, deformed, it may be, by crude speculations on physics, and cramped by imperfect knowledge and a necessarily narrow sphere of observation, but yet always inspired by the spirit of a divine life, centring in the devout recognition of an all-wise and all-present Providence, and in the inexorable assertion of human responsibility. In form, in subject, in the splendour of their imagery, and in the range of their application, they form, if we may so speak, an Hellenic Apocalypse. And if we compare our popular theories of the world and man with the aspirations which they embody, we may well doubt whether we have used the lessons of eighteen Christian centuries as Plato would have used them.

The earnestness of Plato is indeed a strange contrast to our indifference in dealing with the same topics; for the myths were not for him poetic fancies, but representations of momentous truths.

The myths transcend the domain of pure reason, and their moral power springs out of their concrete form. In the first respect, to take an illustration which will make the notion clear, they answer to Revelation, as an endeavour to enrich the store of human knowledge; in the second, to the Gospel, as an endeavour to present, under the form of facts, the manifestations of divine wisdom.

Whatever may be the prevailing fashion of an age, the myths of Plato remain an unfailing testimony to the religious wants of man. They shew not only that reason by its logical processes is unable to satisfy them, but also in what directions its weakness is most apparent and least supportable. They form, as it were, a natural scheme of the questions with which a revelation might be expected to deal,—Creation, Providence, Immortality,—which, as they lie farthest from the reason, lie nearest to the heart. And in doing this, they are so far an unconscious prophecy, of which the teaching of Christianity is the fulfilment.

But more than this: the Myths mark also the shape which a revelation for men might be expected to take. The doctrine is conveyed in an historic form: the ideas are offered as facts; the myth itself is the message. With what often appears unnecessary care, Plato appeals to popular tradition or external testimony for the veracity of his mythical narratives. He knows that their power of influencing life depends directly upon their essential connection with life. If the Myth belongs really to our world, not as a thought, but as an event, it is homogeneous with man as man in his complex nature. In this way, again, Plato is an unconscious prophet of the Gospel. The Life of Christ is, in form no less than in substance, the divine reality of which the Myths were an instructive foreshadowing.

It is well, then, that we should remember that what we look back upon as accomplished events were once looked forward to as aspirations of the heart. The problem of life is not changed by the lapse of centuries, but the conditions are changed. What the problem is, and what the conditions were in old times, and what they are now, Plato himself may teach us (*Phædo*, 85 A. *et seq.*) Socrates said to his friends on the evening of his execution:—

"Do you think that, when I speak of my present fate

as no misfortune, I am a less skilful diviner than the swans, who sing longest and sweetest in the prospect of death, because they are on the point of going to the god whose servants they are? Nay, rather, I am bound by the same service as they are, and devoted to the same god, and my lord inspires me with prophetic insight no less than them, and therefore I ought to depart from life as cheerfully as they do."

And Simmias answers:—

"Still, Socrates, I feel some difficulty. I think, and perhaps you think with me, that it is impossible or extremely difficult to obtain distinct knowledge on such subjects in our present life. On the other hand, it is utterly unmanly to desist from investigating, by every means in our power, whatever is urged about them before we are exhausted by a complete inquiry. For we must gain one of two results. We must either learn or discover the truth about them; or, if this be impossible, we must take the best and most irrefragable of human words, and, supported on this as on a raft, sail through the waters of life in perpetual jeopardy, unless we might make the journey on a securer stay,—some *Divine Word*, if it might be,—more surely and with less peril."

The Word for which the wavering faith of Simmias thus longed, has, we believe, been given to us; and once again Plato points us to St. John.

Dionysius the Areopagite

IF it be true in one sense of men that the dead are sovereign over the living, the saying has a deeper application to literature. A particular phase of thought is taken up into some broader intellectual development, and works its full effect under the changed circumstances; but the writings to which it owed its origin, or in which it first found expression, are forgotten, or, if remembered, lose their true significance.

Few, even among students of theology, read the works of Dionysius the Areopagite, "out of which," to quote the enthusiastic words of their editor, "the Angelic Doctor drew almost the whole of his theology, so that his *Summa* is but the hive in whose varied cells he daily stored the honey which he gathered from them."

The harmonisation of Christianity and Platonism was not effected without a sacrifice. It is impossible not to feel in Dionysius, in spite of his pure and generous and apostolic aspirations, the lack of something which is required for the completeness of his own views. He fails indeed by neglecting to take in the whole breadth of the Gospel. The central source of his dogmatic errors lies where at first it might be least looked for. The whole view of life which he offers is essentially individual and personal and subjective: the one man is the supreme object in whose progress his interest is engaged. Though he gives a magnificent view of the mutual coherence of all the parts of the moral and physical worlds, yet he turns with the deepest satisfaction to the solitary monk, isolated and self-absorbed, as the highest type of Christian energy. Though he dwells upon the divine order of the sacraments, and traces the spiritual significance of each detail in their celebration, yet he looks upon them as occasions for instruction and blessing, suggested by appointed forms, and not supplied by a divine gift. He stops short of that profounder faith which sees the unity of worlds in the harmonious and yet independent action of derivative forces: one, indeed, in their source, and yet regarded as separate in their operation. He is still so far overpowered by Platonism that he cannot, in speculation as well as in confession, consistently treat man's bodily powers as belonging to the perfection of his nature. The end of the discipline of life is, in his view, to help the believer to cast aside all things that belong to earth, and not to find in them gifts which may, by consecration to God, become hereafter the beginning of a nobler activity.

A Christian Philosopher—Origen

THE progress of Christianity can best be represented as a series of victories. But when we speak of victories we imply resistance, suffering, loss: the triumph of a great cause, but the triumph through effort and sacrifice. Such, in fact, has been the history of the Faith: a sad and yet a glorious succession of battles, often hardly fought, and sometimes indecisive, between the new life and the old life.

We know that the struggle can never be ended in this visible order; but we know also that more of the total powers of humanity, and more of the fulness of the individual man, are brought from age to age within the domain of the truth. Each age has to sustain its own part in the conflict, and the retrospect of earlier successes gives to those who have to face new antagonists, and to occupy new positions, patience and the certainty of hope.

In this respect the history of the first three centuries —the first complete period, and that a period of spontaneous evolution in the Christian body—is an epitome or a figure of the whole work of the Faith. It is the history of a threefold contest between Christianity and the powers of the old world, closed by a threefold victory.

The Church and the Empire started from the same point, and advanced side by side. They met in the market and the house; they met in the discussions of the schools; they met in the institutions of political government; and in each place the Church was triumphant.

In this way Christianity asserted, once for all, its sovereign power among men by the victory of common life, by the victory of thought, by the victory of civil organisation. These first victories contain the promise of all that later ages have to reap.

This victory of thought is the second, and not the first, in order of accomplishment. The succession involves a principle. The Christian victory of common life was wrought out in silence and patience and nameless agonies. It was the victory of the soldiers and not the captains of Christ's army. But in due time another conflict had to be sustained, not by the masses, but by great men, the consequence and the completion of that which had gone before.

It is with the society as with the individual. The discipline of action precedes the effort of reason. The work of the many prepares the medium for the subtler operations of the few. So it came to pass that the period during which this second conflict of the Faith was waged was, roughly speaking, from the middle of the second to the middle of the third century.

Origen's whole life, from first to last, was, according to his own grand ideal, "one unbroken prayer," one ceaseless effort after a closer fellowship with the Unseen and the Eternal. No distractions diverted him from the pursuit of Divine wisdom. No persecutions checked for more than the briefest space the energy of his efforts. He endured "a double martyrdom," perils and sufferings from the heathen, reproaches and wrongs from Christians; and the retrospect of what he had borne only stirred within him a humbler sense of his shortcomings.

In Origen we have the first glimpse of a Christian boy. He was conspicuous "even from his cradle;" "a great man from his childhood" is the judgment of his bitterest enemy.

Writings are but one element of the teacher. A method is often more characteristic and more influential than doctrine. It was so with Origen.

The method of Origen, such as Gregory has described it, in all its breadth and freedom was forced upon him by what he held to be the deepest law of human nature. It may be true (and he admitted it) that we are, in our present state, but poorly furnished for the pursuits of knowledge; but he was never weary of proclaiming that we are at least born to engage in the endless search. If we see some admirable work of man's art, he says, we are at once eager to investigate the nature, the manner, the end of its production; and the contemplation of the works of God stirs us with an incomparably greater longing to learn the principles, the method, the purpose of creation. "This desire, this passion, has without doubt," he continues, "been implanted in us by God. And as the eye seeks the light, as our body craves food, so our mind is impressed with the characteristic and natural desire of knowing the truths of God and the causes of what we observe." Such a desire, since it is a divine endowment, carries with it the promise of future satisfaction.

In our present life we may not be able to do more by the utmost toil than obtain some small fragments from the infinite treasures of divine knowledge, still the concentration of our souls upon the lovely vision of Truth, the occupation of our various faculties in lofty inquiries, the very ambition with which we rise above our actual powers, is in itself fruitful in blessing, and fits us better for the reception of wisdom hereafter at some later stage of existence. Now we draw at the best a faint outline—a preparatory sketch of the features of Truth; the true and living colours will be added *then*. Perhaps, he concludes most characteristically, that is the meaning of the words "To every one that hath shall be given;" by which we are assured that he who has gained in this life some faint outline of truth and knowledge will have it completed in the age to come with the beauty of the perfect image.

It seems to me that we have more to learn than to fear from the study of Origen's writings. With all his faults and shortcomings, he is the greatest representative of a type of Greek Christian thought which has not yet done its work in the West. By his sympathy with all efforts, by his largeness of view, by his combination of a noble morality with a deep mysticism, he indicates, if he does not bring, the true remedy for the evils of that Africanism which has been dominant in Europe since the time of Augustine.

Augustine was a Latin thinker, and more than a Latin —an African. He looked at everything from the side of law and not of freedom; from the side of God, as an irresponsible Sovereign, and not of man as a loving servant.

The centre of his whole dogmatic theory is sin.

In his greatest work he writes "Of the City of God," and he draws at the same time the portraiture of a rival "City of the Devil," equally stable and enduring.

We must regard the teaching of Origen as not so much a system as an aspiration. Welcomed as an aspiration, it can, I believe, do us good service.

We are inclined to underrate the practical effect of

wide thoughts and of great ideals. But life is impoverished and action is enfeebled for the lack of them.

"THE spirit of man is the candle of the Lord." The phrase, "over-frequently quoted" by Whichcote, as his opponents alleged, at once brings before us the central characteristic of his teaching. For him reason was "lighted by God, and lighting us to God—*res illuminata, illuminans.*" "What," he asks, "doth God speak to but my reason? and should not that which is spoken to hear? should it not judge, discern, conceive what is God's meaning?" "I count it true sacrilege to take from God to give to the creature, yet I look at it as a dishonouring of God to nullify and make base His works, and to think He made a sorry, worthless piece fit for no use when He made man."

For Whichcote truth was the soul of action. "I act, therefore I am," was the memorable sentence in which he echoed and answered the *cogito ergo sum* of Descartes.

But I act not as my own maker, not as my own sustainer, but as the creature and servant of Him who is original of all and will be final to all; who is "to be adored as the chiefest beauty and loved as the first and chiefest good"; who hath given us "a large capacity which He will fulfil, and a special relation to Himself which He will answer."

"The idolatry of the world," as Whichcote profoundly remarks, "hath been about the medium of worship, not about the object of worship." The testimony of conscience—"our home-God," as he calls it—still remains. Great hopes and great aspirations contend in the human heart with the sense of weakness and failure.

"Heaven," as he tersely says, "is first a temper and then a place." "Heaven present is our resemblance to God, and men deceive themselves grossly when they flatter themselves with the hopes of a future heaven, and yet do, by wickedness of heart and life, contradict heaven present."

"We must be men," he writes, "before we can be Christians."

"The reason is the only tool with which we can do men's work. If God did not make my faculties true, I am absolutely discharged from all duty to Him."

"They are greatly mistaken," he argues, "who in religion oppose points of reason and matters of faith; as if Nature went one way and the Author of Nature went another."

"If you see not well," Whichcote writes, "hear the better; if you see not far, hear the more. The consequence of truth is great; therefore the judgment of it must not be negligent."

"He that is light of belief will be as light of unbelief;" and "of all impotencies in the world credulity in religion is the greatest."

"That is not an act of religion which is not an act of the understanding; that is not an act of religion which is not even human."

It ill becomes us to make our intellectual faculties "Gibeonites"—in Whichcote's picturesque phrase—mere drudges for the meanest services of the world.

"Faculties without any acquired habits witness for God and condemn us;" and in spiritual things the paradox is true, that which is not used is not had.

"When the doctrine of the Gospel becomes the reason of our mind, it will become the principle of our life."

Judgment is a revelation of character: punishment is the unchecked stream of consequence. Every man may estimate his future state by his present. He will then be more of the same, or the same more intensely.

Our greatest zeal is in things doubtful and questionable. We are more concerned for that which is our own in religion than for that which is God's. But true teachers are not masters but helpers; they are not to make religion but to shew it.

Whichcote's teaching represents much that is most generous and noblest in the "moral divinity" of to-day. It anticipates language which we hear on many sides. It affirms in the name of Christianity much that is said to be in antagonism with it.

We can easily imagine with what enthusiasm he would have welcomed now "the infinite desire of knowledge which has broken forth in the world," to use the phrase of Patrick; how he would again have warned us "that it is not possible to free religion from scorn and contempt if her priests be not as well skilled in Nature as her people, and her champions furnished with as good artillery as her adversaries."

With larger knowledge and on an ampler field we are then called upon to exercise his faith; to claim for religion, in the name of the Son of man, all things graceful, beautiful, and lovely; to shew that there is nothing in it but what is sincere and solid, consonant to reason and issuing in freedom.

One remark must still be added which concerns us in

our crises of transition most nearly: "I think that if I may learn much by the writings of good men in former ages ... I may learn more by the actings of the Divine Spirit in the minds of good men now alive." In that confidence lies our strength. The ages of faith are not yet past. The last word of God has not yet been spoken.

The Lesson of Biblical Revision

THE Latin Vulgate can alone in any degree bear comparison with the English Vulgate in regard to the rich variety of influences by which it has been formed.

The other vernacular Versions of Europe—German, French, Spanish, Italian—were the works of single men, and bear their names; but our own Version may fairly be described as the work of the nation, or rather as the work of English Christianity.

In the strictest sense it was not so much a work as a growth, the outcome of life and not of design. Parties most bitterly opposed combined without concert to bring it to its familiar shape. Puritans, Anglicans, Romanists successively enriched the original composite Bible, from which each later one has directly descended. Thus it has come to pass that so many different contributions, unlooked for and unmeasured, have gone to form what we call the Authorised English Version—a version simply "authorised" by the tacit consent of general use and not by any legislative sanction—that no one man, no one party, can lay his hand upon it and say, "It is mine:" nor, again, can any turn aside and say, "I have no part in it." As the result of its history it bears the enduring stamp of manifoldness and holds the prerogative of life.

It was shaped and reshaped in the prison-cell, in the exile's chamber, in the halls of our Universities.

Alone of modern versions, so far as I know, it has been hallowed by the seal, the fourfold seal, of martyrdom.

In virtue of almost a century of continuous change, it refuses every claim to finality. However much our natural affection may be tempted to invest it, even unconsciously, with an absolute authority, we know, as we are now emphatically reminded, that it is no more than a representation, necessarily inadequate, however noble, of texts which are not exempt from the application of the ordinary laws of criticism.

And here it is that a Revised Version will do us good service. It will bring home to us the conviction that the English Bible is not to be regarded essentially as a finished work of literary skill, an unrivalled monument of the fresh vigour of our language, a precious heirloom whose very defects have gathered grace from time; and still less as a fixed code, sacred and unalterable in its minutest points. The very idea of a revision of the Bible which extends to the ground-texts, as well as to the renderings, suggests to us that the Bible is a vital record, to be interpreted according to the growth of life.

Changes of sweet rhythms and familiar words, which, though they may sometimes startle and even vex us, have never been made (this I can say without reserve) except under the fullest and most reverent sense of responsibility, will force us to reflect on the conditions under which God has been pleased to send His message to us, and on the obligations which He has laid upon us by the form in which the message has been preserved.

We shall be constrained to think over forms of expression and contrasted synonyms, which are able to suggest to patient thought lessons of larger and exacter truth.

Perhaps when the first surprise is over we shall learn, as Origen said, that no letter of Scripture is without its meaning.

No superstition can be more deadening than that by which a man is made to leave his noblest faculties unconsecrated by devout and unceasing exercise.

The Bible does not supersede labour, but by its very form proclaims labour to be fruitful. This is a conclusion which we can no longer put out of sight.

The Bible does not dispense with thought, but by its last message it lifts thought to sublimer regions.

There is no doubt a restless desire in man for some help which may save him from the painful necessity of reflection, comparison, judgment. But the Bible offers no such help. It offers no wisdom to the careless and no security to the indolent. It awakens, nerves, invigorates, but it makes no promise of ease. And by this it responds to the aspirations of our better selves.

We cannot—and let me press this truth with the strongest possible emphasis,—we cannot by a peremptory and irresponsible decision satisfy ourselves that such and such changes are "trivial" or "unmeaning" or "pedantic" or "disastrous."

We know that we are bound to take account of them seriously.

The duty may be unwelcome, but we have to face it. And like trials are not rare. Life would be easier indeed if we might once for all surrender ourselves to some power without us. It would be easier if we might divest ourselves of the divine prerogative of reason. It would be easier if we might abdicate the sovereignty over creation with which God has blessed us, and shrink up each into his narrowest self.

It would be easier; but would that be the life which Christ came down from heaven to shew us and place within our reach? No: everything which makes life easier makes it poorer, less noble, less human, less Godlike.

What we need is not that the burden of manhood should be taken from us, but that we should be strengthened to support it joyously: not that our path should be made smooth and soft, but that it should be made firm to the careful foot: not that our eyes should be spared the vision of celestial glory, but that we should see it reflected in Him who, being Man and God, can temper it to our powers.

And for this end the whole Bible has been given us, not a book of texts, immutable and isolated, but a vast history, a clear mirror of manifold truth, to try, to correct, to train us equally for thought and for action.

For this end examples have been hallowed in it most remote from our experience, lest we should be tempted to abridge the grandeur of the whole plan of salvation.

For this end, as I believe, the Hebrew theocratic view of nature and life found a final expression through the forms of Greek language.

For this end *whatsoever things were written aforetime were written for our learning; that through patience and through comfort of the Scriptures we might have hope.*

No one can make another feel what the Bible is: that assurance must come to each from the Spirit of God speaking to the single soul through the Word of God; but we can make our experience the guide of our study, and we can make our hope the inspiration of our experience.

The Bible trains us severally for thought and for action, not for one only, but for both: and we must never forget that we all share, though in unequal degrees, in each part of this twofold existence.

We are all bound, according to our circumstances, to think rightly and to act rightly. In no other way can we offer to God our whole nature : in no other way can we discipline the faculties which are given us as *men*.

No one can take account of the wide world darkened for the most part by gross idolatry, so that a fraction only of mankind even now know the name of the one God : no one can look out upon Christendom, desolated by war and degraded by sin : no one can ponder the differences by which the foremost champions of right and purity and love are separated ; without being at first filled with doubt and dismay.

Can this, we ask, be the issue of the Gospel, this partial spread, this imperfect acceptance, this discordant interpretation of the Truth ?

When we are thus cast down the Scriptures bring us comfort. By the long annals of the divine history of mankind—so long that we can hardly go back in imagination to the earliest forms of religious life which they record—we are taught to see the slowness of God's working, the patience with which He accepts what man in his weakness can offer, the variety of service which He guides to one end ; and hope is again kindled.

And here Nature illustrates the lesson of the Bible. No result has been established more certainly by recent investigations than the gradual passage from lower to higher types of life in the natural world through enormous intervals of time.

So far from this being opposed to revelation, as some have rashly argued, it falls in exactly with what the Bible teaches us of the spiritual progress of men.

Why there should be this marvellous slowness in

THE LESSON OF BIBLICAL REVISION 361

either case we cannot tell. It is enough for us to know that in this respect the whole divine plan goes forward to our eyes in the same way. And if cycles of beings came into existence and perished, if continents were washed away and reformed before the earth was made fit for the habitation of man, we shall not wonder that it was by little and little that he was himself enabled to apprehend his relation to God, and through God to his fellows and to the world.

It is not that evil becomes less hateful when we look fixedly on the world, but that it is found to be less predominant.

If we regard with patience the strangely mixed characters of men and nations there is almost always something in them which we can love, some traits of tenderness, or devotion, or courage, in accordance with the Spirit of God, and so betokening His presence.

Phrases of the Bible startle us by their direct application to our own wants, by their clear revelation of our own thoughts: they cling, as it were, to us: they reach where no friend's voice could reach: they stay where even the counsel of love could find no entrance.

How often it happens that a great sorrow or a great joy, or the slow passage of years, makes sayings clear which were dark before.

There is a natural progress in our understanding the Scriptures. Some things we can see when we are children : some things are opened to us in maturer age : some things remain mysteries to the end. But however slowly we go forward, or however swiftly, voices of Scripture are always with us.

The Bible while it speaks to each one singly never treats him as standing alone. *We are members one of another:* that is the truth which underlies all Christian Morality.

However quiet or obscure the part may be which we play, it is a part in a great drama and not an isolated fragment.

From the first book of the Bible to the last; in the book of Genesis no less than in the book of Revelation, man is seen in direct communion with God. However different the idea of God may be which is presented in the different books of Scripture, varying from the rude and limited conception of the patriarchs to the perfect revelation in the Person of the Lord, in this apprehension of it there is no variation.

THE RELATION
OF CHRISTIANITY TO ART

Does Christianity leave Scope for Art?

NO student of the apostolic writings can fail to find himself sometimes confronted by the question, Does the teaching of the New Testament cover all the interests of human life? and more particularly, Does the New Testament, does Christianity as laid down there in its broad outlines, leave scope for the free development of Art?

There can be no doubt that truth, sympathy, reverence, will characterise all effort which deserves the name of Christian; but it is not at once obvious that in the face of the overwhelming moral problems of life Christian effort can be properly directed to the pursuit of Art.

Thus there is the suggestion if not the distinct appearance of a conflict between man's constitution and the Gospel. He is born with artistic instincts and powers; and these, it may be alleged, are not directly taken into account by the records of the Faith.

Man so Constituted as to seek Beauty

ON the one side it is certain that Art corresponds with essential parts of our nature. Men universally seek particular combinations of form, colour, sound, and the pleasure which these give can be deepened and extended through the study of the principles by which they are ruled. Men can be trained to a keener and finer perception of beauty.

There is then here a force of influence which cannot be overlooked in the discipline of life.

External Nature needs Interpretation

AND more than this, the complex scene in which we are placed requires to be revealed to us. We are at once able to enter into the manifold aspects of Nature which we can recognise when they are pointed out. There is something of disorder and disproportion in the impression which we first receive from the world about us. The "form" of things needs some interpretation; and the particular interpretation which we adopt has helped and will help to make us what we are and what we shall be.

The Interpretation of Nature by Art has a Powerful moral Effect

FOR the physical effects which Art produces exercise a profound and spiritual influence upon character.

It is unnecessary to attempt to make any comparison of the relative power of external nature and society upon the education of the soul. It is enough that both have their due office in moulding the ideal man. Remove the discipline of one or the other, and the man is weaker and poorer, however successfully he cultivates the self-centred virtues on which he has concentrated himself. It may be necessary to "cut off the right hand," or to "pluck out the right eye," but he who is forced to do so enters into life "maimed."

Sense specially needs Discipline

THIS expressive image seems to carry with it a full recognition of the manifold activities of eye and hand, of the power of seeing beauty and setting it forth, as belonging to the completeness of man.

And if under the actual conditions of life it is through sense, which Art uses as its organ, that the most obvious and universal dangers come to men, the natural conclusion seems to be that this fact shews convincingly the paramount importance of the study of Art. In this region we need peculiarly to be trained in order that we may enjoy rightly; and not be called upon to sacrifice that which was capable of ministering to a richer service.

Art not directly recognised in the New Testament

SUCH reflections, indicated in the briefest summary, serve to shew that Art justly claims a permanent place in the highest training of men; but on the other hand it may be urged that, with the exception of music, there is no recognition of the office of Art in the New Testament. One or two illustrations from engraving (Heb. i. 3) or painting (Heb. viii. 5; x. 1) are all that it contains. The imagery of the Apocalypse—as the cubic city (Apoc. xxi. 16)—is symbolic and not pictorial.

And not only so, but it seems as if representative Art were distinctly condemned. It is difficult to give any sense to "the desire of the eyes," which St. John declares to be "not of the Father but of the world" (1 John ii. 16), which shall not include works of sculpture and painting; and at first sight the revelation of the transitoriness of that out of which they spring appears to carry with it the sentence of their rejection.°

The use of Art in the Old Testament not a sufficient Recognition

NOR can any stress be laid upon the partial recognition of the service of Art in the Old Testament. The system of the old Covenant was essentially external. It spoke through symbols. But it might be argued, not unreasonably, that, as Christianity is essentially spiritual, it is likely that it would be independent of all illustrations from Art.

The Principle of Reconciliation

THESE are the elements of the contrast which have to be reconciled. The reconciliation lies in the central message of Christianity, *The Word became flesh.*

By that fact the harmony between the seen and the unseen which had been interrupted was potentially restored. Creation in all its parts was made known as a revelation of Him through whom it was called into being.

But the reconciliation here as elsewhere lies in transfiguration. The passage to life is through death. The old had to pass away that the new might find its proper place.

This truth has even now not been fully mastered; but it will be seen more clearly if we consider the position of Art in relation to Christianity in the apostolic age, and the character of Christian Art in the first four centuries, and the attempt to determine the relation of Christianity to Art, and the peculiar office of Art.

Contrast of Shemitic and Hellenic Tendencies

THE position of the early Christian teachers towards Art was determined under two powerful and conflicting influences. In no other region of human activity were the Shemitic and Hellenic tendencies more directly at variance. Each bore witness to a partial truth; and in the apostolic age each had reached its complete development.

Art Consecrated among the Jews

THE Jew learnt from the records of the Old Testament that it was the divine will that in the unapproachable darkness of the Holy of Holies the costliest works of Art should render service before the revealed Presence of the Lord.

No human eye could rightfully ever again trace the lineaments of those cherubim and palm trees and open flowers when they were once placed in the oracle, but it was enough to know that they were there.

In no other way could the Truth be more eloquently or more solemnly enforced that the end of Art is to witness to the inner life of Nature and to minister to God. The repetition of the forms in the Holy place kept the memory of them fresh in the minds of the priests.

Their significance could not be mistaken. By that offering of the best which he could command simply for the divine glory, Solomon declared to his people for all time the consecration of Art, and he declared not obscurely that it is the office of Art to reveal the meaning of that which is the object of sense.

Circumstances delayed for ages the fruitfulness of the idea; but it remained and remains still; and few can think of all that was implied by the adornment of that august chamber, lighted only by the splendour of a manifested Presence of God or the glow of the kindled incense (Apoc. v. 8), without feeling that it has a lesson for those to whom Art is appointed work. Philosophers and poets have dwelt often upon the veiled statue at Sais: there is an open secret in the sacred gloom of the Holy of Holies more sublime and more inspiring.

Imitative Art treated as Absolute by the Greeks

THE Jewish repression of imitative Art, which the law still hallowed for the highest service, corresponded with the spiritual conception of God, which was the endowment of His "people." Spiritual Religion could not at this stage of its development admit the habitual use of painting or sculpture.

With the Greeks, on the other hand, imitative Art was the characteristic embodiment of the Nature worship which underlay their life. The form of beauty was for them not the symbol but the direct representation of the godlike. The statue was the final expression of the artist's thought, and his consummate skill enabled the spectator to rest in it. Humanity was made the measure of the divine; and under these conditions anthropomorphism became a fatal temptation.

At the same time Greek Art, if premature and perilous in regard to the complete spiritual training of man, witnessed to a part of the truth affirmed in the record of Creation which is most commonly forgotten. The form of man, the visible expression of what he is essentially embodied under the conditions of time, answers to "the image of God," in which he was made.

So far the Greek was right in seeking for traits of divinity in human beauty. The source of error, from which flowed the stream of later corruption, was that he regarded these as fixed and final. He failed, necessarily failed in the way of nature, to claim recognition for the fulness of the truth that man made in the image of God has to grow into His likeness: that all that is noblest in form or present embodiment is preparatory to something yet unseen and higher: that Art in its greatest achievements must be prophetic, must not rest in a victory, but reveal that which is unattained.

The necessary Decline of Greek Art

IT would be difficult to overrate the skill with which Greek sculpture of the best period represents strength in majestic repose, and feeling under sovereign control; but all, so to speak, lies within the figure before us. "The Gods have come down to us in the likeness of men;" and we look no farther.

At first the spiritual, religious, element is supreme, as in all living Art; but with the decay of faith that which is sensuous usurps the place of the spiritual, and Art which takes man as the standard of the divine cannot but fall.

A single illustration will be sufficient to indicate my meaning. This is given in a crucial shape by the treatment of Aphrodite in the earlier and later schools. The physical beauty of the Medicean Venus has lost all the pure sovereign majesty of the Aphrodite of Melos, which is worthy to be an ideal of "woman before the Fall."

It is unnecessary to trace the decay of Greek Art. It retained to the last the gifts of physical beauty, but in the apostolic age it had become the servant of the luxury of the Empire. Starting from a human ideal it became enslaved to man. So far as it had a place in popular worship it brought down the divine to the level of a corrupt life.

Christianity essentially antagonistic to Art as it was

THIS being so the antagonism of early Christians to contemporary Art was necessarily essential and absolute. Before Art could be placed in its true position there was need of a complete change of centre. For this the stern discipline of Judaism had made provision. The lesson of consecration which had been kept in silent witness for long ages could be applied now that "the Word had become flesh." By that fact a new meaning was given to the beauty which the Greek artist had felt for, and an immeasurable scope was opened for the ministry of nature to God, which the Jewish legislator had declared in symbols. But death is the condition of resurrection. There is indeed a continuity through death; but a formal severance from the past was the prelude to the new birth of Christian Art.

Characteristics of Christian Art

CHRISTIAN Art was fashioned on classical models; it inherited the use of classical methods; it incorporated some of the familiar subjects of classical use; but at the same time it embodied, even if only in an elementary form, the power of a new life. It was conventional and it was symbolic. By these characteristics it claimed effectually the office of interpreting the invisible through the visible, of giving predominance to the spiritual idea over the external appearance, of advancing from within outwards, from the thought to the expression.

The means adopted for securing these ends belong, no doubt, to the infancy of Christian Art. Efforts which were arrived at directly and simply in the first stage of the new artistic life, can be secured now without any sacrifice of the freedom or of the fulness of the artist's labours. But this fact does not deprive the earliest works of their distinctive meaning and importance.

Joyfulness of Christian Art

IN spite of appearances the Christian believed that the victory over sin and death was already won; and he gave expression to his conviction. The characteristic words "in pace," which marked the "rest" of the believer, were reflected in all the associations of death.

The painful literalism which deforms many of the monuments of the fifteenth and sixteenth centuries found no place in the fifth and sixth, and still less in earlier times. The terrible pictures which Tertullian drew of the sufferings of persecutors, and the scarcely less terrible descriptions by Augustine of the sufferings of the wicked, were not as yet embodied by Art.

No attempt was made to give distinctness to the unseen world. It is doubtful whether there are any representations of angels earlier than the latter half of the fourth century, and it seems certain that there are no representations of powers of evil, other than the natural serpent, till a later date. By that time the work of early Christian Art was ended.

General Relation of Christianity to Art

THE relation of Christianity to Art is that which it holds generally to life. It answers to a fresh birth, a transfiguration of all human powers, by the revelation of their divine connections and destiny. The pregnant words of St. Paul, "old things (τὰ ἀρχαῖα) passed away: behold, they have become new," have an application here. There is no loss, no abandonment of the past triumphs of thought and insight and labour, but they are quickened by a new power, and disclosed in a new position with regard to the whole discipline of man.

Christian Art is the interpretation of beauty in life under the light of the Incarnation. The ministry of the beautiful in every shape, in sound, in form, in colour, is claimed for God through man.

The Relation slowly Realised

THE realisation of this idea must necessarily be slow, but it is impossible that the facts of the Incarnation and Resurrection can leave Art in the same position as before. The interpretation of Nature, and the embodiment of thought and feeling through outward things, must assume a new character when it is known not only that Creation is the expression of the will of God, and in its essence "very good," but also that in humanity it has been taken into personal fellowship with the Word, through whom it was called into being.

Such a revelation enables the student to see in the phenomena of the visible order Sacraments, so to speak, of the spiritual and unseen, and frees him from bondage to "the world," while he devotes himself with devout enthusiasm to the representation of the mysterious beauty which it contains. The Old Testament teaches us to regard Creation as an embodiment of a Divine thought, marred by the self-assertion and fall of its temporal sovereign: the New Testament teaches us to see it brought again potentially to harmony with God through the Blood of Him who is its Eternal Author and Head (Col. i. 14-23).

The Gospel therefore seeks the service of Art in the sensible proclamation of its message. The spirit must clothe itself in some way, and the dress may help to emphasise salient features in that which it partly veils.

No doubt it is true that the spirit can in any case illuminate that in which it is confined; but it is no less true that it has a necessary tendency to fashion its own shrine, even as the soul "doth the body make."

Conflicting Views as to the Lord's Appearance

THE early controversy as to the outward appearance of the Lord, illustrates this twofold truth. Some argued from the description of "the servant of the Lord," that the Son of man had "no form or comeliness," "no beauty that we should desire Him." And others replied that it could not but be that perfect holiness should become visible in perfect beauty. To the spiritual eye, we feel, there would be no final antagonism in the two statements. And Art by spiritual sympathy is able to guide the spectator to a right vision of that which is not naturally discerned.

Art reveals the Divine End

OR, to present the same thought from the opposite side, as all Art brings the ideal, in some sense, before us in a material form, and preserves for earth a definite place in the present order, so Christian Art is characterised by the endeavour to present "in many parts and in many fashions" that view of Creation wherein it is shewn in "earnest expectation," "waiting for the revelation of the sons of God" (Rom. viii. 19). In other words Christian Art treats its subject as that which has partly lost and is partly striving towards a divine type, not self-complete and not an end, and seeks to make clear the signs of the true character and the true goal of all with which it deals. It is directed not to humanity and nature in themselves, but to humanity and nature as revelations of the Divine.

Christianity does not alter the range of Art

SUCH an effort is obviously of universal application. Christian Art, like Christianity itself, embraces all life. The inspiration of the new birth extends to every human interest and faculty. Christian Art, as Christian, does not differ from classical Art in range of subject, but in its prevailing treatment. It will indeed happen again and again that "the soul naturally Christian" unconsciously fulfils its high office of spiritual interpretation in classical works, but Christian Art exists by and for this. And there is nothing to which the office does not apply, nothing in which it does not find scope for exercise.

The joys and sorrows and energies of men, the manifold forms and varying moods of nature, all have their "religious" aspect, if religion be, as it assuredly is, the striving towards the unity of man, the world and God.

Music which is, as it were, the voice of the society, and architecture which is as its vestment, have in all their applications a religious power.

This Christianity affirms as its postulate, and by affirming determines its relation to Art.

Opposing Influences

THE fulfilment of this universal claim, as has been already said, will be necessarily slow. The conquest of life for Christ is gradual and not without reverses. New forces are not subdued without a struggle, and old forces, which have been subdued, not unfrequently rise up again in dangerous rebellion. More than once the fanatical iconoclasm of a false Judaism and the sensual Nature worship of a false Hellenism have troubled the development of Christian Art.

No struggle indeed has been fruitless; but even now

we cannot dare to say that the office of Art is frankly acknowledged, or the exercise of Art spiritually disciplined.

Unequal Advances of Christian Art

THE development of Christian Art has been gradual, and it has been unequal in different branches. The social Arts, if I may so describe them, Music and Architecture, were soon welcomed by the Church and pursued in characteristic forms.

It is not too much to say that modern Music is a creation of the Church; and the continuous and rich growth of Christian architecture up to the Renaissance in types of varied beauty is in itself a sufficient proof of the power of the Faith to call out and train the highest genius in Art.

The advance of painting and sculpture was checked perhaps in a great degree by the influence of Eastern asceticism. Both were treated as subsidiary to architecture, which was pre-eminently the Art of the Middle Ages; but some of the single statues of the thirteenth century contain a promise, not yet fulfilled, of a Christian Art worthy to crown that of Greece.

Meanwhile a new style of painting was being prepared by the illumination of manuscripts, in which not only scenes and persons but small natural objects, flowers and insects, were treated with the utmost tenderness and care. Here again the Renaissance checked the direct development of the twofold promise over which the student lingers in admiration and hope as he regards at Bruges side by side the works of Van Eyck and Memling.

Disturbing Effect of the Renaissance

THE forces of the Renaissance have not yet been completely assimilated. The wealth of ancient material then poured at once before Christian Artists, hindered their normal progress; but they have moved since along their proper lines, and the Past contains the assurance that "all things" are theirs.

So much at least the history of Christianity fairly shews, that nothing which is human lies beyond its range.

It lays the greatest stress upon practical duties, upon "the good part" of moral discipline, but none the less it finds place for the satisfaction of what we regard as less noble instincts.

The single incident recorded in the Gospels in which the Lord received a costly offering, seems to illustrate the principles which hallow even the simplest gratifications of sense. When Mary lavished the precious spikenard over the Head and Feet of her Master, "the house," St. John tells us, "was filled with the odour of the ointment."

It was natural that the thought of the apostles should find expression by the lips of Judas. "Why was not this ointment sold for three hundred pence and given to the poor?" "To what purpose was this waste?" And the judgment was given: "Verily I say unto you, wheresoever this gospel shall be preached in the whole world, there shall also this, which this woman hath done, be told for a memorial of her."

The fragrance was most transitory, but it was diffusive; the waste was most complete, but it gave clear witness of love, of that highest love of which the chief reward is that it should be known that its object inspired the devotion of perfect sacrifice.

So it is with every work of Christian Art. It aims not at a solitary but at a common enjoyment: it seeks to make it clear that all to which it is directed has a spiritual value able to command the completest service.

Love the Guide of Art

CHRISTIANITY, it has been seen, claims the ministry of Art in the whole field of life. What then is the peculiar office of Art? It is in a word to present the truth of things under the aspect of beauty, to bring before us the "world as God has made it" where "all is beauty." The fulfilment of this office involves the exercise not only of insight but of self-control. Man and nature are evidently disordered. The representation of all the phenomena of life would not be the representation of their divine truth. Love therefore, a looking for the highest good of the whole, will guide and limit the search after beauty to which Art is directed.

The peculiar Office of Art seen most clearly in the Imitative Arts

IN the imitative arts, painting and sculpture, the effort to make visible the truth of God in man and in nature, is immediate and direct. In the creative arts, music and architecture, the effort is to find an expression, an embodiment, harmonious with the truth of things for elementary emotions and wants.

Men in society seek a common voice, a common home: the hymn and the temple belong to the first stage of the state.

But in these arts there is necessarily more freedom and variety than in those which are directly imitative.

Browning's Revelation of Failure in Art

IN three most suggestive studies of painters of the Renaissance, Browning has marked with decisive power the mission of Art, and the grounds of its failure. He has not crowned the series by a portraiture of the ideal artist, but it is not difficult to gather his lineaments from the sketches of the other three.

In *Fra Lippo Lippi* the poet vindicates the universality of Art answering to the fulness of life, and yet plainly indicates the peril which lies in this frank recognition of "the value and significance of flesh." In *Andrea del Sarto* he shews the power of faultless execution neutralised by the deliberate acceptance of a poor and selfish motive. In *Pictor ignotus*, the loftiest ideal and the fullest power of imagination and execution are supposed to be combined, but the artist shrinks from facing a world, sordid, proud, and unsympathising, and buries his work in obscurity.

Fra Lippo Lippi

IT would not be possible to describe the artist's feeling more truly than in Lippi's words:

> *This world's no blot for us*
> *Nor blank: it means intensely, and means good:*
> *To find its meaning is my meat and drink.*

So it is that for him to see the world is to see

> *The beauty and the wonder and the power,*
> *The shapes of things, their colours, lights and shades,*
> *Changes, surprises—and God made them all . . .*
> *. . . paint any one, and count it crime*
> *To let a truth slip.*

If it be said that nature is before us, and that the artist can neither surpass nor reproduce it, the answer is complete:

> *we're made so that we love*
> *First when we see them painted, things we have passed*
> *Perhaps a hundred times nor cared to see ; . . .*
> *. . . Art was given for that :*
> *God uses us to help each other so,*
> *Lending our minds out.*

It is therefore faithless disloyalty to the Creator to seek to "paint the souls of men" by disparaging their bodies. Even if such a thing as soulless beauty were possible, the devout spectator would "find the soul he wants within himself, when he returns God thanks."

These pregnant words describe the manifold field of Art, its peculiar interpretative power, and its moral effect, but in connection with a perfect, an unfallen world. They take no account of the sorrows and failures which come from what "man has made of men;" and the circumstances under which they are spoken give powerful emphasis to the reality of that disorder in life which imposes on Art the necessity of discipline.

There must, indeed, be no violent suppression of any part of true nature in the endeavour to gain the highest lesson of earth, but the divine meaning must be sought through the traces of the divine ideal, so that the artist "makes new hopes shine through the flesh they fray."

Andrea del Sarto

THE failure of Lippi springs from a reaction against conventionality. In the assertion of the divine glory of Nature he overlooks the reality of corruption. The failure and the success of Andrea del Sarto are of a different kind. There is in him no sense of an illimitable progress of Art as it "interprets God to men." "I can do," he says, "do easily,

what I know,
What I see, what at bottom of my heart,
I wish for, if I ever wish so deep.

The last words give the clue to his position. He has deliberately, irrevocably, limited his ideal by an unworthy passion. In earth and in heaven, as he looks forward, he accepts defeat as the consequence: so he chooses. He has fettered himself and strives to think that "God laid the fetter."

But none the less he is conscious that his matchless power was given him for something nobler. He recognises truer greatness in pictures less perfect than his own. The complete fulfilment of his design is his condemnation:

> *A man's reach should exceed his grasp,*
> *Or what's a heaven for? all is silver-grey,*
> *Placid and perfect with my art—the curse!*

He has said of the Madonna, which was but the image of his wife,

> *It is the thing, Love! so such things should be—*

but yet looking back to the early and unsullied days he thinks, addressing Lucrezia, how he
> *could paint*
> *One picture, just one more—the Virgin's face,*
> *Not yours this time!*

Pictor ignotus

THE artist has need of discipline: he has need of devotion to an unattainable ideal: he has need also of un-selfregarding courage. The pathos of earthly passion in the confession of Andrea is less touching than the self-effacement of "the unknown painter," who, conscious of power and purpose, keenly alive to the joy of triumphs which he might secure, yet shrinks from the cold, hard criticism of the crowd, "as from the soldiery a nun," and chooses for his works silent unnoticed decay.

He has failed to acknowledge the reality of his mission. The question for him was not how men would judge him, whether "their praise would hold its worth," but whether he had a trust to discharge, different from that monotonous task which he took to himself, painting

>   . . . *the same series, Virgin, Babe, and Saint,*
>   *With the same cold, calm, beautiful regard.*

It might have been that "merchants would have trafficked in his heart;" but they could not have disguised the heart's teaching. It might have been that his pictures would have lived with those who

> *count them for garniture and household-stuff,*

but no dull eye could have extinguished the light of his interpretation of life.

The work of the artist is a battle, not without loss and suffering, and he must bear its sorrows, just as he must exercise the patient self-control of one who has to recover an image partly marred and defaced, and to keep in vigorous activity his loftiest aspiration.

Beauty answering to a Divine Ideal the Object of Art

ALL nature, all life, so far as it can be presented under the form of beauty, is the field of Art. But the beauty which is the aim of Christian Art is referred to a divine ideal. It is not "of the world," as finding its source or its final measure there, but "of the Father" as corresponding to an unseen truth. The visible to the Christian eye is in every part a revelation of the invisible. The artist, like the poet, sees the infinite in things, and, under the conditions of his works, suggests it.

Positive Value of Artistic Discipline

SO far the artist's pursuit of beauty is limited. The boundaries within which he is confined will not always be the same, but they will always have the same relation to moral discipline. They will correspond with the circumstances of the time. And the discipline of sense has a positive and not only a negative value. It brings into healthy action a power of goodness which a rigid asceticism keeps unused and tends to destroy.

In this way Christianity is able to give back what was lost by the corruption of the old Aryan passion for Nature. All that was at first referred to limited divinities is shewn to be essentially an expression of one Divine Will.

The spiritual signs may be greatly obscured: they may not be in every case distinctly discoverable; but the assurance of the significance and purpose of the whole cannot but illuminate the study of every part.

And while the field of Christian Art is in one sense limited by the recognition of a spiritual destiny of all its fruits, it is, in another sense, unlimited. The understanding of Nature is deepened and enlarged with the progress of life. Every discovery as to the history of creation, sooner or later, places new forces in the artist's hands.

It may be some detail as to the formation of rocks, some law as to the arrangement of leaves and branches, some phenomenon of light or vapour, which has been more firmly seized; and shortly the painter's interpretation of the landscape will offer a fuller truth. The instructed eye will discern the importance of some minute effect, and the artistic instinct will know how to convey it to the ordinary spectator.

The Artist Interprets and Embodies

FOR the artist has both to interpret and to embody. He has to gain the ideal of his subject and then he has to present it in an intelligible shape. He has to give the right effect and to call out the right feeling. He has, as it were, to enter within the veil, and coming forth again to declare his heavenly visions to men.

He is not a mirror but a prophet.

The work of the photographer may help him, but it in no sense expresses his aim, which is not reproduction but translation.

He has abdicated the office of an artist who simply repeats for the mass of men what they see themselves. The artist bids them behold the ideal as it is his privilege to realise it.

He strives to make clear to others what his keener sensibility and penetrating insight have made visible to him.

There is, as in every true poem, an element of infinity in his works. They suggest something beyond that which they directly present : something to be looked for, and felt after, thoughts which they quicken but do not satisfy. So it is that :

> *Art may tell a truth*
> *Obliquely, so the thing shall breed the thought,*
> *Nor wrong the thought.*

Peril of Realistic Art

THIS consideration places in a true light the danger of the popular realism in Art. There is a charm, no doubt, in being enabled to see some scene far removed from us in time or place as it would have presented itself to an ordinary observer ; but exactly in proportion to the grandeur of the subject such a superficial portraiture is likely to be misleading.

The spectator is tempted to rest in that which he

understands at once; and the loftier though vague impression which he had before is lost and not assisted by the external details which profess to give the literal truth.

Or, to put the truth in another light: the divine act was fitted to convey the divine meaning at the time of its occurrence, in relation to those who witnessed it, but a realistic representation could not give the same impression to a different age.

In Scriptural subjects especially

THIS is signally the case with scenes in the Gospel History. The early Church by a right instinct refrained from seeking any direct representation of the Lord. It was felt that the realistic treatment of His Person could not but endanger the living sense of the Majesty which the Church had learnt to recognise. By no effort could the spectator in a later age place himself in the position of the disciples before the Passion and the Ascension. The exact reproduction, if it were possible, of what met their eyes, would not produce on him the effect which they experienced. The scene would require artistic interpretation in order that the idea might be preserved.

Illustrations from the Treatment of the Madonna

A GREAT artist can alone determine what the law of interpretation must be, and even then he will not himself always obey it. Two illustrations taken from the commonest of sacred subjects, the Madonna and the Crucifixion, may serve to bring out the thought which I wish to emphasise.

In the "Madonna della Seggiola" Raffaelle has given an exquisite natural group of a Mother and Child,

THE RELATION OF CHRISTIANITY TO ART

overflowing with human tenderness, affection, and proud joy, and we look no farther: in the "Madonna di San Sisto" he has rendered the idea of divine motherhood and divine Sonship in intelligible forms.

No one can rest in the individual figures. The tremulous fulness of emotion in the face of the Mother, the intense far-reaching gaze of the Child, constrain the beholder to look beyond.

For him too the curtain is drawn aside: he feels that there is a fellowship of earth with heaven and of heaven with earth, and understands the meaning of the attendant Saints who express the different aspects of this double communion.

The Crucifixion

IT may well be doubted whether the Crucifixion is in any immediate shape a proper subject for Art. The image of the Dead Christ is foreign to Scripture. Even in the record of the Passion Death is swallowed up in Victory. And the material representation of that which St. John shews to have been life through death defines and perpetuates thoughts foreign to the Gospel.

The Crucifixion by Velasquez, with its overwhelming pathos and darkness of desolation, will shew what I mean. In every trait it presents the thought of hopeless defeat. No early Christian would have dared to look upon it. Very different is one of the earliest examples of the treatment of the Crucifixion on the Sigmaringen Crucifix. In that life, vigour, beauty, grace, the open eye, and the freely outstretched arm, suggest the idea of loving and victorious sacrifice crowned with its reward. This is an embodiment of the idea: the picture of Velasquez is a realisation of the appearance of the Passion.

Art Ministerial, and not an End

IF the view of Art which has been given is correct, its primary destination is public and not private, and it culminates in worship. Neither a great picture nor a great poem can be for a single possessor. So it has been at all times when Art has risen to its highest triumphs.

But as an element of worship, Art must be seen to be distinctly ministerial. In every form, music, painting, sculpture, it must point beyond the immediate effect.

As long as it suggests the aspiration "to Thy great glory, O Lord," it is not only an offering, but a guide and a support.

When it appears to be an end idolatry has begun.

The Artist a Teacher

THE artist, we have seen, must use every fresh help and discovery: he must make evident new thoughts, or illuminate thoughts which are imperfectly understood. It is clear, therefore, that he cannot follow one constant method in the fulfilment of his office. His work will be accomplished according to the conditions of his time. He will choose that mode of presenting the truth that he sees which is on the whole likely to be most effective. As a teacher with a limited and yet most noble range of subjects, he will consider how he can best serve his age. Nothing short of this conviction can overcome the influence of fashion, or sustain that resolute purpose which bears temporary failure.

Decorative Art

I HAVE touched only upon the highest forms of creative Art. The principles by which these are animated apply also with necessary modifications to the humbler types of decorative art. The problems which these raise are in many respects more difficult and of wider application than those connected with the artistic interpretation of nature and life.

It is no affectation to speak of the moral influence of colours and shapes in the instruments and accessories of everyday life. Here also there is room for a manifold apprehension and embodiment of truth.

If once thoughtfulness of workmanship could be placed in general estimation before richness of material, a legitimate and fruitful field would be opened for domestic art. When Greek Art was greatest, it was consecrated to public use, and the chief danger of modern society is lest the growth of private wealth should lead to the diversion of the highest artistic power from the common service, and at the same time leave the appropriate labours of domestic art unencouraged.

Summary

THIS, however, is not the place to pursue the questions which are thus opened for inquiry. It is enough to have shewn that Christian Art is a necessary expression of the Christian Faith : that the early antagonism of Christianity to ancient Art was an antagonism to the idolatry, the limited earthliness, of which it was the most complete expression; that from the first beginnings of the Faith there were strivings after an Art which should interpret nature and life as a revelation of God, leading the student through the most patient and reverent regard of phenomena to the contemplation of the eternal ; that the consecration of Art, involved in the facts of the Christian Creed, limits the artist only in the sense that a clear exhibition of the ideal saves the beholder from following wayward and selfish fancies.

The works of the greatest masters of the Middle Ages, of the greatest masters of the Renaissance, and the statement holds good still, shew how constantly foreign elements, fragments of the old life, not wholly transfigured, intrude themselves in that which as a whole belongs to a new order. Here, perhaps, traces of sensuousness, there traces of unlicensed satire, reveal disturbing forces in the artist's soul which are yet powerful enough to make themselves felt. But it is true, I believe, without exception, that the noblest works, those on which we look with the deepest gratitude, drawing from them new powers of spiritual vision, new convictions of a spiritual world about us, are those which are most Christian.

www.ingramcontent.com/pod-product-compliance
Lightning Source LLC
Chambersburg PA
CBHW071224230426
43668CB00011B/1298